THE
ADMINISTRATIVE
PROCESS
IN
BRITAIN

THE
ADMINISTRATIVE
PROCESS
IN
BRITAIN

Second Edition

R. G. S. Brown
and
D. R. Steel

Methuen & Co Ltd

First published 1970 by Methuen & Co Ltd
11 New Fetter Lane, London EC4P 4EE
Reprinted with an additional chapter,
and first published as a University Paperback, 1971
Second edition 1979

ISBN (hardbound) 0 416 85890 2
ISBN (paperback) 0 416 85900 3

Printed in Great Britain by
Richard Clay (The Chaucer Press) Ltd, Bungay, Suffolk

'The money to be earned is the solitary attraction. A clerk in a Public Office may not even dream of fame to be acquired in that capacity. He labours in an obscurity as profound as it is unavoidable. His official character is absorbed in that of his superior. He must devote all his talents, and all his learning, to measures, some of which he will assuredly disapprove, without having the slightest power to prevent them; and to some of which he will most essentially contribute, without having any share whatever in the credit of them. He must listen silently to praises bestowed on others, which his pain has earned for them; and if any accident should make him notorious enough to become the suspected author of any unpopular act, he must silently submit to the reproach, even though it be totally unmerited by him. These are indeed the indispensable disadvantages of the position of a clerk in a Public Office, and no man of sense and temper would complain of them. But neither will any man of real mental power, to whom the truth is known beforehand, subject himself to an arduous examination in order to win a post so ill paid, so obscure, and so subordinate or should he win it, no such man will long retain it.'

SIR JAMES STEPHEN

(Parliamentary Papers 1854–55, Vol. XX, *Papers on the Reorganisation of the Civil Service*)

'That is the way I think a permanent secretary should behave, with a rather consistent attempt to consider what the Minister really needs. But I think no man of spirit can do this for long.'

SIR EDWARD PLAYFAIR

('Who are the Policy-Makers?', *Public Administration* Vol. 43 (1965))

For Gordon and Stuart

Contents

Preface to second edition   11
Acknowledgements   17
PART ONE: BACKGROUND
I   The century of Northcote–Trevelyan   21
II   The 1960s: a decade of enquiry   47
III The civil service today: administrators   66
IV   The civil service today: specialists   96
V   The political environment   125

PART TWO: THEORY

VI   People and organization   155
VII Decisions   174
VIII Decision-making in a political environment   197
IX   The politician's contribution   216

PART THREE: PROBLEMS

X   Planning   237
XI   The machinery of government   266
XII Management   295
XIII Ministers and their staff   319
     Guide to further reading   338
     Name index   343
     Subject index   347

Preface to
second edition

This study was originally conceived in the mid-1960s, when one of the authors was directly involved in the machinery of British central government. It seemed obvious that there were serious weaknesses in the central policy and decision-making machine. Skills and energies were being frittered away on relatively trivial matters, while there was a failure to seek out dynamic solutions to major problems. People of very considerable ability seemed unable to break out of an inhibiting organization structure that no longer reflected contemporary priorities. Many suggestions were being made to improve matters, but none of them appeared to offer a complete and adequate solution. Some criticized the civil service for not achieving the impossible, others for not doing a job that it was not allowed to do by the government it served. There was a gap between the assumptions and objectives of efficiency experts, who often paid no regard to the way the civil service was embedded in the political system, and those of political theorists, who tended to give little or no weight to the practical difficulties of organizing a large and complex body of men and functions. There was also a gap between official studies of administrative procedures and academic accounts of the general growth and functioning of public bodies. Although more material was becoming available about the working of central government machinery, much of it was

11

discursive and imprecise or else – a point that applies particularly to the invaluable evidence collected by parliamentary committees – badly in need of interpretation and assimilation.

The most promising method for a systematic analysis of these problems seemed likely to emerge from a growing body of theory and research about organizations which was attracting interest on both sides of the Atlantic. The twenty years since Simon published the first edition of his *Administrative Behavior* had seen increasingly successful attempts to refine the original crudities of management theory and to apply it to different sorts of organizational problems. In this country, Burns, Lupton, Joan Woodward and members of the Tavistock Institute of Human Relations had made considerable additions to the available knowledge, which had become familiar stock in trade of the better management training schools. But there had been little or no attempt to apply their methods of analysis to the problems of British public administration. The main purpose of the study was therefore to see whether an application of the methods developed by Simon and later social scientists might not provide a more satisfying rationale for changes in central administrative machinery.

In 1968 the Fulton Committee published its report on the civil service, accompanied by voluminous evidence from official bodies and private individuals and by a more slender quantity of research. The supporting material contained a mass of information about the civil service, on which the first edition of this book relied heavily. The report itself was less helpful, being imbued with a 'business-managerial' philosophy which failed to contribute to the theoretical understanding of public administration. Its recommendations were fairly opportunist, in the sense that they attempted to deal with immediate problems and pressures, but even at the time they seemed likely to solve some problems at the price of making others less tractable, particularly those concerning coordination and public accountability.

For reasons that we shall come to in the text, the Fulton recommendations were never fully implemented. An intensive and well-documented five years of activity by the newly-created Civil Service Department left the civil service of the 1970s recognizably similar to that of the 1960s. Criticisms continued to be made of its size, its methods and its alleged élitism. When the House of Commons Expenditure Committee investigated the civil service ten years later, the evidence it received was along familiar lines. Unfortunately it did not include the factual documentation that accompanied the Fulton Report.

In the meantime academic writing about the civil service and the government system increased in volume and began to change in character. Increasingly, organization theory began to appear as a component in university and polytechnic courses on public administration; published work reflected that trend. It is no longer necessary to make the case for interpenetration that was a main theme in the first edition of this book. There have also been important developments in thinking about organizations, both public and non-public.

The context of central government administration too has changed substantially since the 1960s. Up to about 1968 the main problems facing British government seemed to be technical ones about the best means of achieving agreed ends. Earlier in the decade Daniel Bell had written a book entitled *The End of Ideology*. In Britain, Conservative and Labour governments behaved in much the same way while in office and accepted much the same conventions. A transatlantic reviewer of the first edition commented on the unbelievable tranquillity of the environment in which the British civil service seemed to operate. This picture of a stable consensus society, administered by a paternalistic élite, is certainly open to challenge in the late 1970s. The debate between the major political parties has become embittered as each claims that the other has moved away from the middle ground. There has been an increase in protest, both from the cause groups which emerged in the 1960s and from the participation movement, covering a great variety of interests, which seemed to draw its vitality from the desire of groups and individuals to protect themselves from government. It would be an exaggeration to talk about the collapse of consensus. But there has certainly been a decline of confidence in our institutions, which has had its effects on the civil service.

In these circumstances, the publisher suggested that it was time for a second edition. The original author (Ron Brown) had by this time become absorbed in other aspects of public administration. David Steel agreed to become joint author of the revised edition. Its contents are the outcome of joint discussion and mutual criticism; but David Steel has been particularly concerned with the revision of Part One and with Chapters XII and XIII, while Ron Brown has been responsible for revising Part Two and Chapters X and XI.

If we had been starting from scratch, neither of us would have followed the pattern of the 1970 edition. In retrospect, even the title does not seem entirely satisfactory, since the book does not attempt to deal with, for example, relationships between central and local government, which are now a very important part of the administrative process. Nor do we say much about administrative techniques like output budgeting or forecasting. But others have written on these topics. It seemed important that the second edition should be a recognizable successor to the first. Its basic scope and structure have accordingly been retained, although we have tried to find more apt titles for some of the chapters.

The book therefore deals with the central government machine, and not with all of that. The focus for discussion is the fairly small groups of administrators who are involved in the formulation and implementation of policy, the operation of the top-level policy-making machine and the major questions of public sector management. These are the senior administrators who work in a near-political atmosphere, who contribute directly to policy decisions and on whose ability in some measure depends the quality with which we as a nation govern our affairs. There are important questions about the middle ranks, who are charged with the detailed working out of policy decisions, including the operation of regional and local offices, and about the junior staff who are in contact with the public, but they are not examined here.

The original material has, of course, been updated. But it has not been entirely jettisoned, partly because many of the problems are unchanged and partly because many readers have found the analysis of the situation at the time of the Fulton Report to be useful: apart from its historical value, it would be difficult to find comparable evidence about the more confused situation that existed in the late 1970s. Some deficiencies in the original text have been corrected, including the over-simplified picture there given of political roles. Changes in the political environment have also been taken into account, as well as developments in, for example, policy science theory. For reasons of space, some of the original material has had to be left out, including some of the detailed accounts of early experiments with the integration of generalist and professional roles and a whole chapter based on research on job satisfaction and morale, which would now be very out of date and probably misleading. In all, seven chapters have been extensively revised.

Two conclusions from the first edition have stood up remarkably well. The first is the continuing need, in the British system of government, for a generalist administrator at the heart of things, without denying the need for specialist and professional skills appropriate to the great variety of governmental tasks. The second is the need for research to establish the relevance and validity of general theory to particular aspects of government administration.

The book is in three parts. The first is a brief account of the changing role of the civil service from the 1854 Northcote–Trevelyan Report to the present day, its present structure, and the political framework within which it operates. Part Two contains a brief introduction to organization theory; some of this is elementary, and will be skipped by the informed reader. In Part Three these theoretical concepts are applied to a number of continuing problems in the structure of government, executive management, policy and planning, and the support required by Ministers. One of the main arguments, about the most appropriate structure for carrying on the distinctive processes of public administration, runs through all this analysis and is brought to a head in the final chapter.

May 1978   RGSB
                                                                     DRS

Shortly after the manuscript of the second edition was completed Ron Brown was taken ill, and he died on 28 June 1978. It has been a great privilege to work with him so closely during the past twelve months, and my hope is that the end-product of our combined efforts will be a continuing reminder of the contribution that he has made over the years to the study of public administration.

July 1978   DRS

Acknowledgements

The first edition of this book could not have been written without the generous assistance of friends and former colleagues in the civil service. Unpublished documents were readily made available and provided useful source material. A number of individual civil servants, who cannot be mentioned by name, were kind enough to read and comment upon parts of the manuscript. Academically the book owed much to the writings of H. A. Simon, D. K. Price and V. Subramaniam and to the advice and encouragement of Rodney White and T. E. Chester.

In preparing this second edition we have been assisted by the comments of colleagues and students who have used the original text. The responsibility for any errors of fact and of judgement that remain is, of course, our own. We are grateful to our secretaries in Hull and in Exeter for the enthusiasm and care with which they have converted our difficult handwriting and amended typescripts into a clear manuscript. As always, a large part of the burden of authorship is borne by the families of the authors and we would like to thank them for their support and assistance.

Extracts from Crown Copyright documents are reproduced by permission of the Controller of Her Majesty's Stationery Office.

PART ONE
Background

I
The century
of Northcote–Trevelyan

Nineteenth-century foundations

A permanent civil service, in the sense of 'full-time salaried officials, systematically recruited, with clear lines of authority, and uniform rules on such questions as superannuation', emerged in Britain early in the nineteenth century.[1] In the eighteenth century there was no clear distinction between political and administrative offices. The civil service of the Crown became established as the growing volume of parliamentary and administrative business made it necessary to place more of the latter in the hands of officials. Civil servants owed their permanent status, at a time when the development of party politics was making their political chiefs less secure, to parliamentary jealousy of Crown patronage: the opportunities for patronage could be reduced by granting security of tenure to officials already in post. The alternative to a career service – a spoils system in which officials were replaced as their political sponsors demitted office – never took root in Britain.

The watershed between politics and administration became fairly clear as posts immediately below the Secretaries of State in the great departments separated into temporary ones held by Parliamentary Under Secretaries (the junior Ministers of today) and those of Permanent Under Secretaries, held by career civil servants who took no part in politics. The office of Permanent Under

Secretary (Assistant Secretary in the Treasury, and Permanent Secretary in other departments not headed by a Secretary of State) became established in most departments between 1800 and 1830. The first Assistant Secretary to the Treasury was appointed in 1805. At this stage vacancies were still filled by patronage. The Campaign for Economical Reform initiated by Burke and Fox had reduced the number of sinecures, but it was not until the 1850s that Northcote and Trevelyan showed the way to a modern career service, immune from nepotism and jobbery.[2] It took the rest of the nineteenth century for their ideas to be fully worked out.

Sir Stafford Northcote (later Chancellor of the Exchequer under Disraeli) was a politician who had been private secretary to Gladstone. The real author of the famous Northcote–Trevelyan Report was Sir Charles Trevelyan, Assistant Secretary to the Treasury, a former member of the already reformed Indian Civil Service and son-in-law of Lord Macaulay, whose ideas permeate mid-nineteenth-century discussions about administrative reform. Their report was the culmination of a series of enquiries into the organization and staffing of government offices. Professor Wheare described it in 1954 as 'this premature vision in the middle of the nineteenth century of the sort of Civil Service we need in the middle of the twentieth century'.[3] Less enthusiastically, the Fulton Committee on the Civil Service, 1966–8, started its report with these words: 'The Home Civil Service today is still fundamentally the product of the nineteenth-century philosophy of the Northcote–Trevelyan Report. The tasks it faces are those of the second half of the twentieth century. This is what we have found; it is what we seek to remedy.'[4]

Northcote and Trevelyan made four main recommendations.

1 There should be a clear separation between 'intellectual' work, performed by graduates, and 'mechanical' duties allocated to a 'lower class' of lesser ability. (It was not until 1876, however, that a real attempt was made to establish a separate lower division by Order in Council. Subsequent enquiries showed that it took a long time to distinguish clearly the work appropriate to each division. After several refinements, a tripartite system of ad-

ministrative, executive and clerical 'classes' was introduced in
1920.)

2 Entry to the service should be at an early age through competitive examinations, the highest being set at the level of a university
degree. (The Civil Service Commission was established in 1855
to test the suitability of candidates nominated by departments.
From 1859 only persons approved by the Commission were
entitled to superannuation. It was 1870 before an Order in
Council provided that all vacancies should be filled by open
competition – and even then posts in the Foreign Office and
the Home Office were exempted.)

3 Separate departments should be made part of a unified service,
in which transfers and promotions could be made between
departments. (Although service-wide conditions of service were
introduced for some grades before 1900, real unification did not
come until Warren Fisher, as Permanent Secretary of the
Treasury, assumed the title of Head of the Civil Service in 1919
and obtained the right to advise the Prime Minister on senior
appointments throughout the service.)

4 Promotion should depend on merit, assessed by reports from
superiors. (It is harder to identify stages in the implementation
of this principle. The growth and recognition of staff associations
has made promotion at lower levels subject to rules, negotiated
with the staff themselves, in which seniority has inevitably and
perhaps defensibly played a large part. But nepotism has long
since ceased to be a factor in promotion.)

The civil service of 1854

By 1854 the permanent civil service was firmly established.
Northcote and Trevelyan took its importance for granted.

It cannot be necessary [they said] to enter into any lengthened
argument for the purposes of showing the high importance
of the Permanent Civil Service of the country in the present
day. The great and increasing accumulation of public
business, and the consequent pressure upon the Government,
need only be alluded to; and the inconveniences which are

inseparable from the frequent changes which take place in the responsible administration are matters of sufficient notoriety. It may safely be asserted that, as matters now stand, the Government of the country could not be carried on without the aid of an efficient body of permanent officers, occupying a position duly subordinate to that of the Ministers who are directly responsible to the Crown and to the Parliament, yet possessing sufficient independence, character, ability, and experience to be able to advise, assist, and to some extent, influence, those who are from time to time set over them.

But the service was still very small. The 1851 census tables show over 40,000 civilians directly employed by central government, but two-thirds were accounted for by the revenue departments and the Post Office. The Poor Law Board employed 84 persons, including 12 inspectors and a clerk apiece. The Public Works Loan Office employed 4 people (disregarding office keepers, messengers and porters), the General Board of Health 26, the Treasury 70, and the Board of Trade 79, compared with nearly 12,000 in the Customs Service. [5]

This was the age of Bentham and of *laissez-faire*. The conventional view was that governments should not interfere with the operation of natural economic laws, and there was little reason to challenge the assumption that these laws were, on the whole, beneficent. Trade conditions were favourable and apparently stable. There were no major wars to upset the equilibrium in the period between the Crimean and Boer Wars, both of which were associated with administrative charge. True, Bentham had taught that the state should intervene to protect the weak (as in the case of children in factories) and to maintain uneconomic institutions of social value, but until the publication at the end of the century of the social surveys of Booth and Rowntree, these categories had not begun to be identified, far less understood. So there was little intervention by governments in social and economic affairs. When they did intervene, as in factories legislation or in the centralized administration of the Poor Law, it was usually to set limits to acceptable economic activity rather than to exert positive influence.

Nineteenth-century administration was primarily regulatory: Parliament said what was to be done and Parliament's wishes were carried out by inspectors (who watched for infringements) and by lawyers (who prosecuted them). The typical job of an administrator was therefore the simple one of preparing legislation and briefing the Minister when the need arose; he had little need for drive or initiative but could spend his life sitting waiting for papers. Compared with the position even at the turn of the century, the functions of government were narrow, both in theory and in practice. Ministers did more of the actual policy work themselves, and civil servants less, because there was altogether less to do. Central coordination was weak and functions of the state could be administered in watertight compartments. The administration of any particular field or service was relatively simple, because there was little in the way of specialized knowledge and techniques. Finally, most government departments were so small that internal management did not present serious problems.

Consequently, it was easy for senior men, commenting on the Northcote–Trevelyan Report, to pour scorn on the capacity of the service to provide work for good university men. Here, for example, is Arbuthnot, Trevelyan's immediate subordinate at the Treasury:

> The officers of our Civil Service cannot in ordinary cases aspire to become statesmen, and to carry out systems of policy. Their humble but useful duty is, by becoming depositories of departmental traditions ... to keep the current business in its due course; to warn Ministers of the consequences of irregular proceedings into which they might inadvertently fall; to aid in preparing subjects for legislation; and possibly to assist by their suggestions the development of a course of reform. [Their function is to obtain] that intimate acquaintance with details, and the bearing of those details upon general principles, which constitute the distinction between the permanent executive officers and the members of Government who are charged with the duty of administration.[6]

This sounds like work that clerical or executive officers would carry out today. There were already some posts akin to those of the twentieth-century administrative class. In evidence to a select committee, Trevelyan had described the work of the eight Principal Treasury Officers – each of whom had to decide, within the section of the work for which he was responsible, when to bring matters forward to the Treasury Board and later to prepare appropriate minutes – in terms which would not serve too badly as a description of the work of a junior Principal working with a committee in many departments today.[7] Because there was less complexity and less need for coordination, we can probably say that there were no equivalents to the modern Under Secretary or above. But there were at least a few Assistant Secretaries, able and willing to discharge the kind of positive role that some writers consider to have emerged only in the twentieth century. The most outstanding was Trevelyan himself, whose part in the Irish Famine, for example, was certainly not that of a 'humble but useful ... depository of departmental tradition'. Another was Edwin Chadwick, Secretary to the General Board of Health, every inch a technocrat, impatient of parliamentary control and anxious to see the development of professionalism, both in administration itself and in supporting fields like structural engineering. Like many other distinguished nineteenth-century civil servants, Chadwick enjoyed great power as secretary of a semi-autonomous board. His comments on the Northcote–Trevelyan Report are considerably longer than the report itself, partly irrelevant, but wholly worth reading because of the insight they give on the outlook of a thoroughly modern administrator in the middle of the nineteenth century.[8]

The administration of 1854 was not *simply* regulatory. Professor Greaves has commented that, in a sense, the nineteenth-century state never existed: the social service democracy of the twentieth century was born before the maladministration and paternalism of the eighteenth century had wholly disappeared.[9] The principle of administering social services through local agencies under the supervision of a central department was introduced by the Poor Law Amendment Act of 1834 and extended by the Public Health Act of 1848. By 1851 the government was a substantial employer of artificers and labourers: nearly 15,000 of them were employed in the ordnance factories and naval dockyards. The Post Office had become a large commercial enterprise with the introduction of the penny post in 1840 and employed another 15,000 people. In 1829 the Home Secretary had become responsible for the Metropolitan Police Force. The Board of Trade was given the duty of collecting and producing statistics in 1832. Although, therefore, it lacked the machinery and the will to control much of the economy, the government had begun to take on some functions characteristic of a modern state. The civil service that emerged from the 'premature vision' in the Northcote–Trevelyan Report was an essential instrument in its development.

Development and growth 1900–39

The principal Northcote–Trevelyan reforms had been implemented and consolidated by the end of the nineteenth century. In the highest administrative classes, at least, there were men of calibre ready to carry out the 1905 Liberal Government's programme of social and economic intervention and to deal with the administrative aspects of the First World War.

The Old Age Pensions Act of 1908, the Labour Exchange Act of 1909 and the National Health Insurance Act of 1911 established government social services of a wholly new kind. The employment and pensions services (augmented in the 1930s by new schemes for supplementary benefits and employment assistance) brought civil servants into direct contact with the public. The National Health Insurance scheme, administered by the new Ministry of Health after 1919, brought the medical profession irrevocably within the government's sphere of interest. Other health services were established and entrusted to local authorities, whose educational services, including the school medical service, were also expanding under the Board of Education (established in 1899). The development of these services required an intimate relationship between government departments and local authorities which would have been recognized by Chadwick, although not perhaps by many of his contemporaries. Sir George Newman wrote that they 'enlarged the purpose of the Civil Service, as guide, philosopher and friend to the Local Authorities and the auxiliary voluntary movements associated with them'.[10] The task of government became one of participation and encouragement and not merely of regulation and restraint.

In the field of trade and industry, government intervention was more reluctant and change was less continuous. During the 1914–1918 war, the Government became involved in the regulation of economic activity, and particularly with the distribution of man-power, on a very large scale. New Ministries were set up, including a Ministry of Food and a Ministry of Mines. Some of them, like the Ministry of Labour and the Department of Scientific and Industrial Research, were to become permanent. But the main policy objective after the war was to return to 'normal conditions' as soon as possible. This meant eliminating many of the regulatory agencies in industry and trade. Retrenchment and economy were also the orthodox reaction to the great depression.

Thereafter, however, there were stirrings of interventionism, accompanying a change in the general economic climate. There were a number of moves to encourage investment in the depressed areas, to rationalize hard-hit industries like shipbuilding and to set up cartels in industry and marketing boards in agriculture. In 1930 the Government appointed an Economic Advisory Council (to replace a Civil Research Committee appointed in 1925) with a high-level composition of Ministers and outside experts. But (as Lord Bridges points out in his book *The Treasury*[11]) there was no consensus of economic opinion about a remedy for the major current evil of unemployment and this body made relatively little impact on actual policy. The government was not yet in a position, or possessed of the necessary techniques, to attempt a systematic management of the economy.

All this was reflected in the numbers of central government employees. In absolute figures, the number of non-industrial civilian staff rose from 229,000 in 1914 to 285,000 in 1928 and 387,000 in 1939. Within this total the staff of the social service departments more than doubled by 1928 and trebled (to 25,000) by 1939, mainly as a result of the expansion of insurance and assistance schemes. Those concerned with trade, industry and transport had also doubled in number by 1928 and nearly quad-rupled (to 43,000) by 1939, three-quarters of this increase being attributable to Ministry of Labour functions. Over the same period, the staff of the revenue departments doubled and that of the Post Office went up by only a third.[12]

One effect of the steady growth in the functions of government was increasing pressure on the time of Ministers and of Parliament. The pressure on parliamentary time was eased by an increase in the amount of business handled by subordinate legislation. In 1929 the Committee on Ministers' Powers was set up 'to consider the powers exercised by or under the direction of the Crown by way of (a) delegated legislation and (b) judicial or quasi-judicial decision, and to report what safeguards are desirable or necessary to secure the constitutional principles of the sovereignty of Parliament and the Supremacy of the Law'. In its report the Committee agreed that it was necessary to use delegated legislation, partly to save parliamentary time, partly as a speedy and flexible way of getting things done and partly because the scope of legislation now extended to technical matters which it was difficult to include in a Bill 'since they cannot effectively be discussed in Parliament'.[13] The amount of delegated legislation has increased enormously since the Committee reported, and more and more business has come to be subsumed under these categories. Quantitatively, most decisions of a legislative character have been taken out of Parliament. There has been some anxiety that they should not, in practice, be left to civil servants. The Committee suggested a number of safeguards, one of which was that Parliament should set up a committee to keep an eye on rules and orders submitted for formal approval. This was not implemented until 1944.

The increased work of government also implied more delegation from Ministers to civil servants. Although new Ministries were set up during and after the war, and Boards were converted into Ministries, there was a limit both to the number of able politicians and to the time they could give to departmental matters. The rest had to be done by professional administrators. A Reorganisation Committee in 1920 described the duties of the administrative class ('those concerned with the formation of policy, with the co-ordination and improvement of Government machinery, and with the general administration and control of the Departments of the Public Service'[14]) in terms that would, not much earlier, have been thought more appropriate to the Minister himself. The 1929–31

Royal Commission on the Civil Service accepted this definition without modification, saying that the need for civil servants to carry out such work had not been challenged in the evidence given to them, and dismissing the whole question of the administrative class in three or four pages.[15]

But this did not mean that civil servants were usurping the Minister's ultimate function of deciding on policy. Sir Warren Fisher told the Commission:

> Determination of policy is the function of Ministers, and once a policy is determined it is the unquestioned and unquestionable business of the civil servant to strive to carry out that policy with precisely the same energy and precisely the same good will whether he agrees with it or not. This is axiomatic and will never be in dispute. At the same time it is the traditional duty of civil servants, while decisions are being formulated, to make available to their political chiefs all the information and experience at their disposal, and to do this without fear or favour, irrespective of whether the advice thus tendered may accord or not with the Minister's initial view.[16]

The relationship between a Minister and his civil servants is discussed in detail by H. E. Dale, a retired Principal Assistant Secretary, in a classic account of the higher civil service just before the war. Of the daily work of a department he says:

> Only a tiny proportion of the mass would embody decisions of importance, taken by the Permanent Secretary or other high official: and those decisions would every one of them be applications of the policy determined by the Government and the Minister, or adaptations to fit into a change of circumstances. The higher the rank of a civil servant and the more closely he is acquainted with the Minister's mind, the more he feels himself at liberty to modify the detailed application of the policy: but no civil servant, whatever his rank, would think it compatible with his duty to take any step inconsistent with it. If he thought such a step to be imperatively required, he would represent his difficulties and ask for in-

structions. There are now many more officials and they do many more things than forty or fifty years ago: but in reality they do no more without the authority of Parliament and Ministers. Bureaux have grown, but not bureaucracy ... This view I think, will be contested by few who know the inside workings of Government Departments.[17]

The administrator appears in Dale's account as a rather ingenious secretary: 'A good official commands the terse and simple style appropriate to a memorandum for the Cabinet or the easy style appropriate to a private letter as readily as he commands the stately language of a circular to Local Authorities.' On a tricky parliamentary question, the Permanent Secretary 'will be satisfied when a draft reply has been framed which is brief, completely accurate, courteous, exhibits the Minister as modestly surprised to find his own attitude so clearly right, and gives no opening for awkward "supplementaries" '. His entire job is to serve his Minister. To do this he needs broad experience, and a mastery of the government machine that can come only with time. Civil service training must be geared to producing this in the officials closest to the Minister.

The ultimate criterion of the system is whether it produces a sufficient supply of men fit for great office. Assistant Secretaries are important in themselves as administrators and advisers of the Minister on their own subject, but it is much more important that they should provide men fit to be Permanent Secretaries and Second Secretaries.

Some people argued that the administrators were not fit for their new responsibility. Some put the blame for the political inertia of the 1930s on the shoulders of a civil service alleged to be lacking in vitality and in social consciousness. This view was expressed polemically by Laski in his last lectures after the war [our italics].

They never met, with any *imaginative insight*, the problems of a society with never less than one million unemployed, and, more often, as many as two million or more. They never *pushed forward* the plans so urgently needed ... They showed no sense of the *urgent need* for re-education at a far higher level ... They did not *compel attention* to the very serious problem of monopolies ... They did not *press the cabinet* into any serious grasp either of the scale of the housing problem or of the *impossibility* of leaving it to be dealt with by private enterprise ... Not all the devotion the Civil Service brought to its work was a compensation for the absence of *imaginative enterprise* on its part at a time when this quality was vital to the national future.[18]

At less exalted levels of policy-making, also, new needs were emerging. These were reflected in the creation in 1920 of a new executive class with responsibility for the day-to-day conduct of government business within the framework of established policy. This included, for instance, the higher work of accounts and revenue collection and the management of regional and local offices, work which required in different degrees qualities of 'judgment, initiative and resource'.[19]

Many of the government's new responsibilities also called for new qualities of management and drive not previously associated with central administration. Increasingly, therefore, staff with specialist and technical qualifications were recruited to the civil service. Problems soon began to emerge in the relationship between such staff and generalist administrators. The report of the 1929–31 Royal Commission was generally complacent about this but it argued that in the Post Office, at least, there were special administrative requirements that needed further investigation. The subsequent report of the Bridgeman Committee put the Post Office on a different basis from other government departments and can be seen in retrospect as the first official questioning of the generalist tradition. Its recommendations included the establishment of a Board system, in which responsibility for advising the political head was shared between administrative and technical officers, and the opening of senior administrative posts to those with technical qualifications and experience.[20]

To sum up, government had by 1939 taken on many new services of a different character from those of the previous century. The increase of work alone led to some delegation of functions from political heads of departments to career administrators. Many of these functions were primarily political in character, and could be discharged by a generalist whose mind was tuned to the politician's. Some, however, called for new kinds of ability which the generalist did not necessarily possess. It was coming to be recognized that special training (and sometimes special forms of administration) were needed in these areas. Both at senior and at middling levels, the criteria by which civil servants were judged were beginning to change.

New demands: the post-war phase

The Second World War provided an opportunity for rethinking the responsibilities of government and for absorbing some of the economic theories that had been gaining currency in the 1930s.

Two decisions of the 1940–5 Coalition Government entailed lasting changes in the role expected of central government. First came the acceptance of the general principles expressed in the Beveridge Report. This put social insurance firmly in the context of a comprehensive social policy, including national assistance, family allowances and other measures to combat disease, ignorance, squalor and idleness.[21] These ideas finally took shape in plans for improved services, whose impact was summed up by Greaves in 1947.

> The regulatory state has given place to the social service state. Public responsibility is now admitted for the securing to every citizen of an important body of his fundamental needs. Free and enforced educational provision is made for him, with much assistance for further training in technical institutes and universities. His care is organized through a national health service. There is local and central responsibility for housing him. An elaborate insurance system has been constructed to meet the contingencies of sickness, accident, and old age. When he is unemployed the community recognizes a responsibility for his maintenance and for assisting him to obtain and train for work.[22]

These activities were not, of course, all carried out by

organs of central government under the direct responsibility of a Minister. The National Health Service, for instance, was administered partly by local authorities and partly by *ad hoc* local bodies appointed and financed by the Minister. But the scale of the new services, and the magnitude of the problems they had to tackle, involved local agents in a continuous dialogue with the responsible central departments.

The second major decision of the Coalition Government was the acceptance in 1944 of government responsibility for maintaining full employment after the war.[23] This commitment implied a continuing intervention in economic affairs. During the war, a high proportion of economic activity had been regulated from the centre through controls, licensing and rationing. Some resources were controlled directly by the Government through the bulk purchase and allocation of raw materials. Others were controlled indirectly through restrictions on investment, manpower and prices. To allow the controls to be operated, the Government collected a great many statistics about industry and trade. The 1945 Labour Government decided to maintain a large part of this machinery as an instrument of peace-time planning. It faced many economic and financial problems and had to deal with conflicts between social and economic priorities. The situation seemed to demand centralized economic planning. It was decided to place parts of certain key industries, particularly transport and fuel, under public ownership.

Direct physical controls were unpopular. Most of them were gradually abandoned as shortages eased. The election of a Conservative Government in 1951 hastened the process, but derestriction and decentralization had already started. Restrictions on the movement of manpower, other than miners and agricultural workers, were taken off very quickly after the war. Building licences were abandoned in 1954 (although not the attempt to control the location of industry through industrial development certificates). The last traces of war-time rationing of consumer goods, and most price controls, had disappeared by 1955.

In place of direct controls, the Government attempted to regulate the economy through financial management of taxation levels and public expenditure. The necessary machinery for economic intelligence and planning was already in embryo. During the war the Cabinet Office had included an Economic Section charged with presenting 'a co-ordinated and objective picture of the economic situation as a whole and the economic aspects of projected Government policies'.[24] This section remained in existence after the end of the war. Herbert Morrison, as Lord President of the Council, became generally responsible for economic coordination and in 1947 Sir Edwin (later Lord) Plowden was appointed Chief Economic Planning Officer, with a mixed staff of businessmen, civil servants, statisticians and economists, in the Lord President's Office. Later in the same year the central planning staff joined Sir Stafford Cripps in the new Ministry for Economic Affairs, and followed him to the Treasury six weeks later when he became Chancellor of the Exchequer. The Treasury then took on a responsibility for economic coordination that it has kept, apart from a brief period in the 1960s. The Economic Section of the Cabinet also reported to Cripps, but was not formally transferred to the Treasury until 1953.

There were at least two other ways in which the Government began to influence economic activities. One of these mainly affected food and agriculture. In an attempt to stimulate home production farmers were guaranteed a market and a price for some of their main products. For a time, too, certain foodstuffs were directly subsidized. The operation of this and similar schemes involved the Government in negotiations about the detailed structure of the industry.

The other source of influence was the state's own economic activity. The expansion of central and local government and the nationalization of key industries gave the public sector a leading position in the labour market. In 1938 less than 10 per cent of the working population had been employed in the public sector, most of it in local government. By 1950 the public sector, including the armed forces, employed over five and a half million people, or nearly a quarter of all employed workers. The nationalized industries and services alone accounted for over a tenth of the total working population.[25] The number of persons paid from public funds of one sort or another became a significant factor in attempts to influence incomes in the country as a whole. The high proportion of graduates employed by public bodies gave the government a direct interest in the deployment of highly-trained manpower. Moreover, the size of the public sector placed a new instrument in or near the hands of a Chancellor of the Exchequer who wished to influence national levels of investment and employment.

The nationalized industries and services (from house coal to hospital care) constituted a very large field where market forces could, if the occasion demanded, be replaced by political decisions about prices and the level of supply. Public enterprises also had a tremendous potential influence on the market as purchasers of commodities. Some departments, like the Ministry of Health, which had to develop a new relationship with suppliers of drugs and equipment, were practically in a monopsonist position. This situation created new opportunities and new problems which had not been solved by the 1960s, when the need for more effective management of these enormous resources in the interests of the economy as a whole was at last fully recognized.[26]

The implementation of these new social and economic responsibilities entailed an expansion of statistical and intelligence services and the development of new consultative machinery. Each of the new social services had its apparatus of consultative, advisory and executive committees, representing professions employed in the services as well as local interests and consumers. In the economic field, consultative machinery was established to provide links between government and industry, including the National Production Advisory Council on Industry, the National Joint Advisory Council and the Economic Planning Board. The last was set up in 1947, comprising six officials from the departments mainly concerned with finance and industry, three employers' nominees and three nominees of the trade unions, to exchange views on economic problems. It was in some ways the precursor of the National Economic Development Council (1962).

The changes were reflected in the size and structure of the central administrative machine. Between April 1939 and April 1950 non-industrial staff directly employed by central government departments, including the Post Office, increased by over 75 per cent from 387,000 to 684,000. The departments concerned with social services and with trade, industry and transport had more than tripled in size.[27]

We have a fairly clear picture of the civil service at this time. The rules about publication by serving civil servants were relaxed and there are several first-hand accounts of the work of departments in the 1950s, notably those by Critchley, Campbell, Dunnill, Sisson and Walker.[28] Many of the academics who came into the service during the war, like Franks and Devons, had already written of their experiences.[29] Later still, valuable information became available in the published evidence to parliamentary committees. By comparing these accounts with Dale's pre-war study, certain trends become discernible.

Delegation to officials

In the first place, it is clear that political chiefs were forced to devolve even more responsibility to their senior administrators. From merely administering legislation, civil servants began to interpret it and to prepare schemes for its implementation. Here, to contrast with Dale, is what Lord Franks had to say about his work as a temporary member of the administrative class in the Ministry of Supply during the war. Although this particular job was abolished after the war, it had its permanent counterparts in many corners of the 'new look' departments.

Once he was clear about what in general was desirable, he would normally go on to find out, through enquiry, consultations, and meetings with experts, what was practicable in the circumstances, establishing the main heads of the workable schemes and identifying the agents, whether members of the Civil Service or of the public, who must carry out the plans, explaining the policy and the steps worked out to realize it, to make sure that each main agent knew his part and its general context and was convinced that his part and the whole scheme was practicable. Having thus established agreement based on understanding, he would give the word to start operations, satisfied at least that action would not be held up by failures of will or intelligence. Even so, he would arrange for progress reports so that difficulties or delays could be ascertained and dealt with before they grew to proportions which would wreck the scheme or its timing and relevance to wider plans.[30]

Immediately after the war the administrative class was re-organized 'to facilitate speedy and efficient transaction of public business by the maximum devolution of responsibility and by the reduction of steps in the administrative structure to the minimum consistent with the needs of sound organization'.[31] The Permanent Secretary remained the official head of the department and, with the assistance of one or two Deputy Secretaries, remained respon-sible to the Minister for all its activities. A new grade of Under Secretary was created, with the responsibility of advising Ministers on major questions of policy, and, generally, for coordinating very large blocks of administrative work. Below the Under Secretaries came the Assistant Secretaries, in charge of divisions and supported by Principals or senior executive officers in charge of branches. All day-to-day work was to be done within the division and only questions of major policy were normally to be referred above Assistant Secretary level.

The 1953–55 Royal Commission on the Civil Service described 'the most significant function' of the administrative class as follows:

> The members of the class must be able to work from a very broad Government aim, first to thinking out a policy for the execution of that aim and satisfying Ministers that it correctly interprets the aim, secondly to putting that policy into legislative form and thirdly to its translation into action, frequently on a national basis … These duties have to be carried out in ways compatible with Ministerial control, the accountability of Ministers to Parliament and their account-ability, in a less direct but very real sense, to public opinion.[32]

What this meant in practice varied from department to depart-ment according to tradition, the type and volume of its work and the calibre of its staff. In some departments, Assistant Secretaries acting under very broad authority would issue circulars, handle discussions with pressure groups and present subordinate legisla-tion to Parliament on their own initiative. In others, there was a tradition of consulting the Minister to 'keep him in the picture' even on matters of detail. But it was rare for a Minister to wish to see much of the more technical or the more routine aspects of his department's work. The assumption was that he would hear soon enough through conventional political channels if something wrong, or inconsistent, was being done in his name.

Sometimes this happened, as in the Ministry of Agriculture and Fisheries in 1954. After persistent complaints about the way some requisitioned land at a place called Crichel Down had been restored to agricultural use, the Minister (Sir Thomas Dugdale) appointed an independent QC to find out how his officials had reached their decision. Sir Andrew Clark's report found that some officials had acted less fairly than they ought (though there was no question of personal advantage to them) and that they had failed to explain to the Minister what they were doing.[33] The Minister took steps internally to prevent the same sort of thing happening again, but the matter was not allowed to end there. The Prime Minister appointed a committee of two ex-civil servants and a distinguished industrialist to advise whether the officials concerned should be transferred to other duties, and Sir Thomas Dugdale himself resigned.

Following this incident, it was felt necessary to reconsider a Minister's formal position in relation to acts of his officials. The Home Secretary (Sir David Maxwell-Fyfe) defined it in the following terms:

1 Where a civil servant carries out an explicit order by a Minister, the Minister must protect the civil servant concerned.
2 Where a civil servant acts properly in accordance with the policy laid down by the Minister, the Minister must equally protect and defend him.
3 Where a civil servant makes a mistake or causes some delay, but not on an important issue of policy and not where a claim to individual rights is seriously involved, the Minister acknowledges the mistake and he accepts responsibility, although he is not personally involved. He states he will take corrective action in the department.

4 Where action has been taken by a civil servant of which
the Minister disapproves and has no prior knowledge, and
the conduct of the official is reprehensible then there is
no obligation on the Minister to endorse what he believes
to be wrong, or to defend what are clearly shown to be
errors of his officers. The Minister is not bound to approve
of action of which he did not know, or of which he
disapproves. But, of course, he remains constitutionally
responsible to Parliament for the fact that something has
gone wrong, and he alone can tell Parliament what has
occurred and render an account of his stewardship.[34]

Perhaps the most serious risk was that a civil servant, through
ignorance, malicious intent or misunderstanding of the Minister's
mind, would put up proposals which did not in fact exhaust the
viable alternatives. This raised important questions of training and
attitude as well as of political responsibility. The best comment
may be Lord Morrison's.

What the reader can be sure of is that the British Civil Service
is loyal to the Government of the day. The worst that can
be said of them is that sometimes they are not quick enough
in accustoming themselves to new ideas, but then it is up
to the Minister to educate them. The greatest danger in
the running of a Government Department is a Minister who
does not know how to handle civil servants; who does not
possess a mind of his own; or who is lazy and finds life easier
and pleasanter by blindly taking the advice of his civil servants
without considering and criticizing it.[35]

Coordination

The second feature of the post-war service was a vast increase
in the complexity of its work. The new responsibilities which
government had taken on could not simply be aggregated in
separate compartments like the nineteenth-century Boards or even
the *ad hoc* social services of the 1930s. The emphasis on economic
management implied qualitative changes in the way the individual
functions of government were discharged. So, to a lesser extent,

did the attempt stemming from Beveridge to see social policy as a whole. The increasing scale of government activity would in any case have meant that decisions taken in one field had significant repercussions in others. If a programme of factory construction was large enough, it implied a shortage of labour and materials for building houses, schools and hospitals. The Central Electricity Generating Board could cause massive problems for the National Coal Board and ultimately for the Department of Employment if it miscalculated its requirements. Lord Bridges put the point clearly in 1950.

> But it is economic factors more than anything else which have compelled Departments to work more closely together. No government can today discharge its responsibilities unless it has a coherent economic policy, and such a policy must be framed after bringing together the views of separate Departments, while its execution demands constant consultation between them.[36]

This, of course, meant that individual decisions had to be taken in the light of incessant consultation, within and across departmental boundaries. Part of the load fell on Ministers and on their immediate advisers as members of interlocking Cabinet and official committees. But perhaps the greatest burden of consultation fell on officials at about Assistant Secretary level in the course of their day-to-day work.

After 1947 the Treasury became particularly significant as a coordinating department concerned with the adoption of uniform standards throughout the public service as well as with the impact of financial and economic policies on one another. Perhaps it should be said that this was coordination of a rather special kind. The objectives of economic policy were negative rather than positive: it was necessary to *avoid* inflation, to *avoid* excessive unemployment and to *avoid* expenditure not absolutely necessary for the purpose determined by Ministers. In regional planning, too, the tests were negative: factory development in congested areas had to be restrained, but other new building could not make more than a limited demand on national resources of materials and manpower. This approach fitted well with the traditional regulatory functions of the Treasury. In circumstances of acute shortage, perhaps it was inevitable. But post-war writers like Greaves and Munro claimed that the Treasury mistook economy for efficiency and never understood the need to find criteria for the developing public services (like health, education and job-finding) different from those appropriate to a nineteenth-century regulatory department. Much later, when positive planning for economic growth had become an agreed objective of all parties, Brittan echoed a fairly general feeling that the Treasury was an unsuitable agent for such growth, because of its departmental philosophy.

> It is largely a well-justified suspicion that the projects of other Departments will cost much more than appears at first sight, and that total Government spending has an inherent tendency to get out of control. This philosophy has been carried over into the Treasury's newest responsibilities, where it has become a perennial fear that the whole economy is likely to become overstrained, that as a nation 'we are trying to do too much'.[37]

Morale

A third feature of the post-war situation was a sharp drop in the public estimation of civil servants. Although not easy to substantiate or quantify, there is a very strong impression that the civil service enjoyed a status and reputation before the war which it lost afterwards. The service became less attractive to potential recruits. Salaries and conditions of service tended to fall behind; other opportunities were opened to school and university leavers; with the result that for most of the post-war period the Civil Service Commission has had difficulty in satisfying its appetite.

The enlarged functions of government must have affected the situation. The civil service was an obvious target for the frustration caused by restrictions and shortages. Moreover, there were more points at which the service impinged on the lives of the public; inevitably, more mistakes were made and they were more visible. With the volume of criticism and the size of their work-load rising in step, it was not surprising that many civil servants began to feel their job to be thankless and unrewarding.

Heterogeneity

The fourth characteristic which, if not new, became more pronounced in the post-war period, was variety and versatility. The new range of services brought civil servants at all levels into contact with a greater variety of people. New patterns of consultation brought representatives of the professions, industrialists, trade unionists, scientists and pressure groups of all kinds into the penumbra of government. Administrators found themselves working with new kinds of specialists, as colleagues and as advisers, and having to learn something of their language and techniques.

Their range of activity also became wider. Some were still engaged in the kind of quasi-political work described by Dale – preparing briefs to be inserted at the right time and the right place in the government machine. At the same time (perhaps in the same department) a colleague might be considering what light social survey techniques could throw on a problem which a committee was investigating. Another might be handling judicial work of rare complexity, like the Principal in the Civil Service Commission who sat for four years with a staff of over a hundred to decide what candidates were eligible for special examinations on the ground that they had received a number of years' 'full time continuous and systematic education'.[38] Others would be more concerned with horizontal relationships, collaborating with people in other departments and outside the civil service to get things done. Others, again, were beginning to look downwards, at management and organization, applying new managerial techniques to the business of conducting large enterprises, like the hospital service, without waste of resources.

And yet, as one reads not what outsiders said the civil service ought to be doing but what civil servants and Ministers say they actually were doing, the overall impression is one of continuity. Critchley's account of an Assistant Secretary's day, written about 1950, is almost identical with Dale's account of his pre-war equivalent, with one conspicuous exception. The pre-war Assistant Secretary tended to work from 10.30 a.m. to 7 p.m. on weekdays and 1 p.m. on Saturdays. Ten years later his successor's hours were 9.30 a.m. to 7 p.m. or 8 p.m. on weekdays, with a few files taken home for good measure, and possibly to 3 p.m. or 4 p.m. on Saturday. Both writers were worried about the effect on quality of increasing work-load.[39]

Notes

1 H. Parris, 'The Origins of the Permanent Civil Service 1780–1830', *Public Administration* Vol. 46 (1968) p. 143.
2 *Report on the Organisation of the Permanent Civil Service* (Northcote–Trevelyan Report) C. 1713 (1854). Reprinted in *Report of the Committee on the Civil Service 1966–68* (Fulton Report) Cmnd. 3638 (1968) Vol. 1, Appendix B.
3 K. C. Wheare, *The Civil Service in the Constitution* (a lecture given to mark the centenary of the Northcote–Trevelyan Report) (London, 1954).
4 Fulton Report, Vol. 1, para. 1.
5 Parliamentary Papers 1854–55, Vol. xx, *Papers on the Re-organisation of the Civil Service*, Appendix, 'Census 1851 – Supplementary Tables on the Civil Service'. See also M. Abramovitz and V. F. Eliasberg, *The Growth of Public Employment in Great Britain* (Princeton, N.J., 1957) pp. 16–18.
6 *Papers on the Re-organisation of the Civil Service*, p. 411.
7 *Select Committee on Miscellaneous Expenditure 1847–48*, xviii, p. 151, quoted in E. W. Cohen, *The Growth of the British Civil Service* (London, 1941) p. 88.
8 *Papers on the Re-organisation of the Civil Service*, pp. 135–228.
9 H. R. G. Greaves, *The Civil Service in the Changing State* (London, 1947) p. 9.
10 Sir George Newman, *The Building of a Nation's Health* (London, 1939) p. 103.
11 Lord Bridges, *The Treasury*, 2nd edn (London, 1968) p. 90.
12 Abramovitz and Eliasberg, op. cit., Table 4, pp. 40–4.
13 *Report of the Committee on Ministers' Powers*, Cmd. 4060 (1932) pp. 21–4.
14 Civil Service National Whitley Council, *Report of the Joint Committee on the Organisation of the Civil Service* (London, 1920).
15 *Report of the Royal Commission on the Civil Service 1929–31* (Tomlin Report) Cmd. 3909 (1931).
16 *Report of the Royal Commission on the Civil Service 1929–31*, Minutes of Evidence, p. 1268 (evidence from Sir Warren Fisher).
17 H. E. Dale, *The Higher Civil Service of Great Britain* (Oxford, 1941) pp. 38–9. The later quotations are from pp. 121, 37 and 220. Dale's description of the relationship between a senior civil servant and

his Minister agrees almost point for point with Lord Morrison's post-war account of the relationship from a Minister's point of view in *Government and Parliament*, 3rd edn (Oxford, 1964) Chap. XIV.

18 H. J. Laski, *Reflections on the Constitution* (Manchester, 1951) pp. 164–5.

19 *Report of the Joint Committee on the Organisation of the Civil Service*, clause 32.

20 *Report of the Committee of Inquiry on the Post Office* (Bridgeman Report) Cmd. 4149 (1932).

21 *Social Insurance and Allied Services*, Report by Sir William Beveridge, Cmd. 6404 (1942).

22 Greaves, op. cit., pp. 221–3.

23 *Employment Policy*, Cmd. 6527 (1944).

24 Sir John Anderson, 'The Machinery of Government', *Public Administration* Vol. 24 (1946) p. 153.

25 Abramovitz and Eliasberg, op. cit., p. 25.

26 See, for example, Sir Richard Clarke, *The Management of the Public Sector of the National Economy*, Stamp Memorial Lecture (London, 1964).

27 Abramovitz and Eliasberg, op. cit., Table 4, pp. 40–5.

28 T. A. Critchley, *The Civil Service Today* (London, 1951); G. A. Campbell, *The Civil Service in Britain*, 2nd edn (London, 1965); Frank Dunnill, *The Civil Service: some human aspects* (London, 1956); C. H. Sisson, *The Spirit of British Administration: and some European comparisons* (London, 1959); Nigel Walker, *Morale in the Civil Service: a study of the desk worker* (Edinburgh, 1961).

29 Sir Oliver Franks, *The Experience of a University Teacher in the Civil Service*, Sidney Ball Lecture (Oxford, 1947); E. Devons, *Planning in Practice* (Cambridge, 1950).

30 Franks, op. cit.

31 *The Administrative Class of the Civil Service*, Cmd. 6680 (1945).

32 *Report of the Royal Commission on the Civil Service 1953–55* (Priestley Report) Cmd. 9613 (1955) para. 413.

33 *Report of the Public Enquiry into the Disposal of Land at Crichel Down*, Cmd. 9176 (1954). This case and its implications are discussed in K. C. Wheare, 'Crichel Down Revisited', *Political Studies* Vol. 23 (1975) pp. 390 – 408.

34 *H.C. Debs*, Vol. 530 (20 July 1954), cols 1284–7.

35 Morrison, op. cit., pp. 335–6.

36 Sir Edward Bridges, *Portrait of a Profession*, Rede Lecture (Cambridge, 1950) p. 23.

37 S. Brittan, *The Treasury under the Tories 1951–64* (London, 1964) p. 38.

38 Civil Service Commission, *86th Report, covering the Reconstruction period* (London, 1954) p. 11.
39 Dale, op. cit., pp. 27–32; Critchley, op. cit., pp. 71–3.

II
The 1960s:
a decade of enquiry

By the early 1960s leaders of British opinion had begun to seek remedies for disorders in the economic and financial management of their affairs. The wage-price spiral continued to rise. Economic growth was checked by stop-go policies. Problems such as imbalance between the regions seemed to be becoming worse. At the same time there was no overall plan to settle priorities within the growing total of public expenditure. There was a feeling that national prestige was waning and it was natural to look for a scapegoat.

Labour supporters blamed the Conservative Government. Academic economists blamed that Government's advisers. Many felt obscurely that part of the trouble lay in the weakness of Parliament. But the main targets of criticism were administrative methods and institutions and the quality of civil servants themselves. Controversies about the civil service that had been smouldering for half a century were re-ignited. It was claimed that senior civil servants were selected and trained in a way that discouraged vitality and creativity. Their social origins, their university subjects and their lack of outside experience combined to make them a narrow élite from whom not much could be expected. They were not interested in management and had no feeling for technology. They were secretive and used the doctrine of ministerial responsibility to conceal their (apparently negative) use of power. As for the real experts, there were not nearly enough of them, and the administrators were careful to keep them away from any position of real influence. 'In sum, there are new functions to be performed. They require new forms of organization and new men with new skills.'[1]

At the centre of the permanent apparatus of government was an enormously powerful Treasury, controlling the budget and all public expenditure, controlling the civil service, influencing pay throughout much of the public sector, responsible for exchange control, short-term financial regulators and, since 1947, for economic coordination and such economic planning as existed. Inevitably, the Treasury was at the centre of most of the storms.

The Treasury under attack

In 1957–8 the Estimates Committee of the House of Commons looked at 'Treasury Control of Expenditure' and found it inconsistent and haphazard. There was no system of control – rather a shapeless bundle of procedures and precedents. The Treasury was solemnly authorizing the loan of naval flags to churches while apparently lacking any means of supervising hospital expenditure running into hundreds of million pounds.[2] The Committee's recommendations led eventually to a largely internal study under the Lord Plowden who had been Chief Planning Officer to Morrison and Sir Stafford Cripps in 1947. The published Plowden Report is a rather unsatisfactory summary of the main points in a series of confidential reports to departments, which provided a framework for a new look at our institutions for controlling public expenditure. Although the main problem was 'how to bring the growth of public expenditure under better control, and how to contain it within such limits as the Government think desirable', the Committee's approach was very broad. 'The kernel of the matter' was 'what the machine of government is trying to do, what its attitudes are, what it regards as important, and its approach to its work on all matters involving public expenditure'.[3] The Plowden Committee was assisted by a well-known management consultant (Mr E. F. L. Brech) and its report stresses the importance of management. This was defined to include:

1 The preparation of material on which decisions are based.
2 The technical efficiency with which larger administrative operations are carried out.
3 The cost-consciousness of staff at all levels.
4 The provision of special skills and services (e.g. organization and methods, training, and the quantitative techniques of statistics, costing, accountancy and operational research).
5 The awareness and effectiveness with which these are used.
6 The training and selection of staff for posts at each level of responsibility.

The Committee found that heads of departments did not give enough time to management compared with their other duties of advising on policy and accounting for expenditure. Nor was management experience shared between departments. The Treasury should therefore build up a management service and develop techniques to help departments, among other things, to relate the value of an activity to the cost of carrying it out. (The consequences of this recommendation will be described in later chapters; they include some notable achievements. But when an official described the Treasury's management functions to the Royal Institute of Public Administration in the year following the report his examples were mainly concerned with office machinery.[4])

The most important outcome of the Plowden enquiry, however, was the 'forward look' at commitments for several years ahead so that major decisions could be taken 'in the light of surveys of public expenditure as a whole . . . and in relation to the prospective resources'. In 1963 the Government published the results of an early survey in the first of a series of White Papers. It became apparent that the country was committed to a level of expenditure that could not be met painlessly unless the whole economy was expanding. Faster economic growth became a major policy objective and a new task for the civil service.

But not for the Treasury. In 1962, as a result of the Plowden enquiry, the Treasury had been reorganized into two 'sides', one responsible for the pay and management of the civil service and the other, under a separate Permanent Secretary, for finance and economics. But many people felt that the Treasury outlook was too geared to passive coordination and regulation. A new central agency was needed to carry out a positive planning role. At the end of 1964 the Treasury lost its responsibility for long-term economic planning to the new Department of Economic Affairs, which published the optimistic and ill-fated National Plan early in the following year. The DEA was a very 'modern' department, with unconventional staffing patterns giving great weight to temporary experts. It was fairly small, with no executive responsibilities of its own, but powerful enough under its first Secretary of State (Mr George Brown) to challenge the Treasury on its own ground.

Whatever was right or wrong with the Treasury, it had become a convenient symbol for all that was supposed to be stuffy and out-of-date in the civil service. It was soon to lose its dominating position in civil service management also. This position had been under intermittent attack for a long time. In 1964 a Fabian group which included many serving civil servants argued that the Treasury was bound to bring a restrictive, uncreative attitude to its personnel work because of its primary concern with economy. Establishment work should be transferred to a reformed Civil Service Commission.[5]

Although the 1963–4 Estimates Committee had taken a fairly kindly view of the way the Treasury had gone about its job since the Plowden reforms,[6] a report on recruitment in the following year hinted at some serious deficiencies and recommended that a committee be appointed 'to initiate research upon, to examine, and to report upon the structure, recruitment and management of the Civil Service'.[7] This recommendation was accepted by the Government, who in February 1966 announced the appointment of a committee, under the chairmanship of Lord Fulton, with very similar terms of reference. Of its twelve members, three were academics, all of them social scientists and known to be sympathetic to the Labour Party, four were senior civil servants, two administrators and two specialists, two were MPs, two were businessmen and the other the leader of a white-collar trade union.

The Committee's report was published in June 1968.[8] Its main finding was that the structure and practices of the service had not kept up with its changing tasks. The blame for this was laid at the door of the Treasury: 'Despite the recent improvement in its management services the Treasury has failed to keep the Service up to date.'[9] One of its principal recommendations, therefore, which was among the three that were accepted by the Government on the day of publication, was that responsibility for central management of the service should be given to a new Civil Service Department under the direction of the Prime Minister. Various arguments were advanced in support of this transfer, some of which were fairly weak, and the main justification appears to have been symbolic, 'to demonstrate that a fresh start is being made'.[10] In this respect the Committee was in tune with the widely-held belief in the 1960s that performance could be improved by structural reforms. This was a period in which there were frequent changes in the structure of central departments and in the distribution of functions between them. At the time when the Committee was sitting, investigations were also taking place into local government, Parliament and the relations between government and the nationalized industries.

The experience of the Department of Economic Affairs, which was wound up in 1969, and of the Civil Service Department itself, which generally has not lived up to the expectations of its advocates, has helped to dent the faith of those who believe in the efficacy of structural change. But that is another question which will be explored in Chapter XI. At this point we are concerned only to test the assertion of the Fulton Committee that the tasks of the civil service had changed. The Committee asked a group of management consultants to examine what civil servants actually did in selected parts of twelve departments. The consultants' general findings were made available separately in Volume 2 of the report. Their work is valuable partly for its descriptive content, and partly because it explains the logic behind parts of the main report. Blocks of work were assessed from a management point of view and, although the consultants (including a Treasury organization and methods man) were forced to acknowledge the effect of the political environment, their recommendations reflect an industrial rather than a public service outlook. Their findings need therefore to be supplemented by first-hand accounts from senior civil servants and politicians.[11]

Civil service tasks

When all the available material is taken into account, it is apparent that new responsibilities did not replace the old ones. However, public interest shifts from one aspect of public administration to another as new functions of government create new demands. In the debate about the Northcote–Trevelyan Report the main concern was about the reconciliation of intellectual qualities with loyalty, integrity and discretion. The Haldane Committee of 1918 was concerned that administrators should reflect and think ahead.[12] Between the wars there were doubts about the ability of 'conservative' civil servants to understand the needs of radical social policies and to serve a Labour Government. During and after the 1939–45 war, the expansion of services directly affecting the public brought anxieties about training and public relations that are reflected in the Assheton Report.[13] Twenty years later, questions were very properly being raised about the drive, the breadth of understanding and the technical expertise of administrators who might be required to make far-sighted proposals, going beyond the life of a parliament or even of a government, in areas of great technical complexity. But as new requirements appeared the old ones were still there – even the nineteenth-century regulatory and office-maintenance functions for which Northcote and Trevelyan tried to recruit the best available material. The demand for effectiveness and competence did not mean that economy and accountability could be neglected. Indeed, practically all that had been lost over the century was the need for the laborious copying of letters before the invention of the typewriter and its female accompaniment. This was recognized by the Fulton Committee, which did not suggest that any of the traditional skills and knowledge of the administrator could be dispensed with. The new requirements that it sought were additional.

It must be accepted that for the administrator to be an expert in running the government machine is not in itself enough.

He must in future also have or acquire the basic concepts and knowledge, whether social, economic, industrial or financial, relevant to his area of administration and appropriate to his level of responsibility. He must have a real understanding of, and familiarity with, the principles, techniques and trends of development in the subject-matter of the field in which he is operating.[14]

The following analysis of the work of the higher civil service at the time of the Fulton enquiry is drawn from many sources. It is tentative and can no doubt be improved, both by including additional categories and by making them more specific, but it is adequate for our present purposes. Although, as will be seen in later chapters, there were to be some further modifications in the 1970s, the functions of senior civil servants have not changed fundamentally and this picture will thus serve as a backcloth for much of the analysis in subsequent chapters.

(a) Working the machine

Someone in a department has to run the Minister's office. In the narrower sense, this is a job for a private secretary. The Minister has to be supplied with papers when he needs them, including material for speeches and letters; he also needs help in deciding which claims on his time have priority. In a broader sense, running the office is the job of the Permanent Secretary and his administrative staff. Before the Minister makes an executive decision, somebody must check that he is statutorily empowered to do so and has not forgotten the precedents of similar cases. If the Minister has ideas about new legislation, he will have to obtain authority from a Cabinet committee, after making sure that the Chancellor of the Exchequer is aware of the financial implications and that there will be no objections from other Ministers about repercussions affecting their territories. This, in essence, is how the system of collective responsibility works. To make it work, and to handle the related consultative and legislative machinery, requires a body of people who have expert knowledge and skill in the machinery of government, who know their own part intimately, several other parts nearly as intimately and have a general knowledge of the whole machine and the principles on which it works. This 'telephone exchange' function of the administrator, stripped of some of its present-day complexity, would be easily recognized by the administrators of the mid-nineteenth century. It has no real counterpart elsewhere.

(b) Representing the Minister

The Minister cannot personally discharge even that part of his duties which involves him as a political figure. He needs representatives who will present his view to interested groups in contact with his department, to subordinate agencies and to representatives of other Ministers at interdepartmental meetings. He needs people who will argue, persuade and bargain on his behalf and apply his general line of thought to detailed issues with which he will never have time to make himself familiar. Such a function can be carried out only by a group of people who, in Sisson's words, 'specialize in the awareness of Ministerial responsibility'.[15] These people do not only speak, write and think in his name; it will often be necessary that they should usurp part of his personality and prepare a speech or a letter for him as he himself would have prepared it.

(c) Formulation of major policy

Once, perhaps, the function of advising Ministers meant little more than the kind of office support described above. Nowadays it means suggesting what action the Minister should take. The process of formulating policy is distinct from taking decisions. It can be described as 'analysing the problems, defining the issues they present, and finding out what methods might be used to deal with them'.[16] This entails making available to the Minister all the special knowledge and techniques that are thought most relevant to the issue under consideration. Since no decisions would be made if *all* relevant considerations had to be sought and taken into account, it also involves the selection and evaluation of different aspects of a problem.

(d) *Deciding minor policy*

Nearly all observers agree that, in practice, all major issues (and many that are not major) are brought before the Minister personally. Nor does it rest entirely with his staff to decide which are major and which are minor. Discretion, however, is involved in the detailed implementation of his decisions. Anyone who has worked in a government department knows of questions of minor policy which are settled by civil servants at about Assistant Secretary or Under Secretary level on their own responsibility. Sir Edward Playfair provides two examples from his own experience.

> I was in charge of the arrangements for what had to be said to everybody in every part of the world about the devaluation of the pound, and I never enjoyed anything so much. It was important, urgent, tied in to great matters, yet not so big and vital that I could not manage it myself ...
>
> For an example of an independent piece of minor policy one needs a situation where something ought to be done by the machinery of politics which arouses no political feelings. You get your Minister's general blessing and go ahead with it. I had a good example of that. It was quite clear that the constitution of the National Gallery and the Tate Gallery wanted bringing up to date, so I asked the Chancellor if I might go ahead with it. He agreed: I negotiated with the Trustees of both bodies, I got everybody squared, I got a Bill drafted, I got it introduced and it all went marvellously.[17]

This sort of activity is different from those already discussed because of the increasingly technical issues involved. It is a significant element in the work load of higher civil servants.

(e) *Management*

There are many definitions of management. The Plowden Committee's definition (pp. 48–9) was very wide. What is meant here is something narrower: management in the sense of getting things done – and getting them done with the human, financial and physical resources available. Policy has to be implemented at various levels. The Minister's own department has to be organized, equipped and staffed. This may involve decisions about the recruitment and training of people with special skills or about statistics and the use of computers to help in formulating policy for a decision. Policy may also have to be implemented through agents, and management skills may be involved in helping them to do something that they do not particularly want to do and may even believe to be impossible with the resources they have. Or the Minister may be directly responsible for a large executive service (for example running social security offices) in which day-to-day service decisions have to be taken in much the same way as in commercial industry. The parallel with industry can never be exact. It is just possible, although rather misleading, to compare a Permanent Secretary with the managing director and his Minister with the chairman of a company. But a body of shareholders normally has a simple and direct interest in one aspect of the company's activities and does not, if things are going well, take the same delight as Members of Parliament in spotting errors of detail. Nevertheless, the modern civil service does have management responsibilities which are perhaps closer to those of industry and commerce than its other functions. The Fulton Committee rightly pointed out that 'the management of the department's executive activities' constitutes the work of most (that is to say not necessarily the top) civil servants.

Taking these functions as a starting point, we can start to translate them into specifications for the composition and design of the administrative machine. It then becomes possible to study problems in public administration as special cases of general problems in organizations and to consider the relevance of research and experience in quite different contexts. We can also identify problem areas where more research is needed and see the lines on which this might be carried out. (In some cases, this may not amount to much more than repeating in a public institution an investigation that has already proved fruitful elsewhere.) Most importantly, it gives us the opportunity to distinguish different components of the public administrative machine and to examine them, as far as possible, both in isolation and as parts of a whole. The tendency in the past (this was in some ways true of the Fulton Report) has been to try and find general solutions for particular problems without taking the trouble to study their repercussions.

It is convenient to distinguish the human implications from the structural implications of this analysis. An organization consists of people arranged in a particular way. The people and the structure interact to produce a form of behaviour. But it is helpful to focus separately on the individuals and on the way they are organized.

A government department which is designed to meet the five main functions described above seems to need personnel who *collectively* possess the following characteristics (the order is not important): personal loyalty to the Minister; easy familiarity with all aspects of the government and parliamentary machines; reluctance to act on proposals until they have been tested from every possible point of view; unwillingness to take risks that might cause embarrassment to the Minister; detachment from any particular policy and willingness to change direction after a change of government; a scrupulous approach to the *mode* of administration (for example above-board contract procedures) and to record-keeping against subsequent challenge; a legalistic awareness of precedent and principle; literary and presentational skills; negotiating and persuasive ability; a sensitive awareness of political mood and climate; the resilience necessary to meet short-term pressures: intellectual and synthesizing ability of a very high order; imagination and far-sightedness; knowledge of modern data-handling techniques; specialist knowledge in depth of each field of administration; knowledge of and sympathy with other people's problems; good judgement; interest, involvement and perseverance in a current field of work; vigour and readiness to initiate, and to press new ideas on political leaders; courage to take decisions and stand by them; cost-consciousness; the ability to lead junior staff.

The list is, of course, an impossible one. It includes personality attributes (intelligence, imagination) as well as knowledge, skills and attitudes that can be cultivated by training and experience. Some qualities, like vigour and caution, or personal loyalty and commitment to the job in hand, are opposites. Others, like imagination and detachment, are on the whole unlikely to co-exist in the same person. It is also clearly impossible that one person would possess all the special knowledge relevant to the consideration of a problem of any complexity. The whole list suggests a need to cast a fairly wide net in order to ensure that all the qualities are to be found among a Minister's senior staff. Instead of looking for the impossible all-rounder, attention has to be given to the organization that links people together.

Similar problems emerge from a list of the structural requirements for such an organization. There are many alternative ways of grouping individuals in an organization, with differing effects on their relationships, behaviour and communication patterns. It is again possible to deduce some particular requirements from the five main functions. The following list is not claimed to be unique or exhaustive. With the possible exception of (6), each pattern was directly or indirectly advocated at some point in the Fulton Report.

1 The organization should be stable: stability and continuity will maximize the benefit of past experience and ensure that proper attention is given to the future implications of a policy.
2 Waste and delay should be eliminated by encouraging specialization, avoiding overlaps, and locating particular knowledge, authority and skill clearly in one part of the organization; each department should be organized along the most effective lines for its particular function and as few people as possible should be involved in each decision.
3 The communication system should be designed to ensure that all available knowledge and skill, from outside as well as inside the organization, is made available as and when the relevant problem is under consideration; consultation should be extensive (and decision-making must therefore be slow); authority patterns should not be so rigid as to inhibit contributions from all participants.
4 Career patterns should be broad, so that experience is pooled and interdepartmental coordination made easier; all departments, therefore, should be organized along similar lines; and finance and personnel work should be centralized.
5 The organization should be designed to respond rapidly to

change, whether political, economic, social or technological.

6 The organization must be designed so that political decisions
  are transmitted quickly and accurately to the point at which they
  are implemented.

7 To encourage new ideas and the acceptance of responsibility,
  the organization should be supportive, and encourage both
  originality and bold decision-making even if mistakes are made
  in the process.

8 Unless every question is going to the top, the department should
  be designed in a way that incorporates some device for resolving
  disputes; there must be a clear line of authority.

Here again, perhaps less obviously, there are inconsistencies. A
system that encourages creativity is unlikely to be either tidy and
economical or good at transmitting instructions and resolving
disputes. Similarly, an organization designed to assemble all
possible material bearing on a problem is unlikely to be designed
for speedy action. Nor is it easy to combine centralized finance
with the devolution of authority, or to combine short, clearly
articulated lines of command with a flexible use of specialist
knowledge. We shall return to these points in Part Two.

The Fulton analysis

As we have seen, the Fulton Committee's general diagnosis was
that the civil service had failed to keep pace with changes in its
tasks. Now that these tasks have been examined, we must consider
the Fulton Report in greater detail. In the Committee's view the
outdatedness of the service was symbolized by the dominant
position of 'the amateur (or "generalist" or "all-rounder")'.

The ideal administrator is still too often seen as the gifted
layman who, moving frequently from job to job within the
Service, can take a practical view of any problem, irrespective
of its subject-matter, in the light of his knowledge and
experience of the government machine ... The cult is obsolete
at all levels and in all parts of the service.[18]

The Committee therefore advocated the development of a more
dynamic and professional civil service. By professional it meant

that civil servants should be skilled in the performance of their work and should have a fundamental knowledge of and deep familiarity with its subject-matter. Such professionalism was to be developed in various ways. First, a majority of the Committee argued that the relevance to civil service work of the subject-matter of a candidate's university studies should be an important qualification for appointment and that, without preventing the admission of 'outstandingly able' candidates from any discipline, the selection procedures should give some preference to those who had pursued relevant courses, for instance in social studies and in science. Once admitted, the Committee argued that administrators should specialize in a particular area of administration and receive training specially geared to their work. After examining various bases for such specialization the Committee proposed that administrative work might be divided into two categories, each having its own substantial and broadly-based body of knowledge: that which was primarily economic and financial; and that which was social. It therefore advocated that civil servants should be recruited to one of these two areas and that their subsequent careers and formal training should be geared to the development of expertise in that field. The Committee called for a general expansion of central training through the establishment of a Civil Service College which would provide major courses in administration and management, together with a wider range of shorter and more specialized courses in both management and vocational subjects, and which would conduct research into problems of administration and the machinery of government.

The Committee's second main attack was on the class structure of the civil service. The system of stratified classes, dividing the service horizontally (between higher and lower in the same broad area of work) had evolved from the Northcote–Trevelyan Report. In addition, there was a rigid vertical demarcation between different skills, professions or disciplines. Each civil servant was recruited to a particular class and this determined his prospects and the range of jobs on which he could be employed. In the view of the Committee this compartmentalized structure impeded the efficiency and effectiveness of the service. It recognized that some movement between classes had always been possible but regarded the procedures as being excessively 'formal and restrictive' and argued that

> rigid and prolific compartmentalism ... prevents the best use of individual talent, contributes to the inequality of promotion prospects, causes frustration and resentment, and impedes the entry into wider management of those well fitted for it.[19]

It therefore proposed the abolition of the class structure and its replacement by a unified grading structure covering the entire civil service. Such a system would remove any artificial barriers in the way of an able civil servant progressing right up the hierarchy. In addition, no post would be the preserve of any group, management being free to appoint to each post the person it considered best fitted by his qualifications and experience to fill it.

This change would benefit two particular groups of staff identified by the Committee as needing special attention. First, the Committee was concerned that specialists, such as engineers, accountants and economists, were unable to exercise the full responsibilities or corresponding authority which they ought to have, both because policy and the financial aspects of work were reserved to administrators and because specialists received insufficient training in management. This defect was to be overcome both by the abolition of classes, thus opening up new jobs to specialists, and by the provision of management training for specialists at the Civil Service College. The second problem area identified by the Committee was in the middle range of administrative posts. It argued that the civil service had suffered from a failure to recruit graduates of average ability who had been unsuccessful in the highly selective Assistant Principal competition and who regarded a career in the executive class, with only limited prospects of transfer to the administrative class, as insufficiently attractive. Believing that the service thus cut itself off from a field of potential recruitment which was expanding fast and which contained many who would formerly have been recruited straight from school, the Committee proposed a larger graduate entry, all of whom would enter on the same training grade although the most able might receive additional salary.

A third criticism made by the Committee was that there was

insufficient contact between the service and the community. This was partly because most civil servants spent their entire working lives in the service and partly because the administrative process was shrouded in too much secrecy. The Committee accepted that a career service should be maintained

> in the sense that most civil servants should enter at young ages with the expectation, but not the guarantee, of a lifetime's employment; and that the great majority of those who come to occupy top jobs will in practice be career civil servants.[20]

However, it argued that civil servants enjoyed too much security of tenure and were too insulated from the outside world. To encourage more movement in and out of the service in mid-career, it recommended that pension arrangements should be made more flexible, that more late entry and secondment should be encouraged, and that the service should be more ruthless in dispensing with those who were no longer needed or useful. It also proposed that an enquiry should be established into unnecessary secrecy.

The service's lack of contact with the community was, in the Committee's view, exacerbated by its social and educational exclusiveness. A survey it commissioned revealed that there had been little change in the administrative class in this respect since the war; 67 per cent of its members in 1967 had fathers in Social Classes I and II, 56 per cent had attended independent and other fee-paying schools, and 64 per cent were graduates of either Oxford or Cambridge universities.[21] A number of the Committee's proposals were therefore designed to make senior civil servants 'more representative, geographically, educationally and socially, of the nation at large'.[22] This was believed to be a desirable objective in itself on the grounds of social justice. However, the Committee does not appear to have considered how far this objective was compatible with its other principal aim of making the service more professional in the performance of its duties.

The Committee's failure to explore the consistency of its recommendations can in part be explained by looking at its composition and the conditions under which it operated.[23] Although the approach of a majority of its members can be described as progressive, there were differences of opinion on many questions and, as is common in official enquiries, great efforts were made to retain unanimity. In particular the Committee was anxious to retain the support of its civil service members and to produce a report that was acceptable to all the civil service staff associations, as it believed that this would increase its likelihood of being adopted. This meant that many of its recommendations had to be couched in general and occasionally ambiguous terms. The Committee also had to work under a very strict time constraint. Both these factors lie behind its decision to produce a short report, amounting to only 91 printed pages, which was clearly intended to advance a set of principles for reform, rather than a detailed blueprint as to how this could be implemented. It also decided, with at least one dissentient, to include some paragraphs designed to toss a number of 'high-explosive bombs' at the civil service in order to justify its proposition that radical changes were needed and to spark off further discussion and investigation.[24]

If one of the Committee's aims was to be controversial there can be no doubts as to its success. For much of the last ten years debate has revolved around its diagnosis and its specific recommendations. Some of these have been implemented; some were rejected by the government either immediately or after further investigation; and others have become inappropriate as political and administrative conditions have changed. In the next three chapters we will examine in more detail the situation at the time of Fulton and assess subsequent developments, both in the civil service and in the environment in which it operates.

Notes

1 It would be tedious to give detailed references for all these comments. They are derived from B. Chapman, *British Government Observed* (London, 1963); Fabian Tract No. 355, *The Administrators* (London, 1964); S. Brittan, *The Treasury under the Tories* (London, 1964); M. Nicholson, *The System* (London, 1967); H. Thomas (ed.), *Crisis in the Civil Service* (London, 1968). The last quotation is from R. Neild, 'New Functions: New Men?', *The Listener* Vol. LXXII (27 August 1964) p. 304.

2 *Sixth Report from the Estimates Committee 1957–58*, H.C. 254–1, 'Treasury Control of Expenditure'.

3 *Control of Public Expenditure*, Cmnd. 1432 (1961).

4 W. W. Morton, 'The Management Functions of the Treasury', *Public Administration* Vol. 41 (1963) p. 25.

5 Fabian Tract, *The Administrators*, op. cit.

6 *Fifth Report from the Estimates Committee 1963–64*, H.C. 228, 'Treasury Control of Establishments'.

7 *Sixth Report from the Estimates Committee 1964–65*, H.C. 308, 'Recruitment to the Civil Service', p. xxxv.

8 *Report of the Committee on the Civil Service 1966–68* (Fulton Report) Cmnd. 3638 (1968).

9 Fulton Report, Vol. 1, para. 21.

10 Fulton Report, Vol. 1, para. 253. One of the arguments in favour of this transfer was that personnel work and the control of expenditure called for two different kinds of expertise. But this problem could have been overcome by the Committee's own proposal for specialization within departments. It is also surprising, if the argument about special expertise is sound, that the first head of the CSD, Sir William (later Lord) Armstrong, had formerly been in charge of the financial and expenditure 'side' of the Treasury.

11 For example, Lord Morrison, *Government and Parliament*, 3rd edn (Oxford, 1964); H. Wilson, E. Powell *et al.*, *Whitehall and Beyond* (London, 1964); Sir Edward Boyle, Sir Edward Playfair *et al.*, 'Who are the Policy-Makers?', *Public Administration* Vol. 43 (1965) pp. 251 ff.; T. D. Kingdom, 'The Confidential Advisers of Ministers', *Public Administration* Vol. 44 (1966) p. 267; R. H. S. Crossman, *The Diaries of a Cabinet Minister*, Vols. 1–3 (London, 1975, 1976, 1977); E. Boyle and A. Crosland with M. Kogan, *The Politics of Education* (London, 1971).

12 *Report of the Machinery of Government Committee* (Haldane Report) Cd. 9230 (1918).

13 *Report of the Committee on the Training of Civil Servants*, Cmd. 6525 (1944).

14 Fulton Report, Vol. 1, para. 41.

15 C. H. Sisson, *The Spirit of British Administration* (London, 1959) p. 13.

16 N. Johnson, 'Who are the Policy-Makers?', *Public Administration* Vol. 43 (1965) p. 282.

17 Playfair, op. cit., p. 263.

18 Fulton Report, Vol. 1, para. 15.

19 ibid., para. 16.

20 ibid., para. 134.

21 Fulton Report, Vol. 3(1), pp. 52, 80, 83.
22 Fulton Report, Vol. 1, para. 288.
23 The dynamics of the Fulton enquiry are discussed by the secretary to the Committee, R. W. L. Wilding, in 'The Post-Fulton Programme: Strategy and Tactics', *Public Administration* Vol. 48 (1970) pp. 399–401. See also the chapter on Fulton in R. A. Chapman (ed.), *The Role of Commissions in Policy-Making* (London, 1973).
24 Wilding, op. cit., p. 400.

main tasks of the C.S.
/ (a) Working the machine
/ (b) Representing the Minister
/ (c) Formulation of major policy
/ (d) Deciding minor policy
/ (e) Management.

III

The civil service today: administrators

The next two chapters outline the main features of the British civil service as it was at the beginning of 1977. Apart from a few notes on the overall size and composition of the civil service, this chapter is concerned with those engaged in administrative work. Specialist civil servants are discussed separately in the next chapter.

Size and composition of the civil service

In January 1977 the size of the civil service was 746,000.[1] Of these, 572,000 were non-industrial staff, the remainder being industrial workers, about three-quarters of whom worked for the Ministry of Defence in establishments such as ordnance factories and naval dockyards. In recent years there has been growing concern about the number of employees in the public sector. The civil service itself, however, accounts for only 11 per cent of the public work-force and 3 per cent of the working population of the United Kingdom. Nor has its size increased significantly since the war. Excluding Post Office staff, who ceased to be civil servants in 1969, the size of the civil service in 1977 was almost exactly the same as in 1950. In contrast, the number of local government employees more than doubled during the same period. However these aggregate figures conceal a major shift in the composition of the service. Whereas in 1950 the non-industrial civil service constituted less than 60 per cent of the total, by 1977 it amounted to more than 75 per cent.

It is this change which has given rise to the popular image of the civil servant as a bowler-hatted administrator working behind closed doors in Whitehall. In fact this picture is misleading. 75 per cent of non-industrial civil servants work outside Greater London, and over 40 per cent work in local offices which have direct contact with the public. The three largest departments, Defence, Health and Social Security, and Inland Revenue, employ more than 50 per cent of the total.

The size of the non-industrial civil service at the end of 1976 was about three and a half times that of 1939 and more than 50 per cent greater than in 1960. A large part of this expansion can be attributed to the increased workload of government and to the creation of additional departments to undertake new tasks. For instance, between 1965 and 1968 there was especially large growth in departments such as the Ministry of Social Security and the Ministry of Labour, both of which had new responsibilities and new schemes to administer. Moreover, aggregate figures for the non-industrial civil service do not bring out marked variations between departments. Thus, while the staff of the Ministry of Defence grew by only 5 per cent between 1960 and 1970, that of the Home Office increased by 74 per cent, the Ministry of Labour (renamed Department of Employment in 1968) by 43 per cent and the Department of Health and Social Security by 40 per cent. More recently, absolute changes have occurred. In 1975 there were major increases in staff in the Department of Health and Social Security and the Inland Revenue to cope with the extra work caused by unemployment and inflation, but the total size of the civil service rose only marginally as these were offset by reductions in defence manpower.

These figures include all non-industrial staff ranging from the most senior civil servants to typists, messengers and cleaners. They can be divided, as in Table 3.1, into staff groups. 75 per cent are engaged in general administrative work. 44 per cent belong to the Administration Group itself and a further 31 per cent are engaged in local and regional casework, such as tax collection, the administration of social security benefits, or in secretarial work. The remaining quarter of the non-industrial civil service belongs to a wide range of professional, technical and specialized occupations, as the titles of their groups suggest. This division between administrators and specialists contrasts sharply with the position in local government. It is not easy to produce comparative figures, but one study estimates that, excluding teachers and policemen, almost 40 per cent of local government staff are employed in professional or technical capacities; if teachers and policemen are included the figure rises to over 60 per cent.[2]

Table 3.1
Non-industrial civil service: principal staff groups
(January 1977)

	Numbers	% of non-industrial civil service
Administration	251,350	44
Inland Revenue*	52,440	9
Social Security*	43,840	8
Professional and technology	43,460	8
Secretarial	28,980	5
Science	18,090	3
Other†	133,840	23

* Mainly the local and regional staff of these departments; senior staff are members of service-wide groups.
† The remaining 23 per cent of the non-industrial civil service are members of smaller general and departmental groups.
(Derived from *Civil Service Statistics 1977*)

The Administration Group

The Administration Group was formed in 1971 by the merger of the three general service classes into which most non-specialist civil servants had been recruited since the end of the First World War.[3] Its structure, extending from the grade of Clerical Assistant (earning in 1977 about £2,000 per annum) to Assistant Secretary (whose annual salaries ranged in 1977 from £8,650 to £11,000), is set out in Table 3.2.

There are three main points of entry into the Administration Group, each with its own level of educational qualification. Applicants for clerical posts must normally possess GCE O levels (usually taken at age 16). Two passes are needed for appointment as a Clerical Assistant and five for Clerical Officer. Executive Officer (EO) recruits must have a minimum of five GCE passes, including two at A level (which is taken at about age 18). In practice, however, many have better qualifications, and an increasing proportion of entrants at this level, amounting to 45 per cent in 1977, are graduates.[4] When the Administration Group was formed, however, it was intended that the normal graduate point of entry should be the Administration Trainee (AT) grade. External candidates at this level, between 120 and 200 of whom are recruited each year, must possess an honours degree. They compete for entry with internal candidates who were originally appointed at lower levels. There are no barriers in the Administration Group to prevent the promotion of an able civil servant irrespective of his point of entry, but in practice most remain in the range of grades linked to their level of educational attainment. Nor is there much skipping of grades in the hierarchy. This does, however, occur in the middle of the structure. Most ATs are appointed to the grade of Higher Executive Officer (A) (HEO(A)) and are promoted to Principal without having to serve in the intermediate grade of Senior Executive Officer (SEO). The remainder proceed more slowly to the level of Principal through the grades of Higher Executive Officer (HEO) and SEO. Promotion from the Principal grade also can either be to Senior Principal or direct to Assistant Secretary.

The number of staff employed in what is now the Administration Group has increased rapidly. Between 1964 and 1973 the relevant grades increased at an annual rate of 2·5 per cent.[5] After a dramatic increase of almost 7 per cent in 1974, expansion has been halted and there has been some drop in numbers. In recent years, growth has been particularly rapid at two points. Between 1971 and 1977 there was a 35 per cent increase in the number of EOs and a 67 per cent increase in HEOs, reflecting among other things the

Table 3.2
The Administration Group
(The number of staff at each level in January 1977 is shown in brackets)

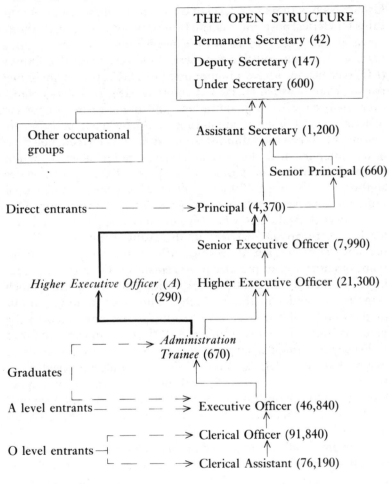

→ Main channels of progression
➤ 'Fast-stream'
– ➤ Main sources of recruitment
Training grades are shown in italics

greater volume of routine work necessitated by the collection of taxes and the administration of social security benefits. This is a continuation of a well-established trend, the number of executive posts having increased by about 30 per cent between 1950 and 1970. The other growth point in recent years has been at the level of Principal, where there has been a 50 per cent increase since 1971. The actual numbers involved in this case are, of course, very much smaller, but this expansion contrasts with earlier post-war experience, there having been little growth in the number of administrative posts between 1950 and 1970. This change not only reflects growth in the scale of government but also a greater complexity in its tasks. For instance, more senior staff have been needed to handle the government's new powers of intervention in industry and to manage and coordinate the work of giant departments such as the Department of Health and Social Security and the Department of the Environment.

Table 3.3

Staff associations representing administrative staff

	Civil service membership	Main grades represented
Association of First Division Civil Servants	6,200	Higher administrative grades (+some senior specialists such as economists and lawyers).
Society of Civil and Public Servants	89,400	Middle administrative grades.
Civil and Public Services Association	178,700	Clerical, typing and machine operator grades.
Inland Revenue Staff Federation	61,000 61,000	Departmental grades in the Inland Revenue.

(Source: Derived from *Eleventh Report from the Expenditure Committee 1967–77*, H.C. 535, Vol. II(I), p. 137)

One of the principal reasons for the creation of the Administration Group was to unify the career structure of administrative staff in the civil service. However, differentiation has not been eliminated entirely, in part because the old class divisions are still reflected in the pattern of membership of the various staff associations which represent administrative staff, as can be seen from Table 3.3.

In addition, there are five other staff associations in the civil service, of which easily the largest are the Institution of Professional Civil Servants, which represents 86,500 specialist and technical staff, and the Civil Service Union, with 44,700 members drawn mainly from the messengerial and cleaning grades. Together these nine associations comprise the staff side of the Civil Service National Whitley Council. This Council provides machinery for negotiation and consultation on matters affecting the service as a whole, including for example the implementation of many of the Fulton Committee's proposals. However, on many important issues the views of the associations diverge, and this has major implications for staffing policy. The changes in the structure of the service have themselves had important repercussions. The absorption of some departmental grades into the Administration Group has led their staff associations to merge with service-wide associations. There have also been a number of demarcation disputes, for instance between the First Division Association and the Society of Civil and Public Servants as to who should represent Administration Trainees and Higher Executive Officers (A).

Open Structure

In 1972 an Open Structure was created at the top of the civil service. It covers about 800 staff at the level of Under Secretary and above (who in 1977 earned salaries ranging from £12,000 to £20,000). Posts at this level are filled by the most suitable people without regard to their academic background or previous employment in the civil service. A unified grading structure, set out in Table 3.2, has been established.

The incorporation of former specialist posts into the Open Structure makes it difficult to gauge changes in the number of administrative posts at this level. What evidence there is suggests that, although there has been some increase over the last ten years, particularly at the level of Under Secretary, the growth has been gradual. It cannot therefore be attributed simply, as some have suggested, to the establishment of larger departments. For instance, the number of Under Secretaries in the area of work which was the responsibility of the Department of the Environment between 1970 and 1976 grew from 45 to 71 between 1965 and 1976, but over half this increase had occurred before unification took place and presumably therefore reflected a heavier workload generally and the greater complexity of most government activity.[6]

Recruitment

The basic features of the system of recruitment to the civil service were established in the latter part of the nineteenth century. Recruitment is the responsibility of the Civil Service Commission which, although it has been part of the Civil Service Department since 1968, enjoys complete independence in individual selection decisions. Traditionally these decisions were based upon written examinations set by the Commission in academic subjects, the assumption being that administrators needed general abilities similar to those called for by academic study. Since the war, however, these examinations have gradually been abandoned in favour of methods of selection based upon interview and various tests, both written and oral, designed to measure general ability and aptitude for administrative work. This change does not, however, mean the abandonment of an academic criterion. As we have seen, there are three main points of recruitment to the Administration Group, at each of which an appropriate level of performance in school or university examinations is normally required.

Methods of selection

Recruitment to clerical posts has generally been delegated by the Civil Service Commission to departments except in cases where there are difficulties. Those possessing the required O levels are selected on the basis of interview alone. However, as this has not always produced sufficient candidates, departments also recruit clerical staff without the minimum qualifications on the basis of special short-answer tests. The recruitment of Executive Officers

(EOs) is also based primarily upon interviews. Since 1976, however, the number of candidates has been so great that the Commission has had to introduce a written qualifying examination consisting of two objective tests of intellectual ability and a set of job-related problems for candidates to solve. The standard of this examination is set to provide a ratio of 3 : 1 between candidates interviewed and vacancies to be filled.[7]

Administration Trainees (ATs) are recruited through a selection procedure still known as Method II, although the alternative system based upon written examinations – Method I – was abolished in 1969.[8] The age limits for candidates to the AT scheme are between 20 and 28 for external applicants and between 21 and 32 for applicants from within the service. External candidates must possess an honours degree in any subject; inservice candidates must have completed at least two years' service, although those with degrees (amounting to 50 per cent of internal successes in 1973) may apply sooner. The selection procedure is in three stages: (a) written qualifying tests, lasting a day and a half, and consisting of a précis, statistical interpretation and constructive thinking exercises and various objectively marked tests; (b) a series of tests and interviews at the Civil Service Selection Board, lasting two days, designed to test candidates' aptitude for the type of work undertaken by administrators in the civil service, such as drafting letters and answers to parliamentary questions and chairing discussions; (c) an interview before the Final Selection Board which is conducted by two civil servants and two outside members under the chairmanship of one of the Civil Service Commissioners.

A small number of administrators are also recruited from outside at higher levels. Between 1968 and 1976 an average of 36 direct-entry Principals have been appointed each year. Candidates are required to have held a responsible post in industry or commerce, at a university or in some professional field. Selection is by tests and interviews at the Civil Service Selection Board and the Final Selection Board. A very small number of direct-entry Assistant Secretaries are appointed to specific posts which call for expertise not normally available in the civil service.

Evaluation

How successful are the civil service's recruitment methods? This question can be answered both quantitatively and qualitatively. On the first count, the civil service has had little difficulty in recent years in recruiting sufficient numbers of staff at all levels, except for certain jobs in the London area (see below).[9] However, this is a marked change from past experience and is largely a reflection of the contraction of job opportunities generally and of a reduction in the number of posts to be filled. For most of the post-war period the civil service has experienced recruitment difficulties at all levels. For instance, in the early 1960s there was an annual short-fall of about 5,000 clerical staff. Similarly, at the end of 1973 there were 3,500 Clerical Officer and 2,500 Clerical Assistant posts unfilled, necessitating the recruitment of staff without the normal educational requirements.

Middle grade recruitment has posed a different kind of problem for the Commission. On a few occasions since the war the number of EO vacancies has exceeded the number of suitable candidates and the gap has had to be met by the recruitment of older candidates, for instance from HM Forces, and by the promotion of clerical officers. In 1973 as many as 2,300 out of 7,500 EO vacancies were unfilled, 78 per cent of which were in London. Subsequently, however, lack of competition in the recession has meant that the Commission's problem has been an excess rather than a shortage of well-qualified candidates. This has led to the already mentioned dramatic increase in the number of graduates recruited at this level, thus removing the basis of the Fulton Committee's concern that the civil service was failing to attract sufficient numbers of middle range graduates.

Recruitment to the AT scheme started in 1971, and all vacancies have been filled since 1973. This marks a sharp change from the past. Since the war the Commission had experienced difficulties in recruiting sufficient numbers of graduates to the more exclusive training grade of Assistant Principal. There was consequently a shortage of staff in the basic Principal grade which had to be met by promotion from the executive grades and by direct recruitment from outside.

The AT scheme was designed both to ensure a larger graduate entry covering a wider range of ability and to improve the chances of promotion for those initially appointed to executive posts. It was therefore planned to recruit 250 or 300 candidates each year, of which a maximum of 175 would be recruited from outside, the remaining posts being reserved for internal candidates. However, as Table 3.4 shows, the balance of external to internal recruits has not been maintained at this level.

Table 3.4
Recruitment to the Administration Trainee Scheme

	Internal	*External*	*Total*
1971	55	125	180
1972	17	133	150
1973	28	199	227
1974	52	190	242
1975	43	185	228
1976	50	120	170
1977	32	111	143

(Figures from Civil Service Commission, *Annual Reports*)

In part these figures point to the success of the new scheme in attracting large numbers of well-qualified external applicants. They also suggest that the recruitment of more internal candidates could have been achieved only at the expense of standards laid down for the scheme and that the old class barrier was perhaps not the only reason why Executive Officers were not promoted in the past. The position has, however, been radically changed by the number of graduates now being recruited at EO level. This has meant that the Commission has only been able to recruit the most able outside applicants into the AT scheme. Indeed the recruitment situation of the service has changed so fundamentally since the scheme was drawn up that an official review was instituted in 1977. At the time of writing its report has not been published, but it seems likely to recommend a smaller entry of 'high-flying' graduates combined with an improved system of training and career development at EO level, which will be the main point of entry for graduates.

Such a scheme is unlikely to satisfy the staff associations representing middle management, who for some time have argued that the AT scheme should be abolished and that graduate recruitment should be confined to EO level.[10] They claim that the Commission has been recruiting the wrong type of person and that it places too much emphasis upon academic abilities rather than on experience of government work. This sort of assessment of a selection procedure is a difficult and subjective exercise, depending very much upon the qualities thought to be needed in a civil servant. Before examining this question in detail it must be stated that in one sense at least Method II generally has a good reputation. Thus, the Davies Committee complimented the Commission upon the accuracy of its procedures, noting that few Assistant Principals recruited in this way failed to have their appointments confirmed at the end of their probationary period and that the proportion who resigned their posts was very small. Moreover, they found some evidence that rankings in Method II were an accurate predictor of later career success.[11]

In other respects, however, Method II has been subject to severe criticism. In particular, concern has been expressed about the sort of people who are successful in the AT competition. For instance, in 1977 the House of Commons Expenditure Committee, during its major enquiry into the implementation of the Fulton Report, was struck by the fact that the increase in the number of recruits into the AT scheme compared with its predecessor appeared to have had little effect upon the social and educational composition of appointees. Thus in 1975 almost 60 per cent of those appointed from outside were graduates of Oxford and Cambridge (compared with 59 per cent in 1968); almost 50 per cent had been educated at independent or other fee-paying schools (compared with 59 per cent in 1968); 78 per cent had fathers in Social Classes I and II (compared with 82 per cent in 1968); and about 50 per cent had degrees in arts or humanities (compared with 54 per cent in 1968).[12] But, apart from recommending that the membership of the Civil Service Commission and its selection boards should be widened so as to remove some of the fears of in-breeding, the

Committee merely proposed another enquiry into Method II.[13] Some of its members, however, were more forthright in their condemnation.

> We recognise 'a bias of the civil service recruiting in its own image', a bias of the civil service paying too much attention to certain literary skills; a bias of the civil service in favour of the rounded individual of the sort created by the atmosphere of Oxford and Cambridge; and a bias of class, caste and cast of mind.[14]

Criticism of the pattern of recruitment to administrative posts in the civil service tends to be based on two arguments. First, it has been claimed that those who are involved in selection either consciously or subconsciously discriminate in favour of candidates with particular kinds of background which, in view of the composition of selection boards, are likely to be their own.[15] In other words it is suggested that 'irrelevant' factors are playing a part in selection decisions. Such a bias would be difficult to prove or disprove and, in any case, alternative explanations of the pattern of civil service recruitment can be advanced.

First, the standards of entry into Oxford and Cambridge are generally higher than those at other universities. Thus, if the civil service aims to recruit the most able graduates it is likely to recruit disproportionately from those two universities. The proportion of graduates in arts and humanities can also be explained in terms of the relative absence of equally attractive alternative careers for such students. In contrast, many scientists and social scientists, for instance economists, are able to compare prospects in the civil service with those offered in industry and commerce, which are frequently more attractive. Further, it can be argued that tradition plays a part. Oxford and Cambridge tutors appear to give students more encouragement to apply than their counterparts elsewhere and this is bolstered by the success rate of those who do apply. Similarly the disproportionate representation of those with middle-class origins may simply reflect the willingness of middle-class children to consider and compete for civil service posts, or the combination in such candidates of those skills and qualities that the civil service seeks. A similar trend is found in countries with such differing social, economic and political structures as Denmark, Turkey, the United States, France and India.[16] In any case, it must be remembered that the university population from which the civil service is recruiting at this level is disproportionately middle class. To this extent the civil service is a captive of the wider social and educational system in which it is placed.

The other argument concedes that the civil service recruits the most able applicants, defined in its own terms, but argues that these are not the people that it needs.[17] It is claimed, not that the selection procedures are biased, but that most civil service work does not require the kind of abilities which the selection procedures test. Thus, it is argued that greater attention should be paid to candidates' awareness and understanding of contemporary problems rather than to their abilities in traditional verbal and literary skills. It is also argued that conscious efforts should be made to ensure that recruits are more representative of the community as a whole. If these views are accepted the remedy then lies not simply in reform of the selection procedures but in redefining the qualities that the Commission seeks in candidates.

The debate about recruitment to the civil service revolves around the issues of social justice and efficiency. On the one hand it is argued that social justice demands that civil service selection procedures should be, and should be seen to be, fair both to external applicants, regardless of class, colour, sex or religion, and to those already employed at lower levels within the service. This may be advocated as a point of principle without regard to its effect upon the efficiency of the service. For instance, the ruling by an industrial tribunal in 1977 against the maximum age limit of 28 for appointment as an EO, on the grounds that it was unfair to women who were likely to be out of work for family reasons in their twenties and early thirties, was based less on an assessment of the needs of the civil service than on the need to promote equality of opportunity in employment.[18]

Alternatively, the case for a representative bureaucracy may be advanced on the ground that greater representativeness would facilitate the work of government by 'making it more sensitive and adaptive to the needs of society and more diversified in the talents and skills which it contains'.[19] Similarly the provision of good promotion prospects to those already working within the service can be justified not only on the ground that it is fair but also because such staff will have a distinctive contribution to make in the posts to which they are promoted since it ensures that at least some senior staff will have had experience of working at lower levels.

In both these respects, therefore, there is not a clear-cut choice to be made between a system of recruitment which is fair and one which is efficient. In practice the two are intertwined in a complex manner. There are thus few in this country who advocate a system of quotas for selection to the civil service as it is believed that this would have an adverse effect upon its efficiency. On the other hand, many are concerned about the present pattern of recruitment not only because they believe it is unfair but also because of the adverse effect it is thought to have on the effectiveness with which the civil service does its work.

Training

Recruitment policy has a major effect upon decisions about training. Given that the civil service recruits to the Administration Group on the basis of general ability rather than the possession of skills and knowledge relevant it its work, its needs have to be met through post-entry training. However, a wide range of training options remains open. Training can take place through practical experience of working in a post under the supervision of senior staff. Alternatively, staff can attend formal training courses which may be mounted internally or by outside institutions such as universities, polytechnics and colleges of further education. Such courses may be 'developmental' in that they prepare a civil servant for the rest of his career generally or they may be job-related in that they provide him with the skills needed in the particular job he will undertake on completion of the course. Still further variety results from decisions about the length of courses, their extent and the stage of a civil servant's career at which training should be provided.

The civil service has traditionally laid great emphasis at all levels on training at the desk under the supervision of a superior officer.

This remains very important, but since 1945 there has been a marked expansion of formal training.[20] Most of this, however, is 'job-related' and is run under the aegis of departments either internally through departmentally-run courses or externally, for instance on day-release at technical colleges. Only in the last fifteen years or so has much emphasis been laid on the need for developmental training. In 1963, however, a Centre for Administrative Studies was opened to provide central training for Assistant Principals. Within a few years a Treasury Working Party concluded that its courses were too short to cover adequately the full range of subjects relevant to management and that this type of training should be provided for a wider range of civil servants.[21] Its recommendation that central training should be strengthened was taken up and developed by the Fulton Committee which proposed the establishment of a Civil Service College.

The Civil Service College

The Civil Service College, which was opened in June 1970, operates in two locations, at a residential centre in Berkshire and a non-residential centre in central London.[22] (Originally there was a second residential centre in Edinburgh but this was closed in 1976 as an economy measure.) The College has three main functions. First, it runs courses which provide general managerial training, principally for staff at the level of HEO and above, including ATs, and which are developmental in their objectives. Secondly, it provides a wide variety of more specialized and technical courses, attended principally by more junior staff, in subjects such as management services and automatic data processing. Thirdly, it conducts research and seminars into problems of administration and the machinery of government. Table 3.5 gives the distribution of its training effort in 1976, illustrating that in terms of student course-days about two-thirds was linked to developmental work.

The College's staff consists of civil servants on secondment from their departments and university teachers employed full time on a contract basis. They provide about 40 per cent of the teaching, the rest being given by civil servants, academics and others brought in for specific courses and occasional lectures. Its first Principal was an academic social scientist, Professor E. Grebenik, who was succeeded in 1976 by a career civil servant, Mrs M. B. Sloman. At this time steps were taken to integrate the College more fully into the Civil Service Department, which has overall responsibility for civil service training, 90 per cent of which still takes place under the aegis of departments.

Table 3.5
Civil Service College: Allocation of training effort

	% *of student course-days in 1975–6*
Administration Trainees and HEO(A)s	22
Senior and middle management	26
Other developmental courses	18
Management services	10
Automatic data processing	18
Other technical courses	6

(Source: Derived from *Eleventh Report from the Expenditure Committee 1976–77*, H.C. 535, Vol. III, p. 889)

Training at AT level and above

The Administration Trainee programme is the largest and most comprehensive part of the College's work. ATs attend the College for two ten-week periods, at the end of their first and second years of service. During the first period they take courses in statistics, economics, law and public administration. Stage II is more closely related to the tasks ATs are likely to perform in the years immediately following attendance on the course. All ATs attend the following courses: Management of Staff, which aims to give them some awareness of the problems involved in dealing with staff and some training in appropriate management techniques; Policy Studies, which consists of an introduction to different theories of decision-making; and Financial Management and

Control of Public Expenditure, which examines some of the economic and financial techniques used in the public sector and the financial aspects of public policy. They also choose, under guidance from their departments, between a course on Government and Industry and one on Social Policy and Administration.

Apart from the twenty weeks they spend at the College, ATs work in a variety of carefully chosen posts designed to enable them to observe and contribute to the working of important areas of civil service work. Between their second and fifth years of service a streaming decision is made to select those who are appointed to the grade of HEO(A) and can expect to be promoted direct to Principal after a further 2–5 years. Under the original scheme, HEO(A)s attended the College for a further period of training, part of which dealt with subjects now included in the Stage II AT course and part of which consisted of a wide variety of options covering different aspects of government work. The last such course was held in 1975–6 and, as part of a general reorganization of the AT/HEO(A) programme, it was planned that HEO(A)s would attend a third ten-week course at the College. The first such course should have been held in 1977–8 but was one of the victims of the cutback in training in 1977.

The College also runs a wide variety of courses for more senior administrators in subjects such as personnel management, economics and social policy. Most of these are of short duration and are attended by only a small proportion of the relevant grade. Some are of a transitional nature in that they are designed to meet the needs of civil servants who were recruited before the development of central managerial training, but others will continue, building upon the AT/HEO(A) programme. At the highest levels, the College arranges short seminars for members of the Open Structure, many of which are also attended by senior officers in local government and the armed forces.

The College has attracted a large amount of criticism, particularly in relation to the courses it runs for ATs. Almost every aspect of this programme has been under attack and on a wide variety of grounds.[23] Some have argued that its courses are excessively academic. This criticism has been voiced by many of the ATs themselves who have resented being taken away from their jobs to undertake courses which in their view have little relevance to their work, and it has also been taken up by some of the civil service unions who argue that practical experience provides a better training than attendance at formal courses. Others, however, have attacked the College's courses for their superficiality and have sought to expand existing components and to add new ones. On other points, too, such as the timing of the College's courses and their staffing, the only point of agreement appears to be dissatisfaction with present practice.

In large part this dissatisfaction arises from the failure at the time of the foundation of the College to define its role unambiguously. As we have seen, the AT programme comprises less than a quarter of the College's training effort, and its energies have been diffused over a very wide range of courses for civil servants at almost every level. The range of its activities led one review of civil service training to comment that it had been expected 'to combine the roles of All Souls and an adult education centre, with some elements of technical education and teacher training thrown in for good measure'.[24] In this and other respects the College presents a marked contrast with its French counterpart, The *École Nationale d'Administration*.[25] *ENA* is an élitist institution dedicated to the recruitment and training of top-level non-specialist administrators and all its efforts are therefore directed towards their needs. The training provided by *ENA* is both very much longer, lasting two and a half years, of which seventeen months are spent on academic study, and also of much greater depth than that provided by the College. This contrast is all the more striking when it is remembered that entry to *ENA* is dependent upon passing academic examinations in many of the subjects it teaches, examinations which are of such high standard that almost all its recruits have attended special preparatory courses. Thirdly, performance in *ENA*'s final examinations has an effect upon career prospects, as successful trainees choose in order of merit from among vacancies in the service.

In this respect *ENA* has some similarities with a military staff college. The concept of a staff college is ill-defined, but most commentators stress the link between training and careers in that selection for courses of training either follows upon or precedes

promotion and that performance in training directly affects
subsequent prospects. The Civil Service College's role, however,
is very different. The only training programme attended by all
staff in a particular grade is that provided for ATs, and not even
in this case does performance have a direct effect upon subsequent
advancement. At higher levels attendance at the College depends
upon departmental nomination and is not a condition of further
promotion. This aspect of civil service training policy was singled
out by the Expenditure Committee in 1977 for criticism. It
advocated the abandonment of the AT scheme and its replacement
by a higher management training course for Assistant Secretaries,
attendance at which would be a condition of promotion to posts
at Under Secretary level.[26]

In summary, therefore, the College's present predicament is that
it is attempting to be 'all things to all men'. Many of its difficulties
stem from ambiguities in the Fulton Report which the Government
did nothing to resolve when it originally decided to set up the
College. On the one hand, the Fulton Committee wanted to
increase the efficiency of the civil service by making it more
professional, and thus it advocated development of training both
in general management and in the areas in which it proposed that
administrators should specialize (principally 'social' and 'economic'
administration). At the same time, however, it disliked the
exclusiveness it found in the senior levels of the service and was
therefore anxious that the benefits of the new professionalism
should be extended to staff at all levels. The College had therefore to attempt to produce a corps of super-administrators without
being able to devote more than a fairly small proportion of its
resources to this task. The College's difficulties also reflect a lack
of agreement in this country, both in the civil service and outside,
as to the relative value of formal training and practical experience,
which itself reflects an underlying disagreement as to whether
administration is an art or a science. Hardly surprisingly, there
is even less agreement as to the content of training programmes.

The controversy surrounding the AT programme has led the
College to make drastic revisions in it even in the short time it
has been in operation. Further changes may result from the current
official enquiry into the AT scheme and from the 1977 proposals

of the Expenditure Committee. If a long-term solution is to be found, a decision has to be taken as to priorities in civil service training. To do this, however, wider questions about the sort of qualities needed in administrators and the best means of obtaining them need first to be answered.

A career service

One of the distinctive features of a British civil servant is his permanence. Most civil servants are appointed when they are young and remain in the service until retirement age. Thus 72 per cent of the higher civil service in 1971 had spent their entire working lives in the service.[27] At lower levels about 75 per cent of SEOs and even 25 per cent of EOs in 1977 had been in the service for twenty years or more.[28] It has already been noted that only a relatively small number of staff are appointed other than to the main recruitment grades. For instance, in 1973 only 10 per cent of those at the level of Principal had been recruited directly from outside.[29] Nor is there much movement in and out of the service. In 1968 a scheme for the interchange of administrators was launched to promote secondments between the civil service and industry and other organizations for periods of about two years. However, the numbers involved are very small. In October 1975 only 23 civil servants were seconded to industry, local authorities and elsewhere, and only 56 outsiders were on secondment to the civil service.[30]

Not only are there few late entrants into the civil service, there are also few early leavers, whether as a result of resignation or dismissal. All civil servants have to complete a period of probation, but only a tiny proportion fail to cross this hurdle. After this they can be dismissed as a result of disciplinary proceedings or on grounds of inefficiency. Since 1971 this has also been possible 'in the public interest' and can occur for structural reasons, for instance if the age distribution in a particular group of staff has led to a serious promotion blockage, or on grounds of limited efficiency when it is in the interests of the service as a whole for an individual to be retired early because he can no longer cope adequately with the requirements of his grade. Dismissal is, however, a rare occurrence. Thus in 1976 only 235 members of the Administration Group (i.e. 0.1 per cent of the total) were dismissed.[31]

There is also little voluntary resignation. At one time it was difficult for a civil servant to move into other employment without losing his pension rights. Since 1972, however, with the introduction of a new Civil Service Superannuation Scheme, the accrued pension rights of anyone with five or more years' service can be transferred to a new employer, whether in the public or private sector, or preserved for payment at retirement age with an appropriate increase to take account of inflation during the intervening period. However, only a few take advantage of these provisions. Between 1971 and 1976 voluntary wastage varied between 5·1 per cent and 8·5 per cent of the non-industrial civil service, and a very high proportion of the leavers were young people occupying junior posts.[32] In 1976 50 per cent of those who left were under 25 and about 70 per cent of the men and 65 per cent of the women had completed less than three years' service. The vast majority of civil servants go on to normal retirement ages. The reluctance of civil servants to resign may in part be a reflection of their generous pension arrangements. One of the effects of the new scheme was to extend pension rights to all civil servants, many of whom (amounting to 29 per cent of non-industrial staff in 1967) had in the past held appointments which did not qualify for pension purposes. The scheme is also non-contributory and inflation-proofed, which makes it very attractive, particularly in times of high inflation.

The maintenance of a career service can be justified on various grounds. First, it is felt that the security given by permanent status is necessary to protect a civil servant whose skills may not be readily marketable in the outside world on the contraction or winding-up of his department. At higher levels it is also considered that security of tenure helps to ensure independence of advice to Ministers. In certain posts – those, for instance, which involve the handling of confidential information provided to the government by firms and individuals – it is necessary to maintain trust in the integrity of the service. For this reason, Under Secretaries and above must obtain special permission before taking up business appointments within two years of leaving the service.[33]

An essential condition for the maintenance of a career service is its political neutrality. Some restriction is placed on the freedom of all non-industrial civil servants to participate in politics. At present all officials above clerical levels are barred from national politics, but they may, with departmental permission, engage in local political activity. In 1978 an official committee recommended that such severe restrictions were needed only for a much smaller group of staff whose work was of a particularly sensitive nature.[34] Under its proposals, however, strict limits would still apply not only to officials in close contact with Ministers but also to those dealing with members of the public on such matters as tax and social security.

Career prospects

An essential condition for a career service is that recruits are assured of reasonable career prospects. Traditionally, a civil servant could look forward to several more or less automatic promotions in accordance with the normal expectations of the class to which he was recruited. At the very top, promotions have always been made on merit, but at lower levels it was assumed that all members of a class were equally well qualified, and promotion tended to take place in accordance with seniority rules agreed with the staff associations. A number of changes, however, have been made in recent years to modify this position. One of the aims behind the creation of the Administration Group was to facilitate the promotion of the able civil servant, whatever his point of entry to the service. The seniority rules have also been modified to enable good quality EO entrants, both graduates and non-graduates, to obtain early and rapid promotion both into the AT scheme and to HEO.[35] The qualifying periods for promotion have generally been shortened and, except in special circumstances, the minimum age for promotion has been abolished. In addition, provision has been made for staff to skip certain grades, for instance in the fast stream of the AT scheme.

At the top of the service, the creation of the Open Structure has opened the most senior posts to those who had not previously been members of the Administration Group, appointments being made solely on grounds of personal suitability, without regard to a candidate's method of entry to the service or his occupational stream.

However, these changes have not fundamentally altered traditional career patterns. It is still possible to predict fairly accurately the career prospects of particular civil servants, and most posts continue to be filled according to the traditional rules. In part, more radical changes have been prevented by the pressure of the staff associations, who have been concerned to protect the interests of the majority of 'average' civil servants. In any case, some of the changes have not had the effect that was intended. It has already been noted that the number of internal appointees to the AT scheme has fallen far short of the agreed figure; partly, perhaps, because of the reluctance of many EOs to move to London where most AT posts are located, but also, in the view of the staff associations, because of the over-academic nature of the AT competition.[36] On the other hand, a much higher proportion of ATs have been fast-streamed than was originally envisaged. In the original agreement it was intended that only one-third of each intake would be fast-streamed. In practice, however, for the two intakes for which all streaming decisions have been taken this proportion has been as high as 80 per cent.[37]

Nor has the creation of the Open Structure made very much difference to the nature of appointments to the highest posts in the civil service. Although, as we will see in Chapter IV, 40 per cent of its posts are filled by people who were previously employed as specialists, almost all of them are in posts which are a natural specialist extension of their earlier careers. At the very top of the service only two of those serving as Permanent Secretary or Second Permanent Secretary in 1977 had held non-administrative posts earlier in their careers.

Thus it is clear both that promotion remains a predictable process, with only a few opportunities for exceptional progress upwards, and that there is little lateral movement between occupational groups at the most senior levels. The post-Fulton reforms in the structure of the civil service have removed some of the formal barriers to both vertical and horizontal movement but they have not led to many such appointments being made. This is not altogether surprising. Given that there is some logic behind the structure of the service in terms of the level and type of abilities needed at different points in the hierarchy and in different types of post, the abandonment of traditional career patterns could only be at the expense of efficiency. On the other hand, the removal of the obstacles which prevented such movement even in exceptional cases can be justified both in terms of fairness to individual civil servants and the contribution it makes to improving the quality of civil service work.

Although the career patterns of most civil servants are fairly predictable, this is not to say that they all spend their working lives in a narrow range of posts. Many Executive Officers do spend their entire careers in a special field of administration, becoming specialists in the management of local offices, in the interpretation of a tax or insurance code, or in the application and development of management techniques. But other executive and nearly all administrative civil servants move among a succession of posts, sometimes fairly rapidly, gaining general rather than specific experience. For instance, in 1977 the average tenure of a post at Under Secretary or Assistant Secretary level in the Department of the Environment was two and a half years, and in the Treasury it was only one and a quarter years and one and three-quarter years respectively.[38]

The advantages of this system were reiterated by the Civil Service Department in 1969 when it rejected the type of administrative specialization proposed by the Fulton Committee.[39] In practice, however, specialization of a different kind is well established. Most administrators spend their working lives in the departments to which they were originally allocated by the Civil Service Commission (or if there is a transfer of functions – say from the Department of the Environment to the Department of Transport – they often follow a block of work to its new home). Thus, examination of one post-war intake of Assistant Principals reveals that, sixteen years after recruitment, 87 per cent of those remaining in the service were in either the same department or its functional successor. Although the range of functions of most departments is very wide, there is usually some functional coherence, and an *esprit de corps* is generated by departmental loyalties among colleagues who work together over long periods without necessarily spending long in any one post.

The only civil servants for whom departmental specialization is not the norm are those who are destined to occupy the most senior posts. Those who seem likely to go all the way to the top tend to be identified fairly early and to be given opportunities for really wide experience in different departments. There is some truth in the gibe made by a former civil servant that 'the more they think of you the faster they move you about'.[40] Such breadth of experience is secured by the intervention of the Civil Service Department which is responsible for career management over the service as a whole and is consulted about the filling of the highest posts. Although there is great variety in the career patterns of those in the higher civil service, a high proportion of them have served in more than one department and many have worked at some stage in one of the 'central departments' (Treasury, Civil Service Department and Cabinet Office).[41] Less than one in six of those occupying Permanent Secretary or Second Permanent Secretary posts in 1977 had spent all their careers in the same department. However, 80 per cent of them had experience in at least one of the 'central departments'. In this way an attempt is made to ensure that the most senior administrators do not become too closely identified with a particular departmental viewpoint, and that they have experience of looking at departmental problems from the perspective of the government as a whole.

Conclusions

Career management thus reinforces the generalist character of administration in the civil service which is founded on patterns of recruitment and training. This aspect of staffing policy has been maintained in recent years despite severe criticism from the Fulton Committee and from some of the staff associations, alleging that generalists are no longer capable of performing the tasks of government effectively and that this policy has produced an élite of senior administrators who are cut off both from the majority of civil servants and from the rest of the community. The latest onslaught has come from Labour members of the Expenditure Committee in 1977.

> They [civil servants] come to the civil service ... with what Balliol men used to refer to as the unconscious realisation of effortless superiority ... Their self-anointed superiority brings them almost immediately up against their obvious and almost complete lack of experience, the lack of which does not improve as much as it might with their work, experience or training. In short, there is conflict between their superior intellect and the little that they have to offer in a practical way.[42]

That far-reaching changes have not been made in the principles of recruitment, training and career management in response to this sort of criticism is not merely evidence of the First Division Association's instinct for self-preservation and of its strength in relation to the other staff associations. It also brings into question the main charges that have been levelled against the generalist administrator. Some critics have argued the case for greater social and educational representativeness and for the provision of better opportunities for the promotion of junior staff purely in terms of justice. But most believe that reforms along these lines would improve the effectiveness of the civil service. It is this latter claim which has been rejected by those in charge of the service in recent years.[43] Their view is that the case for the generalist administrator is still basically sound and that many of the reforms proposed by the service's critics could only be implemented at the expense of efficiency. It is argued that too much stress can be laid upon the possession of formal qualifications and too little on the sort of knowledge and understanding gained from a general education and practical experience.

Underlying this argument is a particular view both of the nature of administration and of the effects of the political environment in which the civil service operates. The view of the Civil Service Department is that the skills required in administration can in large part be acquired only by experience, and that in senior posts the need is for staff of high intellectual and verbal ability who have wide experience of different kinds of government work.[44]

The generalist has also been defended on the grounds that he is able to offer Ministers, most of whom have had little previous experience of the work of their departments, the sort of support they need, and that the conventions of individual and collective ministerial responsibility point to a need for officials who appreciate the implications for their work both of parliamentary scrutiny and of a system of decision-making which attaches great importance to securing agreement between departments.

These factors not only account for the maintenance of the generalist character of administration in the civil service. They also have a major effect upon the role of specialists, which will be examined in the next chapter. However, the critics of the generalist have not been silenced, as the report of the Expenditure Committee in 1977 illustrated. In this continuing debate it is essential that changes in the staffing pattern of the civil service are assessed in their full political and administrative context. Some changes can be and have been introduced without far-reaching consequences, but more radical reforms would need to be accompanied by major alterations in the relationship between Ministers and officials and between the executive and the legislature. The whole question of the recruitment and training of administrators is therefore of particular importance; it will be explored further in Chapter XIII.

Notes

1 This figure, and most of those in this section, comes from the Civil Service Department's *Civil Service Statistics 1977* (London, 1977). Its figures for the non-industrial civil service relate only to home civil servants and have therefore had to be adjusted from other sources.

2 B. C. Smith and J. Stanyer, *Administering Britain* (London, 1976) p. 178.

3 The structure of the Administration Group is outlined in the Civil Service National Whitley Council's report, *Fulton – the Reshaping of the Civil Service: Developments during 1970* (London, 1971) pp. 33–6. The Government's response to the Fulton recommendations in general is set out in a memorandum submitted by the Civil Service Department to the enquiry conducted by the General Sub-Committee of the Expenditure Committee into the civil service; *Eleventh Report from the Expenditure Committee 1976–77*, H.C. 535, Vol. II (I), pp. 1–49.

4 Civil Service Commission, *Annual Report for 1977* (London, 1978) p. 8.
5 These figures are based upon *Civil Service Statistics 1977* and the Fulton Report, Vol. 4, 'Civil Service Manpower Statistics', pp. 195–256.
6 The increase in the number of posts at Deputy Secretary level and above is set out in the Expenditure Committee, op. cit., Vol. III, pp. 1173–4. On the Department of the Environment, see A. Clark, 'Ministerial Supervision and the Size of the Department of the Environment', *Public Administration* Vol. 55 (1977) pp. 197–204.
7 Civil Service Commission, *Annual Report for 1976* (London, 1977) p. 8.
8 The system of recruitment is described in the Civil Service Commission's publication, *Appointments in Administration 1978* (London, 1977).
9 These figures are based upon the annual reports of the Civil Service Commission and on the Fulton Report, Vol. 4, loc. cit.
10 The views of the Society of Civil and Public Servants and the Civil and Public Services Association on the AT scheme are set out in their evidence to the Expenditure Committee, op. cit., Vol II (II), pp. 505–8.
11 *Report of the Committee of Inquiry on the Method II System of Selection*, Cmnd. 4156 (1969).
12 ibid., pp. 115–17; and Expenditure Committee, op. cit., Vol. II (I), pp. 235–8.
13 Expenditure Committee, op. cit., Vol. I, paras 13–15.
14 ibid., p. lxxxiv.
15 ibid.
16 V. Subramaniam, 'Representative Bureaucracy: a re-assessment', *American Political Science Review* Vol. LXI (1967) p. 1010.
17 See, for example, the evidence of the Society of Civil and Public Servants and the Civil and Public Services Association to the Expenditure Committee, op. cit., Vol II (II), pp. 496–508.
18 Civil Service Commission, *Annual Report for 1977* (London, 1978) p. 10.
19 This argument is examined with some scepticism by Nevil Johnson in his 'Recent Administrative Reform in Britain' in A. F. Leemans (ed.), *The Management of Change in Government* (The Hague, 1976) pp. 286–8.
20 The development of training since the war is outlined in the Fulton Report, Vol. 4, pp. 513–33.
21 Fulton Report, Vol. 5(1), 'Report of a Working Party on Management Training in the Civil Service', p. 60.

22 The history of the College can be traced in its annual reports, published by HMSO, which include the Principal's Report to the Advisory Council. See also the papers by B. C. Smith, R. Mair and E. J. Razzell, in R. A. W. Rhodes (ed.), *Training in the Civil Service* (London, 1977).

23 See R. A. Chapman, *Teaching Public Administration* (London, 1973) pp. 35–7, and *Civil Service Training*, Report by R. N. Heaton and Sir Leslie Williams (London, 1974) pp. 14–26.

24 *Civil Service Training*, op. cit., p. 14.

25 The work of *ENA* and its relevance to Britain is discussed by Anne Stevens in Rhodes (ed.), op. cit., pp. 64–78.

26 Expenditure Committee, op. cit., paras 20–30.

27 P. Sheriff, *Career Patterns in the Higher Civil Service* (London, 1976) Table 17, p. 59.

28 *Civil Service Statistics 1977*, Table 5, pp. 32–3.

29 *Third Report of the Civil Service Department 1971–73* (London, 1974) para. 75.

30 Expenditure Committee, op. cit., Vol. II (I), pp. 17–18.

31 *H.C. Debs*, Vol. 939 (18 November 1977) cols 369–70.

32 *Civil Service Statistics 1977*, pp. 6–7.

33 In 1975 a standing advisory committee was set up to advise on such applications. See *H.C. Debs*, Vol. 894 (3 July 1975) cols 495–6.

34 *Report of the Committee on Political Activities of Civil Servants*, Cmnd. 7057 (1978).

35 Expenditure Committee, op. cit., Vol. II (I), pp. 16–17.

36 Expenditure Committee, op. cit., Vol II (II), pp. 505–8.

37 This figure relates to the 1971 and 1972 intakes and is based upon information provided by the Civil Service Department. The proportion of external ATs who were fast-streamed was almost 90 per cent.

38 Expenditure Committee, op. cit., Vol II (I), p. 56.

39 See Civil Service National Whitley Council, *Fulton: A Framework for the Future* (London, 1970) pp. 15–17.

40 J. Sleigh, 'Civil Service Selection', *New Statesman* (29 April 1977) p. 560.

41 Sheriff, op. cit., Table 15, p. 57.

42 Expenditure Committee, op. cit., Vol. I, p. lxxix.

43 For example, see Sir Douglas Allen's evidence to the Expenditure Committee, op. cit., Vol II (II), pp. 808 ff.

44 Expenditure Committee, op. cit., Vol. III, pp. 871–4.

IV
The civil service today:
specialists

Emergence of a need for specialists

The Northcote–Trevelyan Report of 1854 contained only a passing reference to the recruitment of specialists, saying that so long as there was a suitable choice of subjects the principles of open competition were 'not inconsistent with the appropriation of special talents or attainments to special departments of the public service'. The Superannuation Act of 1859 made special provision for the appointment of officers whose qualifications were 'wholly or in part professional or otherwise peculiar and not ordinarily to be acquired in the Civil Service'.[1] At this time the main groups of specialists were inspectors and surveyors. Half a century later, the MacDonnell Commission found civil service lawyers, doctors, engineers, architects, surveyors and natural scientists in addition to the inspectorates of constabulary, schools, etc.[2] The scientists were augmented after the foundation of the Department of Scientific and Industrial Research in 1915. The Institution of Professional Civil Servants (IPCS) was established in 1919 to represent the interests of specialist civil servants, although it did not really become a major organization until the Second World War. By that time, new functions of government were demanding new forms of expertise, and inevitably more civil servants with external qualifications were being recruited.

By 1955 about 25 per cent of the non-industrial civil service were professional, scientific or technical staff and this proportion has been maintained since then. In 1977 60 per cent of those working at the salary level of Principal and above were specialists and just over 40 per cent of the posts in the Open Structure were held by staff with a specialist background.[3] The rapid growth in senior posts in part reflects pressure from the IPCS for higher status and better promotion prospects. But it also reflects the increasing importance of specialist contributions to management and policy. For example, from 1964 until 1976 a Chief Scientific Adviser was attached to the Cabinet Secretariat, and since 1967 a distinguished academic statistician has been in charge of the Central Statistical Office which is an integral part of the Cabinet Office. Increasingly, also, experts have been appointed by Ministers as temporary civil servants to advise on particular problems.

The growing complexity of government organization and decision-making has also created a demand for new specialist skills among administrative civil servants. Executive Officers are often specialists in management services (for example, organization and methods or automatic data processing), in stores or contract procedures or in a branch of social security or taxation law. They handle conveyancing and litigation work in the Treasury Solicitor's Office and in the Land Registry, where they 'virtually run practices in their own right'. Although since 1975 there has been a Government Accountancy Service its numbers are small and administrators still carry out the bulk of government accountancy.[4] Senior administrators also frequently develop competence in a specialized field. For instance, one Assistant Secretary in the late 1960s had spent nearly twenty years on Organization and Methods and Work Study. The relatively few administrators with degrees in science and technology tend to be concentrated in 'relevant' departments; so do the larger number of those with degrees in economics. But there is a clear distinction between specialization by a member of the Administration Group, who is always liable, in theory at any rate, to be transferred to other work, and membership of a specialist group whose work in government 'is just one of a number of career opportunities for the exercise of their qualifications and skills'.

The term 'specialist' is applied in the civil service to a wide variety of staff. Some, such as doctors, architects and lawyers, are members of established professions with their own regulatory bodies. Others do not have formal professional status but range from those with high-level qualifications, such as economists and scientists, to those who are technically qualified, for example draughtsmen or experimental officers. In the past, specialist staff were organized into separate classes based upon different types of specialism and upon the level of their qualifications. Following the Fulton Report this class structure was to some extent rationalized. Specialists are still organized separately from administrators, but there are now two large occupational groups. The Professional and Technology Group contains over 40,000 staff and includes engineers, architects, surveyors and draughtsmen, and their supporting technical staff. The Science Group comprises 18,000 scientific staff, ranging from those with O level qualifications to senior staff at salary levels equivalent to an Assistant Secretary in the Administration Group. The remaining specialists are either members of smaller occupational groups, such as the Economist and the Statistician Groups, or of service-wide classes such as accountants, medical officers and psychologists. The largest employer of specialist staff is the Ministry of Defence, which has 60 per cent of the Science Group and a similar proportion of the Professional and Technology Group. The other major employer of specialists is the Department of the Environment, where 50 per cent of the non-industrial staff in 1976 were specialists, two-thirds of whom worked for the Property Services Agency as architects, engineers, surveyors, etc.[5]

Status of specialists

Traditionally, specialist civil servants have worked outside the main stream of administration. The first serious discussion of their proper place in the administrative system occurs in the report of the 1929–31 Tomlin Commission, to whom the IPCS had represented (unsuccessfully) that specialist advisers in all departments should have the right of access to the Minister on important questions involving technical considerations.[6] Specialists resented the idea that their views would reach the Minister only through an intermediary who, as a non-professional, might misrepresent them. They also resented the monopoly of senior posts in most departments by the administrative class.

Since the 1930s the trend has been towards an enhancement of the opportunities and status of specialists. For instance, following the 1932 Bridgeman Report, technical staff at the Post Office, then a government department, were given a major voice at policy levels and senior posts were filled by promotion of the best man available. During and after the Second World War special consideration was given to providing an attractive career for government scientists, with the result that their position, for instance in the Ministry of Defence, has not noticeably been one of inferiority to the administrator. However, most specialists remained in a subordinate position, and by the 1960s this gave rise to serious problems in places such as the Ministry of Public Building and Works and the Highways Division of the Ministry of Transport, where large numbers of professional staff were working under the financial and policy direction of administrators. Although there were experiments with new patterns of organization that gave more senior posts to professional staff and integrated them more fully into the 'line' structure, these did not satisfy the IPCS.

> The role of the specialist, however, is still largely subordinated to that of the administrator ... Despite interesting developments in some departments, the general position of specialists is still grossly unsatisfactory ... It would be wrong to perpetuate or deify the wholly unwarranted mystique that it is only a member of the administrative class who can understand the machine and advise on policy ... No man should be effectively debarred at any level because of his speciality, whether it be science, engineering, medicine, law, administration or any other branch.[7]

This argument was taken up by the Fulton Committee, which claimed that 'many scientists, engineers and members of other specialist classes get neither the full responsibilities and corresponding authority, nor the opportunities they ought to have', and proposed various reforms designed to remedy this situation.[8] During the last ten years some steps have been taken in this direction but, for a number of reasons, the relationship between specialists and generalists is basically unchanged. Thus in 1976 the IPCS argued that 'the pre-Fulton attitude on the role of the specialist remains firmly entrenched'.[9] Before examining the reasons why traditional attitudes have been maintained, the changes that have occurred in the structural relationship between specialists and generalists and in the career opportunities open to the former must be outlined.

Structural changes

The traditional civil service structure is one of separate, though broadly parallel, hierarchies.[10] Below the Minister, and radiating from the Permanent Secretary, are a number of 'policy' divisions and branches. An administrator in one of these branches who needs advice on a technical problem will refer it to a specialist officer of approximately equal rank. The latter is a member of his own hierarchy, leading up to a chief professional officer who carries general responsibility for the quality of professional advice provided by his staff. For example, the original way of dealing with post-war school building was for the 'policy' (schools) branch to put technical aspects of building plans to an architects branch, consisting solely of professionals, whose job was to advise on specific points and to check that local authority plans conformed to the regulations; the architects had no concern with policy. The 'policy' branch also consulted HM Inspectors of Schools on educational aspects and, at that time, another administrative branch which dealt with building controls and priorities. This procedure proved to be cumbersome and frustrating in practice; it could not have coped with the rapid expansion of school building after 1949. In that year, coinciding with the appointment of a new chief architect, the separate branches were combined into a single architects and building branch, headed jointly by the chief architect and an administrator, who shared responsibility for all aspects of school building. Resident inspectors were attached so that the three principal skills needed for control of a national school building programme were represented in the combined branch. The work of the integrated branch was outstandingly successful. However, it was nearly ten years before the idea of 'joint responsibility' was applied in other departments. One such experiment was in the Ministry of Transport which, following comment by the Estimates Committee in 1962, had been reviewing the organization of its highway engineering staff.[11] Recruitment difficulties and poor morale seemed to be associated with the engineers' relationship with administrators, which was on traditional lines. A committee recommended that steps should be taken to improve the standing of engineers and to involve them more closely in administrative work. In particular it was recommended that the Ministry's highways organization should be headed by a Chief Engineer and a Deputy Secretary jointly (previously responsibility had rested only with the administrative Deputy Secretary). Below that level, it was envisaged that there would be mixed divisions of administrative and professional staff, some headed by 'twins' and others by an engineer or an administrator alone. These recommendations were implemented in stages from the end of 1963. Two years later the former chief engineer was put in sole charge of the administrative and professional aspects of highways with the title of Director General, Highways. Below him were a number of divisions, some with professional heads, some with administrative heads and some with both.

This sort of development was endorsed by the Fulton Committee, which criticized parallel hierarchies on the grounds that they led to delay and inefficiency because of the need for constant cross-reference between the hierarchies, and that they prevented specialists from exercising the full range of responsibilities normally associated with their professions and exercised by their counterparts outside the service. It therefore recommended that

Where administrators and specialists are jointly engaged in a common task, there should be a single integrated structure under a single head, who should be the man with the most appropriate qualifications for the job. Below him administrators and specialists should be integrated in teams or unified hierarchies, in which the individual posts are filled by administrators or specialists according to the requirements of the task.[12]

Arising out of this recommendation the Civil Service Department undertook a review of the structural arrangements in ten departments which employed significant numbers of specialist staff. Its report, completed in 1970, found that most departments were sceptical of the benefits of integrated hierarchies and, although the principle of the Fulton recommendation was reiterated, albeit in a less specific form, departments were given little encouragement to make major alterations in their structure.[13]

It is not surprising, therefore, that despite major changes in the overall structure of departments, few significant developments have occurred in the pattern of official hierarchies since 1970. Greater flexibility has been introduced in the deployment of staff, particularly in some of the departmental agencies and multi-disciplinary project teams that have been created, but in general the pre-eminent position of the administrator in financial and policy matters has been maintained. For instance, although the Rayner Report on Defence Procurement and Civil Aerospace, which was accepted by the Government, called for a structure which would get away from parallel hierarchies, the arrangements actually adopted in the Procurement Executive, set up in 1971 as an agency within the Ministry of Defence, basically place financial responsibility in the hands of administrators both at senior levels and in project teams.[14]

The only major example of structural reform since Fulton occurred in the Ministry of Public Building and Works (MPBW) and has been developed by its successor, the Property Services Agency, which was created in 1972 as an agency within the Department of the Environment.[15] The PSA provides, equips and maintains a wide range of buildings and installations for government departments, the armed services, the Post Office and other clients, and manages a large part of the government's land and property at home and overseas. It employs nearly 23,000 staff, 70 per cent of whom are members of the Professional and Technology Group. Its structure reflects the reorganization which took place in MPBW in 1969 when parallel hierarchies were replaced, at Under Secretary level, by a series of units responsible for meeting the needs of a particular client or group of clients. From Under Secretary upwards, policy, financial and executive control were unified, with these senior posts being filled on an open basis. No changes, however, were made in the structure below the level of Under Secretary. The PSA has developed this structure, with executive responsibility resting with the Chief Executive and through him with the Deputy Chief Executives and their Directors, each of whom answers for an identifiable block of work. Separate chains of command still generally exist below the level of Under Secretary.

Career prospects for specialists

One object of these structural changes has been to remove artificial and restrictive barriers to communication between people engaged on a common task. Another has been to improve the status and morale of professional staff by blurring the distinction between generalist and specialist roles and enabling specialists to have greater influence over policy and management. Thus, one consequence of the structural changes in the highways organization of the Ministry of Transport was to open up senior posts to professionals. It was also made clear that the post of Director General would be filled by the most suitable person, regardless of his background; since 1965 it has been held first by an engineer and then by an economist.

This was the kind of flexibility that the creation of the Open Structure, covering more than 800 posts at the top of the service, was intended to achieve.[16] Moreover, to ensure that specialists are able to compete effectively for these posts, a Senior Professional Administrative Training Scheme (SPATS) was instituted in 1972 to provide specialists who show potential to reach senior posts with an opportunity, early in their careers, to broaden their experience in the wider fields of administration and management. Those selected for the scheme, most of whom are at Principal level, attend a three-month course in administration and management at the Civil Service College, followed by up to two years in an administrative post, normally in their own department. They then return to their specialism better equipped for responsibilities they may assume later in their careers. Steps have also been taken to provide early promotion for specialists so as to allow them to compete for Open Structure posts at a comparable age with members of the Administration Group.

At lower levels, various steps have been taken to introduce greater flexibility in the filling of posts. First, a number of 'opportunity posts' have been designated, mainly in the range of Executive Officer to Assistant Secretary, for which members of more than one occupational group are automatically considered. By September 1975 there were nearly 3,500 such posts, of which 40 per cent were completely open in the sense that any suitable official could be considered, the rest being open to members of certain agreed groups only. Secondly, it is now possible for a civil servant to transfer laterally between occupational groups, normally between grades at a roughly equivalent level, either on a temporary or permanent basis. Such moves could be made in the past but only after a complex process of re-certification by the Civil Service Commission.

The effect of these changes, however, has not been very great. Although 40 per cent of those in the Open Structure have a specialist background, nearly all of them are working in posts in their own discipline or profession. For instance, in the Department of the Environment in September 1976 about two-fifths of posts in the Open Structure were held by officials who had entered in a specialist grade. However the four Permanent Secretaries all had administrative backgrounds, and although there were seven specialists among the sixteen Deputy Secretaries, six of them were employed in posts directly related to their previous occupations. Thus, an engineer was employed as Chief Water Engineer, a planner as Chief Planner and an architect as Director General of Design Services. Although each of these posts involves wider policy responsibilities than their titles might suggest, it nevertheless appears that in this case the introduction of the Open Structure has made little impact upon the dominance of members of the Administration Group in the fields of policy advice and general management, and the experience of DOE is typical.[17] Nor have any of the other developments been on a large scale. The annual intake into the SPATS scheme is only about 25, and during the first four years only 78 officials finished both parts of the scheme.[18] Moreover, whereas promotion within the Administration Group has generally been faster than originally envisaged, equivalent opportunities have not been provided for specialists, and there is thus a marked difference in the age structure of equivalent grades in different occupational groups. Similarly, the number of opportunity posts is very small in relation to the total number of posts in the civil service (less than 0·2 per cent) and in 1976 only 300 of their incumbents differed in background from their predecessors. The number of officials who have taken advantage of the possibility of lateral transfer has also been very small. For instance, in 1975 there were 164 such moves, only a third of which involved transfer across the specialist/administrator boundary.

Pre-eminence of the generalist

That these reforms have not been more far-reaching is not altogether surprising. Officially a cautious attitude has always been adopted towards those who advocate a more influential role for specialists. Thus, in its evidence to the Fulton Committee, the Treasury argued that

> Most scientific and professional officers would still make their careers in their own field and indeed wish to do so; and most senior scientific and professional posts would still need to be filled by men trained in these disciplines. At the same time, those who had spent their careers in general management and administration would tend to look to the general policy posts in the higher Civil Service. Moreover, at these levels, a high degree of expertise in government administrative processes and the working of a very complex machine is essential. The civil servants concerned have acquired a knowledge in depth of public administration which, as a profession, is as exacting in its demands as any other.[19]

The traditional relationship between the specialist and the generalist administrator has therefore generally been maintained.

In this respect British practice is unusual.[20] In France, for example, the specialist *technicien* is himself a member of an administrative élite: key posts at the Ministry of Transport are filled from engineers in the *Corps de Ponts et Chaussées*. In Australia, the professional enjoys higher status and salary than the general administrator and some posts, like those at the head of the Departments of Health and Works, are reserved for him. In the United States a high proportion of senior posts are held by scientists and engineers; specialist heads of bureaux carry more weight than generalists with Congressional Committees.[21] The higher status of the specialist in these countries is linked with calibre and qualifications. Traditionally, the Australian and American civil services have not been able to attract general graduates of the standard recruited in this country. On the other hand, the French *École Polytechnique* and the *École des Ponts et Chaussées* attract high quality applicants who are aiming at careers in public or private enterprise after a period in the civil service. Their graduates are trained in administrative law, economics and report-writing in addition to their engineering speciality; it is misleading to compare them with a newly recruited engineer in the British Department of Transport. A status pattern which is reinforced by recruitment and training tends to be self-perpetuating.

Another factor in accounting for the subordinate position of the specialist in Britain is political tradition. The key figure in the British tradition is the amateur gentleman-politician, who takes decisions by applying common sense and political judgement to the advice of experts.

> In these circumstances the volume of work demands that a Minister should be supported by a body of staff which can bring to bear on the work of the Department the same type of considerations that the Minister would himself bring and act for him under his general direction in matters either of a minor policy or quasi-judicial nature.[22]

Sir Ernest Barker suggested long ago that the key to understanding the British system was the historical fact that political reform preceded administrative reform in this country; parliamentary politicians tended to fashion their secretaries and assistants in their own image.[23] On the Continent, in contrast, the administrative machine was developed initially as an instrument for carrying out the will of an absolute monarch (or, later, of the doctrinaire politician) who needed experts, e.g. jurists and engineers, to implement policies and looked to political friends (in a *cabinet*) rather than to career civil servants for advice on policy itself. In new countries like Australia and the United States, political questions were relatively unimportant at formative periods of administrative history compared with the problem of exploiting and dominating natural resources. It was natural to give senior positions to the possessors of relevant specialist knowledge. These differences and their effects are discussed with insight by Subramaniam.

> Even now, Australian ethos finds it difficult to recognize policy-advising as a special skill, requiring special modes of selection and training. The same compulsions of economic development work in favour of the specialist in the other young democracies such as Canada and New Zealand and in Soviet Russia too, where the engineer administrator is as common a phenomenon as in America.[24]

One of the main criticisms of those such as the IPCS who wish to see the position of specialist staff change is that their present role is no longer appropriate in modern conditions. They point to changes in the background of many Ministers, with the gentleman-amateur increasingly being replaced by experienced party politicians, and argue that the practice of appointing special advisers, many of whom are experts in their fields, is an indication that Ministers no longer feel able to rely upon advice given by generalist administrators. One cause of this change has been the growth of government involvement in social, economic and technological matters, most of which are complex to understand and require expertise and relevant experience to master. Moreover, the 'knowledge explosion' of the last thirty years has encouraged new and esoteric specialisms with which the administrative generalist simply cannot keep abreast. Finally it is claimed that the diminishing stature of Britain in the world has made it more important to deal with urgent problems on technical grounds alone, without worrying too much about political consequences which are often fairly remote. Such a view lies behind the recommendation of the Central Policy Review Staff in 1977 that changes should be made in Britain's overseas representation with career diplomats being replaced in many posts by civil servants with specialist expertise and experience in relevant home departments.[25]

On these grounds, therefore, it has been argued that the relationship between specialists and administrators in the civil service needs to be reassessed.[26] However, as has been shown earlier in this chapter, despite considerable pressure for reform little change has actually occurred. It is also interesting to note that at the same time as the position of the administrative generalist in Britain has been under attack, in other countries such as the United States and Australia some have been arguing the need for just such an institution. Similarly, in British local government – where traditionally specialists have occupied the highest posts – as more emphasis has been placed upon the coordination of services and on overall financial management, so a greater role has been advocated for generalist staff.[27] The question of the relative contribution of specialists and generalists to different types of government work therefore needs closer examination.

Role of the specialist

The special problems of public administration are concerned with deciding what to do and getting things done in a political context. There is no difficulty about the role of professional staff who are carrying out strictly professional work at a long remove from the political decision centres. The scientist pursuing research in the National Physical Laboratory, the medical officer conducting clinical examinations in connection with social security benefits and the lawyer undertaking prosecutions for a government department are all doing work which is only fortuitously in the public sector. It would not, in principle, make much difference to the scientist's work if he was employed by an industrial firm; the medical officer and the lawyer could easily be acting in the same way for a private insurance company.

Policy and the expert

At the other end of the spectrum are civil servants who have been recruited, either as a group or as individuals, because their specific knowledge and experience is essential to the formulation or execution of policy at the highest level. Many of these are specialists in the sense used in this chapter. Economists provide a good example. Although a few economists had been employed earlier, for instance in the Treasury, the need to improve the quantity and quality of economic advice available to the government was symbolized by the creation in 1965 of the Government Economic Service. Originally it had an establishment of only 45, many of whom were academics on temporary secondment from universities, but by 1975 it had grown to 317, most of whom were career civil servants. Its members are now concentrated in the Treasury and other 'economic' departments such as Industry, Trade, and Prices and Consumer Protection (which share a common economic section) and Environment and Transport (again with a common economic division). Similarly, many of the staff of the top level policy advisory unit, the Central Policy Review Staff (CPRS), have been economists, and its present head, Sir Kenneth Berrill, was formerly an academic economist and head of the Government Economic Service. The influence of these economic advisers during the last fifteen years has been considerable, not only on policy questions but also in pioneering and establishing new procedures for settling priorities and planning public expenditure. It is not possible to pick out particular decisions in which the influence of economic advisers has been crucial, but the fact that Ministers have continued to make such appointments and the survival of the CPRS despite departmental opposition is indicative of the importance politicians attach to this type of assistance.

This has not prevented many of those recruited on short contracts from claiming on leaving the civil service that they had not been fully used, nor from implying that they had been the victims of some sort of administrative conspiracy to keep them in the dark.[28] The paradox is explained in a paper by a former head of the Government Economic Service. Sir Alec Cairncross showed how the increasing importance of economic thinking has made it difficult to be a successful administrator without some knowledge of economics; hence the emphasis on economics in the training given to administrators. At the same time, the academic who enters government service as a specialist economist soon learns that economics alone does not take him very far in the complicated issues on which he is expected to advise; he 'has to acquire the ability to judge a situation from limited and uncertain evidence just like any other administrator'. Moreover, there is very often no clear distinction between his role and the administrator's. In economic departments both economists and administrators are functioning as advisers on issues of economic policy, and the final decision rests with the Minister. On the other hand, there may be a difference in approach.

> Inevitably, when economists enter government service their interest tends to be concentrated on policy decisions rather than on the way they are taken. Administrators, on the other hand, are often more interested in the process of getting decisions taken and implemented ... It is, at any rate, not infrequent for the economist to feel that the administrator doesn't even understand the question and is too willing to blur it by considerations of procedure, while the administrator in his turn has to cope with economists who are unaware that the question has already been studied times without number, that their views are irreconcilable with those of the responsible department, or that what they are urging is in flagrant contradiction with some recent ministerial pronouncement.[29]

This problem is, of course, exacerbated when the economist is only in Whitehall on short-term secondment.

The central position of economists in recent years can also be gauged from the eminence of many of those who have been appointed to senior positions. Sir Alec Cairncross was Professor of Applied Economics at the University of Glasgow immediately prior to joining the Treasury in 1961, initially as Economic Adviser to the Government, and he left in 1969 to become Master of St Peter's College, Oxford. Others who have worked in government since 1964 include Lord Balogh and Lord Kaldor, Professor Robert

Neild, Sir Kenneth Berrill, Mr Michael Posner and Professor Christopher Foster, all of whom are academic economists of very high standing. Lord Balogh was seconded from Balliol College, Oxford from 1964–8 to serve as Economic Adviser to the Cabinet with direct access to the Prime Minister. Lord Kaldor, a Cambridge economist, acted for two periods as adviser to the Chancellor of the Exchequer: on a part-time basis from 1964–8 and full-time from 1974–6. The arrival of staff of this calibre, most but not all of whom have been politically sympathetic to the Government, has brought a new fluidity to the top administrative structure. It is impossible to believe that men of such reputation and standing would allow an administrator to intervene between them and the Prime Minister, Chancellor or Minister concerned.[30]

Much the same can be said of the senior industrialists who have been brought into Whitehall since 1964. The then Labour Government recruited a number of industrial advisers into the Department of Economic Affairs to provide a bridge between economic planning and private industry, including men such as Mr (later Sir) Frederick Catherwood, formerly Managing Director of British Aluminium, and Mr (later Sir) Campbell Adamson (subsequently Director General of the Confederation of British Industry).[31] In 1968 it also established a panel of businessmen, headed by Sir Robert Bellinger, to review particular areas of work with a view to finding savings in manpower. Their enquiries continued after the change of government in 1970. In addition, the Conservative Government appointed a team of six senior business executives, led by Sir Richard Meyjes, formerly Marketing Co-ordinator of Shell International, to advise it on the machinery of government and on the introduction of new managerial techniques, and a former Managing Director of Boots, Mr (later Sir) Arthur Cockfield, was brought in as adviser on tax policy to the Chancellor. Although some of these industrialists, like the economists, expressed disappointment that their advice was not always adopted, there can be no doubt as to their proximity to Ministers.[32] Indeed, it would have been impossible to attract such people – perhaps the nearest British equivalent to the American 'in-and-outers' – except on the basis of personal and unrestricted access to Ministers. Any 'administrative' objection to such direct contact between expert and Minister would have been derisively ignored by both.

What goes for economists and industrialists also applies to other senior professional officers, many of whom combine professional distinction with long experience in Whitehall. For instance, the Chief Scientific Adviser between 1964 and 1971 was Sir Solly (later Lord) Zuckerman, a Fellow of the Royal Society since 1943 and a member of many important advisory bodies throughout the post-war years. Similarly, the Chief Medical Officer from 1960 until his retirement in 1973 was Sir George Godber, an eminent physician who had joined the Ministry of Health at the age of 31. Economists, statisticians and those of the legal officers who are concerned with the preparation of legislation are indeed in a rather special position at all levels, because their work is so closely involved in the formulation of policy. But headquarters scientists, medical and nursing officers and senior members of the inspectorates share their importance in some measure.

In the social service departments, policy has long been determined in a dialogue between expert and administrator. In these exchanges, administrators have often played a more modest part than might have been supposed. It may be helpful to illustrate this with an example from a field rather different from that of grand economic or industrial strategy.

An illustration: police establishments

The Home Secretary is responsible for approving the number up to which each police force in the country can recruit. This is, in principle, a matter of political judgement. On the one hand there is public concern about a rising crime rate and a decreasing proportion of crimes cleared up. It is easy to interpret such figures as indicative of a need for more policemen. (It is also an advantage for those who represent the police in pay negotiations if they can point to authorized establishments which are considerably higher than the actual number of policemen willing to serve on current pay and conditions of service. Within police forces, too, promotion is slow and growth may be welcomed because of the new senior posts it implies.) On the other hand, there are obvious objections to over-policing. Policemen are expensive and they are paid with public money which could be used for other purposes. Nor is there any way of calculating accurately the marginal contribution of an additional policeman to the campaign against crime. The Home Secretary, therefore, has the difficult but essentially political task of assessing the claims of specific demands on a general pool of resources without a great deal of solid factual information to guide him.

In theory, he exercises this judgement with the assistance of administrative civil servants, who formulate a policy based partly on general considerations that are susceptible to lay judgement and partly on advice from the appropriate professional staff – HM Inspectors of Constabulary – who inspect each police force annually before certifying that it is 'efficient', and so eligible for police grant. In practice, the Inspector (himself these days a man with long police training and experience) plays a most influential part throughout. It is he who assesses in the first instance what the 'realistic' (that is to say desirable) establishment should be for the forces he inspects. He advises the Chief Constable on the scale of increase for which he should apply. As the Home Office told the Estimates Committee in 1963, 'It would be a very foolish Chief Constable who did not accept advice'.[33]

The Chief Constable still has to persuade his local authority to accept the increase and the local authority then has to persuade the Home Secretary. But in the normal way the question has already been settled at professional level. The Home Office officials routinely check proposals when they receive them, to make sure that they do not violate agreed conventions about, for example, the ratio of senior to junior posts, and then refer to the Inspector for 'advice'. As for the local authority share in this procedure, we may quote the address of the then Home Secretary (Sir Frank Soskice) to the 1965 annual conference of the Association of Chief Police Officers.

> I have officially asked a number of Police Authorities whose existing establishments, in the light of the advice of Her Majesty's Inspectors of Constabulary, appear to be substantially below a realistic level, to review the establishment of their Forces in consultation with the Chief Constable and

to propose whatever revision appears to be necessary for the adequate policing of the areas ...

As you know, the initiative for proposing increases in establishment normally comes from the Chief Officer and the Police Authority, and I am glad to say that in most areas Police Authorities loyally support their Chief Officer's needs in this respect. Only in a few cases does financial stringency dissuade the Authority from putting forward necessary proposals for increases in establishments, and then of course it is the function of the HM Inspectors of Constabulary to report the facts to me, so that I can consider my own responsibility in the matter, bearing in mind that the Police Act requires me to exercise my powers in such manner and to such extent as appears to me to be best calculated to promote the efficiency of the Police.

Fortunately, a solution is usually found by consultation and it is rarely necessary for me even to consider withholding the Exchequer grant; but it is clearly my duty to go to this length, if need be, to ensure that no Police Force in this country is deprived of essential manpower merely for want of an adequate establishment.[34]

The only meaning that can be given to the word 'essential' in the last sentence is 'essential in the eyes of the Inspector of Constabulary'. If a decision has to be taken in a situation of uncertainty, it is necessary to arrive at a working assumption. The Inspector is at the crucial point where uncertainties harden into 'facts' that are unlikely to be challenged later. The question for the Home Secretary is whether, on other grounds, the 'essential' requirements can be accepted or not. He has to decide whether it is consistent with other objectives of the Government of which he is a member.

One such objective is the orderly management of public expenditure. If public expenditure has to be squeezed, as has often been the case in recent years, an arbitrary limit may be set on the resources allocated to additional policemen. The Home Office administrators are expected to check that the financial implications of any specific proposal can be contained within this total.

Another test is political acceptability. It is possible, although unlikely, that the Home Secretary might have to defend himself against criticism in Parliament or in the press for authorizing an increase in police establishment. (It is more likely that he would be attacked for turning a proposal down.) Whatever his decision, he would want to be satisfied that it was defensible in political terms and again he would expect his administrators to relate general principles to the particular case. In practice, of course, the HM Inspector of Constabulary would normally know of an unfavourable financial or political wind and would not inspire applications at a time when they were certain to be turned down.

The limits to the Inspector's influence are set by the way Ministers carry out their individual and collective responsibilities and not by his formal relationship to administrators. He settles 'technical' aspects of questions regardless of whether he carries executive authority or is merely an 'adviser' – although he must of course be in a position to be consulted, which means having a close working relationship with whoever does carry administrative responsibility.

The Inspector of Constabulary has his equivalent in other social service departments which administer professional services. The Department of Education and Science has its HM Inspectors of Schools. The Department of Health and Social Security has its medical, dental and nursing officers as well as its social work service. In each case the professional officer is prominent wherever policy is in the making. He is in touch with professional people in the field. He is present when the relevant professional interests come to bargain with the department. He plays an active part in the department's advisory system, preparing papers, guiding discussion and chairing working parties. The true measure of his influence on policy and day-to-day administration will become apparent if and when departmental working files are available for research. Clearly there will be cases where structural arrangements are in need of overhaul, where the professional is too remote or where his calibre is simply too poor. But most of the visible and anecdotal evidence confirms his key role.

A general hypothesis can be formulated that, given reasonable calibre and a workable link with the main channels of communication in his department, the professional officer (whatever his formal status) will effectively decide policy questions within limits set by current conventions about what is financially and politically tolerable.

Technical management and the administrator

Most of the enduring quarrels between specialists and general administrators have arisen not where exclusively professional work is being done on the periphery of government business nor at the apex where professional advice is an essential element in the formulation of policy, but rather at the intermediary levels, where professional officers providing professional services, or managing technical projects, complain that they are not left alone to get on with their job without administrative interference.

In some departments, the system of joint decision-making outlined earlier in this chapter has had the desired effect of bringing administrators and professionals closer together. For example, writing in 1966, Regan concluded that the new arrangements adopted in the Ministry of Transport had given engineers a broader perspective on financial and political aspects of their work, while a closer personal relationship had made it easier for administrators to seek engineering advice without risking loss of face.[35] But, even in this case, the IPCS felt that professional staff were being allotted an advisory, auxiliary role, with the main policy and financial decisions reserved to the administrative members of the hierarchy. This criticism has been levelled against most departments which employ large numbers of specialist staff. The IPCS is particularly critical of the situation in the Property Services Agency.[36]

As we have seen, one of the main tasks of the PSA is the provision and maintenance of accommodation for other government departments. It is thus a vast executive building organization. In some ways it is an historical accident that it is part of a government department and not an *ad hoc* or even a private contractor. If comparable work was being done outside the civil service, there would almost certainly be a more streamlined organization in which professional staff took executive decisions in their own name. In local government an organization of this type would be headed by a professional chief officer who was also chief adviser to the appropriate committee. This contrast was brought out by a recent enquiry appointed by the government to advise on standards of design in government building, which was generally critical of the position of professionals in the PSA.

The fundamental difference between PSA and other organisations concerned with large building programmes arises from an assumption that, while the design and management of individual buildings lies properly within the province of professionals, many parts of the total process of obtaining buildings (e.g. taking clients' instructions, planning and managing building programmes, allocation of professional resources, budgeting, cost control, etc.) are not considered primarily a professional responsibility and are therefore taken out of the professional sphere of control, into the hierarchy of administration.[37]

Nor is this situation found only in the PSA. It is repeated in other departments where civil servants are engaged in the supervision and execution of complex technical work. In these areas the traditional civil service command structure may not seem particularly appropriate. It is thus necessary to consider what the distinctive contribution of administrators is to this sort of work and how far it is associated with factors peculiar to the civil service.

The general administrator's contribution to technical management can be divided very roughly into three aspects. First, he performs a *secretarial function*, including tasks such as the preparation of ministerial briefs and parliamentary papers, the drafting of letters and the routine administration of personnel, accounts and common services. It is clearly desirable that specialist staff should not be burdened with these details; but there is no obvious need for an administrator who is primarily a secretary to share executive control with a professional director. Secondly, administrators have traditionally been responsible for *financial control*, including the preparation of estimates, arguing with the Treasury over proposals and ensuring that they are covered by available finance, controlling expenditure during the year and providing explanations (ultimately for the Public Accounts Committee) of any over- or under-spending. There does not seem to be any reason, however, why specialist staff should not accept financial responsibility for schemes in the same way as their counterparts in local government and private industry, providing of course that they accept the conventions of public accounting.

Neither of these functions is therefore sufficient to justify the generalist's pre-eminence. What is crucial is his part in giving *final approval* for a scheme. The exact nature of this role is often difficult to assess. The IPCS feels that administrators frequently interfere in matters beyond their competence, causing wasted effort and delays.[38] However, there frequently seems to be some confusion in discussing this subject. The word 'approval' is ambiguous. It can imply that the person giving approval is a superior, with the right to veto, or it can denote the mere giving of assent by an interested party (for example, a consultative committee) with no hierarchical implications.

Often, when the administrator appears to be approving a scheme he is not assessing its technical merits but confirming that it is financially within the budget – or he is acting secretarially by making sure that its official acceptance is conveyed to the appropriate people in the appropriate form and noted on the appropriate files. To do either of these things, he may have to ask questions that seem ignorant and trivial to the professional. But sometimes he is doing more than that.

In the public sector decisions depend partly on technical considerations and partly on economics and politics. Thus the choice between two types of nuclear reactor is made not just on the basis of their relative efficiency and safety but also in terms of their effect upon the balance of payments and upon employment in particular parts of the country. It is this need to take account of the wider economic and political implications of technical decisions which lies behind the role of the general administrator. Moreover this applies even to decisions which appear to be entirely technical. For instance, for the Property Services Agency (which remains part of a government department), there is a constant possibility of parliamentary interest in particular projects on grounds of suitability, extravagance, aesthetic appearance, the rectitude of tendering procedures and so on.[39] Liability to parliamentary scrutiny makes it important that there are staff who are involved in quite detailed work and who are also familiar with the principles of lay control and who know the working of the parliamentary machine and the Minister's mind. The strongest argument for joint responsibility at project level is that schemes must, if they are to be viable, command the assent of administrators who apply a lay mind and a knowledge of the administrative machine to match their partner's professional expertise. If two types of skill are needed for the pursuit of an activity, it will probably be more effective if they are applied simultaneously through joint working.

But are two types of skill necessary? Or, to put it another way, could not one person possess both skills and therefore fill both roles? One problem, frequently encountered in organizations which are headed by specialists, is that those performing administrative tasks soon get out of touch with developments in their specialism and therefore cease to be able to provide the specialist contribution to decision-making themselves. But, unlike the situation in many other countries and in local government in this country, there is also a feeling that specialists are unsuitable for administrative work in the civil service. Underlying this belief is a particular view of the nature of the administrative process. Thus an official working party in the 1960s on the role of the professional engineer regarded administration as

the analysis and co-ordination of ideas and proposals, the relation of these to political and economic conditions and the expression of proposals and decisions in a form in which they can be assimilated and carried out by the government machine.[40]

This view has also been advanced by writers, such as C. H. Sisson, who see government as a process of arbitration among special interests.[41] Administration is a matter of making adjustments where interests conflict. The committed specialist is therefore incapable of filling the administrative role. Others, like the authors of the Labour Party's evidence to Fulton, feel that coordination and adjustment are relatively less important in these days than purposive and committed management.[42] Summing up a long reasoned argument on the subject of specialists and generalists, Professor F. F. Ridley endorsed this view.

> One might ... expect the professional to be a little more
> impatient of administrative difficulties and, indeed, public
> opinion, more anxious to get things done, even at a cost.
> Perhaps too much emphasis is placed on avoiding friction:
> it may be less important to have a smooth-running machine
> than a machine which actually gets somewhere. But that
> obviously brings one back to one's own philosophy of
> politics.[43]

Thus in the end it is the nature of the administrative process
which determines the role of the administrator, even in the management of technical matters. As long as importance is attached to
the maintenance of a collegiate system of government and
to political accountability, so there will be a need for general
administrators in senior posts. Their broad education and experience of working in different fields enables them to take a detached
view of departmental problems and to relate them to the needs
of the government as a whole. They also appreciate the full
implications of the fact that decisions are being taken in the name
of a Minister who is accountable to Parliament and the public.
These features of the administrative process are, of course, themselves the result of basic principles of the constitution such as
individual and collective ministerial responsibility. It is their
absence in local authorities which, along with other factors such
as the operational nature of their work, accounts for the different
relationship between specialists and generalists at the local level.
Moreover, if the 'committed specialist' was to replace the general
administrator in the civil service, change would be inevitable
elsewhere in the executive and in its relationship with the
legislature.

Given that within the present political and administrative environment of the civil service it is not possible to combine the
roles of the specialist and the administrator, the problem of
integrating their work successfully is inevitable. The drawbacks
of traditional parallel hierarchies have been well documented,
particularly in areas with a high technical content. Nor are joint
hierarchies without their problems. It is clear that great strains

may be involved for the partners in joint responsibility. Roles may be easier to define in principle than in practice and some people may prove to be temperamentally unsuited to joint working. To a certain extent these problems can be eased by ensuring that specialists receive some training in administration and that administrators develop some expertise in the field in which they are working, either by specializing themselves or through training; but they cannot be eliminated entirely. Staffing patterns can also be varied to meet the needs of different kinds of work. But the problems will never be solved entirely, and the debate on the relationship between specialists and administrators is certain to continue for a very long time.

Conclusions

The number of special techniques relevant to government has increased markedly over the last sixty years. Decision-making has become more difficult, and governments are engaged in many fields where technical competence is of supreme importance. Consequently more and more specialists have been employed. Over the years they have gradually taken on policy-making and managerial as well as advisory functions and their status has been recognized by creating more specialist posts at senior levels with access to Ministers.

But the framework in which general administrators represent the lay Minister and are involved on his behalf at every level of administration, except in research establishments, has been slow to change. The Fulton enquiry gave the IPCS a fresh opportunity to press for more status, authority and opportunities for its members. Its case was strongly supported by the Committee's management consultancy group, which was not convinced that the special problems of public administration were such as to justify the differences which were noted between the civil service and private industry.

The sweeping terms of the Fulton Report should not exaggerate the extent of the changes the Committee was suggesting. In a quiet way, experts and specialists had enjoyed a great deal of influence behind the façade of 'expert advice; administrative decision'. In the newer departments, like Technology, the façade had been crumbling too. The main skirmishes have been in fields of executive management where administrators, afflicted by over-frequent postings, were uncertain of their role and unable to keep out of matters of detailed technical management. At policy-making levels, at least in the social service and technological departments where technical issues predominate, the administrative role has on the whole been relatively modest and could be best described as secretarial.

Nor have the changes that have occurred since Fulton fundamentally altered the position. This may disappoint the IPCS, which is properly concerned about the career prospects of its members, but it is clear that without a radical change in our political system it would not be possible to establish an administration which was entirely professional, even if professional training was altered to include more basic administration than it does now and civil service professionals enjoyed fuller opportunities to gain administrative experience early in their careers. So long as the doctrines of individual and collective ministerial responsibility are held, there will be a need to relate different technical fields to one another and to the social and political environment. Professionals can do this, but only at the cost of ceasing to be specialist.

The problem about professionals is the same as the problem about excessively 'departmentalized' administrators. Policy and priorities are normally evolved as a result of a dialogue. There may have to be several stages in the dialogue before a sectional pressure (for example, for better quality school baths) can be given its place in the current political scale of values. If the school baths department is staffed by professional educationalists (or by administrators who have spent all their working lives listening to professional educationalists), the settlement of priorities must take place somewhere else, either in the Treasury or in the Minister's private office. And no professional worth his salt is going to be completely satisfied with the share of resources allocated to him as a result of the process!

Notes

1 *Superannuation Act 1859*, section IV.
2 *Fourth Report of the Royal Commission on the Civil Service, 1912–14*, Cd. 7338 (1914).
3 *Eleventh Report from the Expenditure Committee 1976–77*, H.C. 535, Vol. II (II), p. 547.
4 ibid., pp. 620–2.
5 ibid., Vol II (I), pp. 280, 289.
6 *Report of the Royal Commission on the Civil Service 1929–31* (Tomlin Report) Cmd. 3909 (1931) paras 172–7.
7 Fulton Report, Vol. 5, p. 287, paras 5–7.
8 ibid., Vol. 1, para. 17. The point is further developed at para. 197.
9 Expenditure Committee, op. cit., Vol. II (II), p. 532.
10 The position of specialists is summarized in a paper by the then Deputy Secretary General of the IPCS in F. F. Ridley (ed.), *Specialists and Generalists* (London, 1968) pp. 13–56.
11 *Seventh Report from the Estimates Committee 1961–62*, H.C. 227, 'Classified Roads'.
12 Fulton Report, Vol. 1, paras 161–2.
13 Printed as an annex to the evidence of the IPCS to the Expenditure Committee, op. cit., Vol. II (II), pp. 556–64.
14 ibid., pp. 535–6.
15 ibid., Vol. II (I), pp. 285–7; Vol. II (II), pp. 532–5.
16 ibid., Vol. II (I), pp. 15–16; Vol. II (II), pp. 539–51; Vol. III, pp. 871–4.
17 ibid., Vol. II (I), p. 280; Vol. II (II), pp. 546–7; Vol. III, pp. 968–70.
18 ibid., Vol. III, p. 873. The other 128 officials who had completed the training element were awaiting posting to an administrative post.
19 Fulton Report, Vol. 5, p. 5, para. 13.
20 F. F. Ridley (ed.), op. cit., *passim*.
21 D. K. Price, *The Scientific Estate* (Cambridge, Mass., 1965) pp. 59–63.
22 Fulton Report, Vol. 5 (Association of First Division Civil Servants) p. 105, para. 3.
23 Sir E. Barker, *The Development of Public Services in Europe 1660–1930* (London, 1944) Chap. 1.
24 V. Subramaniam, 'The Relative Status of Specialists and Generalists', *Public Administration* Vol. 46 (1968) p. 337. See also his 'Specialists in British and Australian Government Services: a Study in Contrast', ibid., Vol. 41 (1963) pp. 357–73.
25 *Review of Overseas Representation*, Report by the Central Policy Review Staff (London, 1977).
26 In addition to the evidence of the IPCS, see for instance B. Chapman, *British Government Observed* (London, 1963); Fabian Society, *The*

Administrators (London, 1964); Conservative Political Centre, *Change and Decay* (London, 1963).

27 For example, see Lord Redcliffe-Maud and B. Wood, *English Local Government Reformed* (London, 1974) pp. 166–8.

28 For example, S. Brittan, 'The Irregulars', *Crossbow* Vol. 10 (1966) p. 30. This question was raised with varying degrees of resentment and understanding in evidence to the Fulton Committee; Fulton Report, Vol. 5, pp. 856–72, 982–93 and 1093–1105.

29 Sir Alec Cairncross, 'The Work of an Economic Adviser', *Public Administration* Vol. 46 (1968) p. 8.

30 The importance of Balogh and Kaldor as advisers emerges clearly from R. H. S. Crossman, *The Diaries of a Cabinet Minister*, Vol. 1 (London, 1975).

31 Their role is discussed in C. Adamson, 'The Role of the Industrial Adviser', *Public Administration* Vol. 46 (1968) pp. 185–90. See also Sir Eric Roll, 'The Department of Economic Affairs', ibid., Vol. 44 (1966) p. 8.

32 See J. Bruce-Gardyne, *Whatever Happened to the Quiet Revolution?* (London, 1974) pp. 128–30.

33 *Eleventh Report from the Estimates Committee 1962–63*, H.C. 292, 'The Home Office', p. 129.

34 *Police Review*, 18 June 1965.

35 D. E. Regan, 'The Expert and the Administrator: Recent Changes at the Ministry of Transport', *Public Administration* Vol. 44 (1966) p. 160.

36 For example, see its evidence to the Expenditure Committee, op. cit., Vol. II (II), pp. 532–5.

37 Quoted in the Expenditure Committee, op. cit., Vol II (II), p. 534.

38 ibid., p. 533.

39 See the views of its then Chief Executive, J. G. Cuckney, 'The Commercial Approach to Government Operations', *Management Services in Government* Vol. 29 (1974) p. 127.

40 'Report of Working Party on the Role of the Professional Engineer' (unpublished), quoted in the Fulton Report, Vol. 5, p. 328.

41 C. H. Sisson, *The Spirit of British Administration* (London, 1959).

42 Fulton Report, Vol. 5, pp. 653–4.

43 F. F. Ridley (ed.), op. cit., p. 209.

V

The ⌃ political environment

'A fundamental feature of our parliamentary system'

The public servant works within a framework of political institutions. British civil servants work under the direction of a political Minister who is in turn accountable to Parliament, to his colleagues in the government and, more remotely, to the political party of which he is a member. Each line of accountability imposes its own discipline on the Minister and limits his department's scope for manoeuvre. Civil servants are constantly aware of the political implications of their work and many of them spend much of their time servicing the political machine by preparing answers to parliamentary questions, briefs for debates and material for the Minister's correspondence.[1] They are, of course, exposed to many influences that do not arise from the central political machine. They have to deal with the public, and with the interest groups and cause groups that make up their special 'publics'. They have to bargain with colleagues in other departments, notably in the Treasury. These relationships have developed outside the parliamentary system. But in an important sense they are conditioned by it; in the last resort a dissatisfied group can appeal to political levels and this possibility sets the tone for relationships lower down. Without Parliament there would be no final sanction for the weight given to impartiality, fairness and consistency in the daily work of government departments.

At the heart of this framework lies the convention of ministerial responsibility. It is the means by which Parliament controls Ministers both individually and collectively. It also determines the relationship between Ministers and their officials. Its importance has been reiterated on many occasions. Thus in 1966 the Prime Minister declared that

> Civil servants, however eminent, remain the confidential advisers of Ministers, who alone are answerable to Parliament for policy; and we do not envisage any change in this fundamental feature of our parliamentary system of democracy.[2]

However, since this doctrine was first established, great changes have occurred in the scale of government and in the nature of its tasks. It is not surprising, therefore, as we saw in Chapter I, that the operation of the convention has been modified. This chapter will examine the contemporary relationship between Ministers and civil servants, taking account of some of the most recent developments such as the growth of 'giant' departments, British entry into the EEC, and changes in Parliament which affect the work of the civil service, notably the creation of the office of Parliamentary Commissioner for Administration and the establishment of new committees to scrutinize the administration.

Civil servants and Ministers

Formally, the Minister *is* the department, whose members are his agents and are appointed only to carry out the functions entrusted to him. The Minister alone is accountable to Parliament and this has a profound effect upon his relationship with his civil servants and on the way in which they approach their work. However, in practice, the scale of contemporary government is such that only a small part of the department's work is done with the knowledge and specific approval of the Minister. This fact has given rise to frequent allegations from politicians of both parties that civil servants have conspired to conceal information from Ministers and even that on occasion they have deliberately frustrated the wishes of their political masters.[3] Such charges are not easy either to prove or to refute. The relationship between Ministers and their officials is a complex and subtle one, varying with different personalities and circumstances. It is also almost entirely a confidential one. However, on the evidence available, most of these allegations do not appear proven and usually they reflect weakness on the part of Ministers or disagreements between them, the civil service being a convenient scapegoat for ministerial failings. On the other hand the role of civil servants in departments is of very great importance and it extends a long way beyond the mere implementation of ministerial decisions.

Some generalizations can be made about the respective roles of Ministers and civil servants. At the outset it is important to realize that the Minister is not merely a superior civil servant and that he is likely to approach problems in a different way. He is recruited, trained and promoted through very different channels. He is likely to have little or no previous knowledge of his post and if he is ambitious he may hope not to remain in it for very long. The Treasury had fourteen different Chancellors of the Exchequer between 1945 and 1977 and there were no fewer than eight Secretaries of State for Education and Science between 1964 and 1977, the longest tenure of office being that of Mrs Margaret Thatcher between 1970 and 1974. On the whole, a Minister is more likely to be interested in positive action in the short term than in long-term strategy. He is unlikely to be well-disposed to decisions that are going to be unpopular or difficult to explain. In contrast, the experienced career official is more aware of problems of continuity and more concerned with the risk of a policy going sour in the long term. Some appearance of conflict between them is therefore unavoidable if advice is to be tendered frankly and Ministers made aware of all the consequences of their proposed actions.

In the last resort, the civil servant must do what he is told. In the last resort, too, a Minister who is determined to get rid of a senior civil servant whose advice he finds uncongenial can do so, although it is not easy – he has to persuade the Prime Minister first and would be unwise to attempt it for trivial reasons.

In practice, a Minister can depend on habits of loyalty.

The Minister's immediate influence on his department owes a good deal to his strategic constitutional position. Some questions are bound to come to his personal attention, simply because he provides an essential link with the political system. He must concern himself with his department's contribution to his party programme. For this he will have to answer not to Parliament as such but to the Prime Minister, his ministerial colleagues and the appropriate backbench committee. He must also become aware of any reference to his department in Parliament. He or one of his junior Ministers answers parliamentary questions, replies to criticisms in debates and introduces new legislation or statutory instruments. A reply to any letter from an MP is also, as a rule, signed by a Minister personally. Through all these means a sample of his department's work is exposed to his attention and possible criticism.

Apart from parliamentary business, the Minister is like the head of any other concern. He sees papers that his senior advisers think he ought to see. A good deal will depend on the training and experience of the civil servants and on their ability to anticipate the Minister's wishes. They know the pressures on his time and see their job partly as protecting him from being deluged with paper.[4] No question of any importance, however, is likely to be settled in the Minister's name before he has seen the papers and had a chance to intervene.

Indeed, most questions of any importance will be referred through him to Cabinet or one of its committees. He will have to be brought in as a final big gun in disputes with other departments or powerful outside interests. He will be informed about fairly minor questions that seem likely to have political repercussions. A new Minister will be consulted on many questions that will be settled much lower down once his mind is known. Finally, the Minister will see papers (and arguments as detailed as he likes) on questions in which he has expressed a particular interest. It is his ability to select issues on which he can have an influence that is one of the tests of the calibre of a Minister.

The amount of detail that is given to the Minister on any question will vary for all these reasons. Normally, the department will present him with as brief a summary as possible, including a highly compressed description of the problem, a note of the main factors in which he is likely to be interested (including, for example, repercussions in his own constituency) and an outline of the main arguments. Even if the arguments are fairly evenly balanced, the paper will end with a definite recommendation. Usually this summary is the top document on a file which the Minister, if he has time and inclination, can read to see what sort of detailed arguments have been put forward in earlier discussion. If he is busy, he need read only the top document. If he wishes to proceed as suggested all he has to do is to add his initials. Most Ministers will initial most documents most of the time. But he may disagree with the recommendation. He can ask for fuller information, covering points that seem to him to have been missed out. He may call in the Permanent Secretary and other civil servants and instruct them to look at other possibilities. The process is a subtle one of mutual influence, which it is very difficult to describe except in the context of a particular question and of particular personalities.

The vast majority of decisions, however, will not and cannot be seen by a Minister personally. These are not just routine questions. Many near-ministerial decisions are given by senior civil servants who decide whether a concession should be made to a pressure group, whether a piece of legislation should be reviewed in consultation with other departments, or whether a problem should be referred to a committee before recommending any particular way of dealing with it. The test of these decisions is not just that the Minister can defend them in Parliament if challenged. The test is that each decision should, as far as is humanly possible, be the one that the Minister himself would have taken if he had been able to take it personally. Ministers thus expect their senior assistants to be able to think in terms of their own priorities. They even expect to be warned about political reactions to a proposed policy. Experience of a particular field sometimes makes civil servants more aware of impending trouble than the Minister himself.

However, increasingly in recent years Ministers have felt the need to bring in personal advisers whose appointments terminate when the Minister leaves office. In 1977 there were 26 such advisers, 6 of them working in a special policy advisory unit in the Prime Minister's Office and the rest in 13 other departments.[5] A common element shared by all these advisers is their total commitment to their master. Their precise roles, however, vary according to the wishes of particular Ministers and the age and experience of each adviser. Some are acknowledged experts in their fields and have been influential on many issues of departmental policy. Others are young, with little political or other experience, and have tended to provide general support, such as briefing on Cabinet business and liaison with backbenchers and party head-quarters. The number of special advisers is, however, too small for the basic relationship between a Minister and his career officials to be altered. He still depends upon his career officials for political advice on a wide variety of questions and expects complete loyalty from them.

A further complication has been the increase in the workload of government. Such a trend has existed for a long time but it has accelerated markedly in the last ten or fifteen years. Not only has this meant that both Ministers and senior civil servants have to work harder. It has also led to changes in the structure of central departments. In the past most departments were relatively small and were headed by a single Minister who was supported by one or two Parliamentary Secretaries and who was able to establish close contact with all his senior officials. Now, however, many departments have large ministerial teams, in some cases five or six Ministers at three or four different ranks, and although the senior Minister is constitutionally responsible for the entire department he publicly delegates responsibility for particular areas to his subordinate Ministers.[6] The number of senior civil servants can also be very large. For instance, in April 1976 the Department of the Environment had 93 officials at the level of Under Secretary and above. This makes it much more difficult for officials to main-tain close contact with Ministers and thus for them to perform the role outlined above. It also casts doubts on the continuing validity of the doctrine of ministerial responsibility.

The problems caused by the increase in the size of departments were highlighted by the enquiry into the failure of the Department

of Trade and Industry to avert the collapse of the Vehicle and
General Insurance Company in 1971. In its evidence, the Department stated that well under 1 per cent of its business was referred
to Ministers. Largely for this reason, the Tribunal exonerated all
the Ministers and laid the blame on the shoulders of a named
civil servant.[7] Were its views generally to be accepted the doctrine
of ministerial responsibility would effectively be at an end. However, the Tribunal's verdict was also affected by the technical
and unusual nature of the government's responsibilities in relation
to insurance companies and, even in the debate on its report, the
traditional doctrine was reasserted.[8]

When the relationship between Ministers and civil servants is
examined in detail the crude differences between a good Minister
and a good civil servant begin to melt away. The Minister is a
political animal. But one of the jobs of his administrative entourage
is to help him to handle his political business creditably. They
are bound to become, in some measure, political animals too and
to transmit their political sense through to their own subordinates.
The administrative system is a mirror of the political one. This
convergence at the highest levels of government is found throughout the world. Posts are held by career officials in Britain which
in the United States would be held by political appointees. Conversely, in the Fifth Republic, French civil servants have been
appointed to many posts normally regarded as political. British
Prime Ministers have also frequently reallocated functions between
junior Ministers and civil servants, and they intermingle on many
committees.

Despite the appointment of special advisers, much of the work
of career administrators is still taken up with assisting and representing Ministers in a primarily secretarial capacity. Between a
secretary and his chief there can be no disagreement in public.
Their relationship would become impossible if those at the
receiving end of an administrative decision knew that the person
they were dealing with had previously argued against the very
policy he was now defending. This was one of the reasons why
the Government attempted to prevent the publication of those
parts of the diaries of the late Richard Crossman which revealed
the opinions of individual, named civil servants.[9]

The practice of confidentiality, and the extent to which individual civil servants remain anonymous, varies from department to department and from situation to situation. As part of their normal jobs, civil servants have to consult outside bodies and give evidence to parliamentary committees but they are expected not to express personal views differing from those of their Minister. Professional civil servants are often invited to address meetings as individuals, and some (for example, the Chief Medical Officer of the Department of Health and Social Security and the Chief Inspector of Constabulary) present their own views on policy in published reports. Administrative civil servants lecture to bodies like the Royal Institute of Public Administration. Individual civil servants are generally found both revealing and helpful by an outside enquirer, so long as he is not obviously wasting their time, or trying to penetrate the mysteries of an essentially political decision. Kingdom tells the story of a young American who wanted to study departmental files in order to find out what part the Chancellor of the Exchequer, the Minister of Health and their respective advisers had played in the decision to impose National Health Service charges in 1951: 'Wherever he went in London he received literally nothing but courtesy.'[10]

Recently a number of developments have occurred to reduce the secrecy which surrounds the processes of government and to improve methods of consultation with the public. Parliamentary developments, to be examined in the following sections of this chapter, have had the effect of making civil servants and their actions more visible to the public. British entry into the EEC in 1973 has had similar consequences. The amount of work in Brussels and the inability of Ministers to be in two places at once has made a substantial delegation of power to officials essential. Moreover, in Brussels British civil servants work alongside officials representing other countries who are accustomed to greater independence of action from their political masters and are less inhibited from making public statements.[11]

The government has also taken steps towards wider and more open consultation. One significant development has been the publication of policy ideas for discussion before the government is committed to them, in the form of a Green Paper. The first such document, on regional employment premiums, was published in 1967 and it has been followed by many others on subjects such as the reorganization of the National Health Service, select committees of the House of Commons and local government finance. In 1976 the Prime Minister also announced that the Government intended to publish more of the background material on which policy decisions were based.[12]

None the less, the reticence of British government and especially of the civil service has frequently been criticized. The Fulton Committee recognized that there was a need for confidentiality at some stages of decision-making but felt there was a need generally for much greater open-ness. It was impressed by Swedish practice, where government files are open to the public except when there is a security risk and except for working material on which policy decisions are in process of being taken.[13] Recently a considerable amount of attention has been paid to the Official Secrets Acts which make it an offence for civil servants to communicate unauthorized information to the press and for the press to publish such information. In practice the law is frequently ignored, but it still remains a significant barrier to a freer flow of information. In 1972 a committee of enquiry recommended that the Official Secrets Acts should be repealed and proposed that civil servants should be free to communicate information unless it fell into one of a number of reserved categories, for instance if it related to defence, foreign relations or the currency, or if it had been entrusted to the government by a private individual or concern.[14] This recommendation has been accepted by the Labour Government but no legislation had been introduced by the end of 1977. In any case although the Official Secrets Acts set the general climate of secrecy, strictly they relate only to unauthorized disclosure. Perhaps more important is a willingness on the part of Ministers to be more open themselves and to authorize the release of more information about their plans and their reasons for adopting them.

Greater open-ness has serious implications for the relationship between Ministers and civil servants. If civil servants are to be given greater personal autonomy and their freedom to explain departmental policies in public is to be extended, a point could soon be reached at which it was no longer tenable for Ministers to be held responsible for all the actions and utterances of their officials. A change in attitude would also be needed by MPs and by the press who at present see it as their duty to make political capital out of human errors and to upbraid a Minister with the sins of his servants.

Parliamentary Commissioner for Administration

It was largely the belief that the Minister's own accountability to Parliament was no longer sufficient to protect the victims of departmental error and maladministration that led to the institution of the office of Parliamentary Commissioner in 1967.

In the late 1950s considerable interest began to be taken in the Scandinavian Ombudsman, who investigates complaints by citizens against the administration. In 1961 a private organization, Justice, produced a report on existing procedures for protecting the citizen against arbitrary administration. The report recommended the institution of a Parliamentary Commissioner to deal with complaints of maladministration, as well as greater use of tribunals to allow citizens to appeal against administrative decisions.[15] The idea was taken up by the Labour Party and the first Parliamentary Commissioner for Administration started work on 1 April 1967.

The Commissioner's function is to investigate cases of alleged maladministration referred to him by Members of Parliament. He thus complements the work of MPs in dealing with constituents' complaints, providing them with 'a new and powerful weapon' in addition to their earlier rights to question Ministers in the House and to raise matters in adjournment debates. The Commissioner and his staff have the power to call for papers, including all internal files, and witnesses, even the Minister himself if he was involved. The Minister can instruct him not to publish all the information to which he has access but no departmental files can be withheld from him. The Commissioner's findings are reported to the MP who had referred the case to him and to the House of Commons which in 1967 set up a Select Committee to consider his reports. Since 1972 the Commissioner has published quarterly reports giving in an 'anonymized' form the results of all the cases he has investigated. Occasionally special reports are published on important cases.

The Commissioner's jurisdiction is limited in two important ways. First, he can only investigate complaints against government departments and a small number of other public bodies which are specified in the Parliamentary Commissioner Act. He is also precluded from investigating complaints which relate to personnel matters in the civil service and the armed forces. Originally this constituted a major limitation, but since 1967 separate ombudsmen have been created for local government and the National Health Service and a Police Complaints Board has been established to take part in the investigation of complaints against the police. Arrangements have been made for handling complaints which cross the boundaries between the jurisdiction of the different ombudsmen. The most controversial area still excluded from the Commissioner's terms of reference is personnel questions. On a number of occasions the Select Committee has advocated the removal of this restriction but the government has disagreed, arguing that it would interfere with established procedures for resolving internal staff disputes.[16]

Secondly, the Commissioner is only permitted to investigate allegations of 'maladministration'. He is not allowed to question policy, which remains subject to general parliamentary control; nor is he able to question the merits of discretionary administrative decisions, provided they were taken legally and after an appropriate administrative procedure. However, the Act did not define the term 'maladministration' and this has enabled the Commissioner gradually to extend his jurisdiction, spurred on in this direction by the Select Committee. The first Commissioner, Sir Edmund Compton, tended to be very cautious, which led *The Times* in 1967 to head an editorial on the new office 'Ombudsman – or Ombudsmouse?'. In 1968 he was encouraged by the Select Committee to investigate 'bad decisions', on the grounds that if a decision was thoroughly bad there must have been an element of maladministration in the way it was taken, and 'bad rules' which caused hardship each time they were applied. Although this recommendation was accepted by the Commissioner, in practice it appeared to have little effect, at least until 1971. The second Commissioner, Sir Alan Marre, however, took a wider interpretation of his terms of reference and in a number of cases he criticized decisions on the ground that they were unreasonable.[17] One such case was the TV licences case of 1975. A large number of complainants alleged that the Post Office and the Home Office had acted unlawfully and unreasonably in attempting to prevent licence holders from holding overlapping licences, obtained before an announced increase in licence fees came into force. The legality of this action was successfully challenged in the courts. The Commissioner's investigation was confined to the administrative arrangements adopted by the Home Office which he found to have caused needless distress and confusion. In reaching his conclusion the Commissioner reported that he had directed his mind to the question 'whether, within the framework of their view of the law, the Home Office's actions have been administratively sound and reasonable'.[18] In doing so he must have been very close to weighing the merits of their decisions.

The principal reason lying behind this restriction on the Commissioner's jurisdiction is a concern that he should not infringe upon the responsibility of Ministers by substituting his decisions for theirs. Thus, in his report for 1977, the Commissioner defended his present jurisdiction, arguing that

> It is no part of my function to substitute my judgement for that of a Minister or one of his officials if I see no evidence of 'maladministration' either in the way the decision was taken or in the nature of the decision itself.[19]

In any case, the Commissioner's recommendations are not binding upon departments. Generally, however, they have rectified injustices identified by the Commissioner. On occasion, with the support of the Select Committee, he has had to apply some pressure, but almost invariably he has had his way in the end.[20] For instance, it took the Inland Revenue twelve months to agree to waive additional tax that had arisen in one case as a result of unreasonable delay on the part of officials in answering letters and then only after the Chairman of the Board of Inland Revenue had appeared before the Select Committee.[21]

One consequence of both these restrictions has been the high proportion of cases which the Commissioner has to reject as lying outside his jurisdiction. In 1976 he dealt with 863 cases and rejected over 60 per cent of them, either because a central department was not involved, or because they did not relate to administrative functions, or because they concerned personnel matters. It has also led to widespread public misunderstanding and disappointment. In 1971 Sir Alan Marre commented that many complainants still looked to the Commissioner 'to reverse decisions by departments (including Ministers) simply because they disagree with the decisions and not with the way they have been taken'.[22] This is not surprising, as most complainants are motivated by a feeling that a decision or a regulation is unfair rather than by concern with the propriety with which it was taken or applied.

The gradual extension of the Commissioner's interpretation of maladministration can perhaps be seen in the increasing proportion of cases in which he has found an element of maladministration. In 1970 maladministration was found in 23 per cent of cases investigated; in 1973 in 37 per cent; and in 1976 in 43 per cent of cases. These occurred mainly in departments where fairly junior staff have substantial dealings with the public, notably the Department of Health and Social Security and the Inland Revenue. In 1976 the Commissioner upheld 57 complaints against the former and 26 against the latter. Most of them related to delay, failure to apply rules, inadequate correspondence, wrong advice or decisions made without taking account of the available evidence. Remedies applied by departments after the maladministration had been pointed out varied from an apology (to a taxpayer whose file was lost) to an extra-statutory payment (to a woman who had lost pension rights as a result of wrong information about her national insurance position).

The office of Parliamentary Commissioner has been in existence for more than a decade and some assessment of its effectiveness can therefore be made. On the debit side must be placed the lack of impact it has made upon the general public, many of whom are unaware even that there is an ombudsman; this can partly be attributed to the restrictions which have been placed upon access to the Commissioner and on his jurisdiction.[23] Against this must be weighed the not insignificant number of cases he has investigated and injustices he has succeeded in having put right, amounting between 1967 and 1977 to 3,000 and 830 respectively. Many of these would not otherwise have been remedied, as other channels of redress had already been tried before the Commissioner was approached. It is also necessary to assess the influence that the Commissioner has had upon the executive generally. The cautious way in which the first three holders of the office, each of whom has been a former civil servant, have performed their duties has ensured that the office has not had the adverse effect upon 'the prompt and efficient despatch of public business' which was predicted in the early 1960s.[24] Nevertheless the possibility that decisions will be referred to the Commissioner has various implications for officials and for the way in which they perform their duties. These will be discussed in the final section of this chapter.

Parliamentary committees

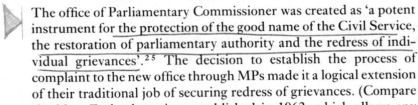

The office of Parliamentary Commissioner was created as 'a potent instrument for the protection of the good name of the Civil Service, the restoration of parliamentary authority and the redress of individual grievances'.[25] The decision to establish the process of complaint to the new office through MPs made it a logical extension of their traditional job of securing redress of grievances. (Compare the New Zealand version, established in 1962, which allows any citizen to approach the Commissioner direct on payment of a small fee.) The establishment of a Select Committee on the Parliamentary Commissioner for Administration was designed to consolidate the link with Parliament and to involve some backbenchers more closely in problems of administration. It occurred at the same time as the House of Commons was setting up a number of new and specialized committees to review particular blocks of administrative work.

  For some time three committees had been in existence which enabled MPs to interrogate civil servants and enquire into details of administration. These were the Public Accounts Committee, established in 1861; the Estimates Committee (1912); and the

Select Committee on Nationalised Industries (1956). In the early 1960s a group of academics and House of Commons officials, known as the Study of Parliament Group, began to advocate the establishment of further committees which would specialize in particular areas of government and thus increase the effectiveness of parliamentary scrutiny of the executive. Their recommendations were taken up by the Labour Party and, spurred on by an influx of young and enthusiastic MPs in the 1964 and 1966 elections, the Government decided in 1966 to establish two new select committees on an experimental basis, one to deal with a subject, science and technology, and the other to cover a single department, the Ministry of Agriculture, Fisheries and Food. An important feature of these new committees was that they would examine witnesses and hear evidence in public.

This experiment lasted until 1970.[26] The Select Committee on Science and Technology operated throughout this period, but that on Agriculture was disbanded in 1969. Committees on Education and Science (1968–70), Race Relations and Immigration (1968–70), Scottish Affairs (1969–70) and Overseas Aid (1969–70) were also appointed during this period. In 1969 the Government announced that it was conducting a review of the operation of these committees. It had before it a report of the Commons Procedure Committee which drew attention to the adverse effect that the new committees had had upon the work of the Estimates Committee and which advocated its replacement by a new Select Committee on Expenditure with a larger number of members and wider terms of reference.[27] The 1970 General Election intervened before the completion of this review, and it was the Conservative Government which published a Green Paper in 1970 which accepted the case for setting up a Select Committee on Expenditure, although not on the scale of the original proposal, and advocated the retention of a limited number of 'subject' specialized committees but the abandonment of the experiment with 'departmental' committees.[28] A committee system along these lines was created in 1971 and, with only minor modifications, has been in existence since then. In the 1977–8 session of Parliament, the following committees, whose main function was to scrutinize the activities of central departments were in existence:

Table 5.1
Scrutiny Committees in 1977–8

Committee	Number of members	Subcommittees
Public Accounts Committee	14	
Expenditure Committee	49	General; Defence and External Affairs; Environment; Trade and Industry; Education, Arts and Home Office; Social Services and Employment.
Nationalised Industries	15	A; B; C.
Overseas Development	9	
Parliamentary Commissioner for Administration	8	
Race Relations and Immigration	10	
Science and Technology	14	General Purposes; Technological Innovation; Japan.

The Public Accounts Committee is the traditional watchdog of public money. It considers reports from the Comptroller and Auditor General on irregular and unusual features of government expenditure and makes recommendations after examining papers and witnesses, usually the Comptroller and Auditor General and the Permanent Secretary of the department concerned, if it chooses to do so. The scope of its work is indicated by some of its recommendations in 1976–7, covering subjects such as the four-fold increase in the cost of building Liverpool's new teaching hospital; the substantial losses incurred by the Professional and Executive Recruitment Service, particularly in relation to the number of clients for whom it found jobs; and the lack of adequate monitoring of the Department of Industry's financial assistance to a number of workers' cooperatives.[29]

Whereas the Public Accounts Committee looks at expenditure

already incurred, the Expenditure Committee takes as its starting point the government's forward projections of public expenditure which are set out in an annual White Paper. Unlike its predecessor, the Estimates Committee, it can examine expenditure other than that contained in departmental estimates, and it has the power to consider the policies which lie behind particular heads of expenditure. The Committee operates through six subcommittees, each of which enjoys a considerable degree of autonomy. In its first five years of existence the Committee has produced a vast number of reports covering a very wide variety of subjects. They can be placed in three broad categories: technical appraisals of the way in which the government controls public expenditure and of the assumptions behind that exercise; examination of spending on particular functions of government, for instance Employment Services and Training, and Urban Transport Planning; and examination of the operation of particular departments, such as the Ministry of Defence and the Department of Education and Science.[30]

The nature of the Expenditure Committee's enquiries has not, however, been very different from those of its predecessor. In general it has not sought to challenge the government on policy questions. However, occasionally the Committee has shown a willingness to examine issues which are politically sensitive in that decisions have just been taken or are about to be taken by the government. Thus, the Trade and Industry Subcommittee undertook an enquiry into the Government's rescue plan for Chrysler UK Ltd shortly after it had been announced, and the Defence and External Affairs Subcommittee is at the time of writing conducting an enquiry into the report of the Central Policy Review Staff on Britain's overseas representation, in advance of a government decision on its recommendations.

It is not possible to outline the nature of each of the committees, which vary considerably both in the sort of issues they have examined and in their working methods. In any case, our concern in this chapter is with the impact that they have upon government. At the outset it must be stressed that the committees operate within constraints laid down by the government. This can be seen very clearly in a comparison of the experience of the first two specialized committees. The Select Committee on Agriculture decided that its first task should be to look at the quality of the Ministry of Agriculture's assessment of the effect on agriculture if Britain joined the Common Market. This raised questions, previously regarded as confidential, about the basis on which a Minister reached decisions. Indeed, as the late J. P. Mackintosh (himself a political scientist interested in parliamentary reform, and a member of the Committee) made clear, such was the main aim of some of its members.[31] Moreover, the Committee came into conflict with the Foreign Office over its wish to go to Brussels to see if the official picture was correct and to see in detail why the Foreign Office had declined to approve an extra assistant for the agricultural attaché to the British delegation there. The Foreign Office refused to grant the second request but eventually agreed to a meeting in Brussels on a basis that did not compromise official negotiations. The Committee's report on all this did not, in the end, make major criticisms, but it claimed (probably rightly) that it had succeeded in getting information published about the Common Market that would not normally have been available.[32] According to Mackintosh, the Government reappointed the Committee in 1967 only after considerable delay and after 'press-ganging' nine new members to restrain the original sixteen. The Committee then turned its attention to the equally difficult subject of import replacement and had not completed its work when the Government peremptorily ordered it to close down. After a struggle an extension was granted which allowed the review to be completed.

The Select Committee on Science and Technology presents a marked contrast. Its membership has been relatively stable and a high proportion has had some previous connection with science and technology. Its first report dealt in great detail with the nuclear reactor programme and was welcomed by the Minister of Technology. Since then it has produced a large number of reports on subjects such as defence research, tracked hovercraft, the UK computer industry and the development of alternative sources of energy. Some of its reports have been highly critical of the government, but they have mainly been concerned with technical matters which lie outside the mainstream of party politics. They are also relatively self-contained. By contrast, the effect on food prices of joining the Common Market is of considerable political interest. If the Agriculture Committee had discovered weaknesses in the machinery for briefing the Minister of Agriculture it would have been easy for opponents of the Government to make political capital out of it. This sort of investigation poses a much more realistic threat to the doctrine that the Minister is personally accountable to Parliament. It also strikes at the doctrine of collective responsibility, since the views of the Minister of Agriculture may not coincide with the policy that finally emerges from the Cabinet.[33]

Ultimately, therefore, the government can disband committees which are troublesome; this reflects the fusion of the executive and the legislature in Britain and accounts for the marked differences in the power of committees of the House of Commons in comparison with their counterparts in the US Congress. In Britain the government also has more subtle means of influencing the behaviour of committees. It determines their membership and can exclude MPs likely to cause trouble. It is also important to remember that a high proportion of MPs aspire to ministerial office and therefore do not want to fall out with the leaders of their party, whereas US Congressmen usually have ambitions within Congress, and will seek for instance, the chairmanship of an influential committee.

It is not only for these reasons that parliamentary committees have tended to keep away from broad questions of policy. The selection of subjects for investigation is a very delicate matter on various accounts. Again, the reaction of the government is crucial; firstly, committees look to the government as the main source of information. At one level this has presented few problems; only on very few occasions has the government actually withheld information sought by a committee or prevented it from hearing particular witnesses.[34] More serious is the question of how ready the government may be fully to confide in committees and to release the information they really need, whether in written memoranda or oral evidence; a problem which is exacerbated by lack of expertise in cross-examination on the part of many MPs. It is for this reason that committees increasingly in recent years have appointed advisers, some of whom have been experts in the field of particular enquiries, to assist them in assimilating evidence and framing questions.[35]

Secondly, the choice of subjects for investigation usually reflects a committee's hope that its report will have some influence upon the government. Occasionally a committee may be able to place an issue on the political agenda. For instance, the enquiry by the Employment and Social Services Subcommittee of the Expenditure Committee in 1972 into facilities for private patients in the National Health Service was a major factor in bringing this question, which had lain dormant for many years, to the forefront of political debate, and eventually led to the enactment of legislation in 1976.[36] Generally, however, committees have to work within a framework set by the government, thus selecting subjects on which Ministers shortly have to take decisions but at the same time being careful not to intrude upon sensitive areas. Similarly, to enhance their impact, committees are likely to attach importance to producing a unanimous report and will therefore generally avoid subjects of intense partisan disagreement.

The impact of committee reports is difficult to gauge. The government does publish its observations on reports, normally in the form of a White Paper, but there is frequently a considerable delay before this occurs. Its reaction may range from agreement to specific action, through non-committal acceptance to outright rejection. But even in the first case it is difficult to assess how far its decision was influenced by the views of the committee and how far by a host of other factors which may have been involved. It is certainly hard to identify many decisions which would have been different had select committees not been in existence and the conclusion of one recent survey was that

It is hardly to be questioned that the increased effort put in by select committees and by their agents and witnesses, resulting in so large a quantity of evidence and recommendation, has had but a modest impact on the course of public policy, on patterns of expenditure, and on levels of spending.[37]

It appears, therefore, that the main achievement of the new committees has been the publication of papers and evidence submitted to them, rather than in their specific recommendations. The practice of holding public sessions has resulted in good press coverage and in more informed public discussion of frequently complex issues. At the same time, MPs on the committees have been able to familiarize themselves with particular topics and to study them more intensively than is possible in a full-scale parliamentary debate. There is a risk, however, of overloading both the parliamentary and the administrative machines. It has been noted earlier that the creation of the new specialized committees in the 1960s had an adverse effect upon the Estimates Committee, and a number of MPs argue that committee work has detracted from the floor of the House.[38] More serious, perhaps, are the implications of these committees for the government. It is to this question and to the effect of the Parliamentary Commissioner upon the government that the last section of this chapter is devoted.

Administrative implications

The most immediate effect upon the executive of these parliamentary developments is to create more work. Papers for a committee have to be prepared and witnesses have to be briefed. Both have to be done with some care, in the knowledge that written and oral evidence will be published. This burden falls primarily on the shoulders of civil servants. Between 1970 and 1974 only fourteen Ministers appeared before the Expenditure Committee and the four other specialized committees. During the same period, however, over three hundred civil servants gave evidence.[39] A much larger number were, of course, involved in briefing those who did appear and in preparing written memoranda. The burden varies between departments and at different times, but there can be no doubt that on occasions it can be seriously disruptive. This effect is exacerbated by the fact that most committees expect to receive evidence from very senior personnel, frequently the Permanent Secretary. The more senior the witness, the more extensive is the briefing he must receive and the greater the opportunity costs in terms of other work which has to be postponed.

Time and effort are also needed to deal with complaints referred to the Parliamentary Commissioner for Administration. The Commissioner has described in detail his method of conducting investigations.[40] His first step, after confirming that a complaint is not outside his jurisdiction, is to ask the Permanent Secretary of the department concerned for comment, which usually contains 'a full statement of the facts known to the department and of the department's view of the case, often with supporting evidence'. Even in cases that are taken no further, there is a good deal of work involved in assembling details of a perhaps complicated history going back a year or more. But in most cases this is followed by an examination of departmental files, discussion with the officials concerned, and discussion of a 'results' report with the Permanent Secretary, who has to consider at that stage whether to advise the Minister to prohibit the publication of any information contained in the report. Any official mentioned in the original complaint must also be given the opportunity to comment. Nor need that be the end of the matter, since MPs can still question the Minister about the Commissioner's findings. Since the complaint may concern advice given informally or on the telephone (a characteristic of many cases in Social Security or Inland Revenue) it may be difficult to recall incidents of which there is no record. A secondary effect of the investigations may therefore be to make departments keep more detailed records of trivial occurrences against the possibility of an inquisition by the Commissioner. The correction of a relatively small number of injustices and the gain in public confidence arising from the Commissioner's investigations need, therefore, to be weighed fairly carefully against the costs in administrative time, disruption of normal work during an enquiry and possibly greater reluctance on the part of staff dealing with the public to step outside safe limits in an effort to be helpful.

Detailed record-keeping has always been a feature of public departments and these recent developments are additional to the work involved in dealing with MPs' correspondence, material for parliamentary debates (always painstakingly voluminous, since it covers all points that MPs are likely to raise, and largely consigned, unused, to oblivion after the debate) and answers to questions in the House. The number of such questions is substantial. In a typical week in 1976, 77 questions received an oral answer and 787 a written reply. The cost of answering each of the former was estimated to average £26 and the latter £16.[41] Kingdom has recalled the saying:

> a civil servant's time divides into three parts: doing his own work, interfering with other people's work, and saying what he is doing ... The last is a very necessary part of democracy but one feels it is on the increase and it can seem to take up a lot more than a third of the time ... What happens, one wonders, if it rises to a point where there is no time for anything else – when your whole doing consists of saying what you are doing. Is it something like the curious problem of what happens in the end when two snakes start swallowing each other by the tail?[42]

A second effect of these developments has been to increase the control exercised by Ministers and senior civil servants over their departments. In part this occurs because of the increased flow of information they receive. In assembling details of a case being investigated by the Commissioner and in mastering a brief prior to giving evidence to a committee, senior personnel become acquainted with details of work of which they would otherwise know little. The Commissioner's investigations can make the Minister's task easier by exposing irregularities and weaknesses the Minister himself would have wanted to put right had he been aware of them. The existence of the Commissioner and of parliamentary committees also adds to the apparatus of sanctions that obliges administrators constantly to bear in mind how their actions will look if exposed to parliamentary scrutiny.

On the other hand, these developments have modified the relationship between Ministers and civil servants, adding to the sense of unease felt by many civil servants about their duties and loyalties. The Commissioner's investigations have opened up the process of decision-making within departments and although his reports do not name officials, in some cases it is relatively easy to identify who was responsible for particular decisions with the aid of a copy of the *Civil Service Yearbook*. This consequence of the Commissioner's work was strongly criticized by George Brown as Foreign Secretary in 1968 in the debate on the Sachsenhausen Case; but an attempt by the Government to prevent the Select Committee interrogating any official other than the Principal Officer did not succeed.[43] Although the Permanent Secretary is almost invariably called at some time in every enquiry, civil servants at all levels down to Assistant Secretary often give evidence to select committees. They have therefore become more visible to the general public, and at the same time it is difficult for them under skilful cross-examination to avoid expressing personal views, on a wide variety of questions, which may not accord fully with those of their Minister. The effect of these developments has therefore been to modify the traditional convention of ministerial responsibility under which Ministers are the sole spokesmen of their departments, their officials remaining largely anonymous. However, as yet, it has not been replaced by any other set of 'rules and understandings'. Indeed, in 1978 the Government rather blandly restated the traditional position.[44]

Along with the other developments discussed earlier in this chapter, these institutional changes have disquieted many senior civil servants, as was reflected in the decision of their staff association, the First Division Association, to set up a committee in 1969 to enquire into the professional standards expected of civil servants. Its report, published in 1971, identified various situations which officials faced in their daily work where they sought guidance as to how they should behave.[45] A common factor in each of these situations was anxiety as to the nature of a civil servant's loyalty to his Minister.

Since 1971 a number of further developments have occurred which are potentially of even greater significance for the role of senior officials. Their ability to serve both political parties impartially has been brought into question by the appearance of differences in the parties' views on a number of major issues, which are probably greater than at any time since 1945. The relationship between the executive and the legislature has been altered, some would argue irrevocably, by the experience of minority government in 1974 and again after 1976. Entry into the EEC has implications, for instance in the role of the courts in controlling executive action, which are not yet fully appreciated.

In addition, the confirmation by referendum in 1975 of EEC entry challenged the supremacy of Parliament, and it seems likely that this device will be used again. Lastly, the 1977–8 session of Parliament was dominated by debate on the setting-up of assemblies for Scotland and Wales which, if they come into being, will fundamentally alter the way in which the system of government as a whole operates.

It is not easy to predict the long-term significance of these and other developments in contemporary British politics. It may be that after the next general election the traditional pattern will be restored. However, if even a few of them become permanent features, some reconsideration of the relationship between Ministers and officials will be inevitable. And, in turn, the abandonment or modification of the doctrine of ministerial responsibility would have major implications for various aspects of civil service staffing, such as the maintenance of a career service and the role of the generalist, which, as we saw in Chapter III, depend for their existence upon a particular constitutional environment.

Notes

1 In its evidence to Fulton, the First Division Association estimated that its members spent between a fifth and a quarter of their time on functions directly related to the parliamentary system. Fulton Report, Vol. 5, p. 119.

2 *H.C. Debs*, Vol. 724 (8 February 1966) cols 209–14.

3 For example, see the Labour Party's evidence to the Fulton Committee (Fulton Report, Vol. 5, p. 655); J. Haines, *The Politics of Power* (London, 1977); J. Bruce-Gardyne, *Whatever Happened to the Quiet Revolution?* (London, 1974).

4 The problems of coping with this paperwork are discussed in R. H. S. Crossman, *The Diaries of a Cabinet Minister*, Vol. 1 (London, 1975) pp. 21–2, 78–9.

5 The role of special advisers is discussed further in Chap. XIII. See also R. Klein and J. Lewis, 'Advice and Dissent in British Government: The Case of Special Advisers', *Policy and Politics* Vol. 6 (1977) pp. 1–25; J. E. Mitchell, 'Special Advisers: A Personal View', *Public Administration* Vol. 56 (1978) pp. 87–98.

6 For example, in April 1976 the Department of the Environment had ten Ministers at four levels (Secretary of State, Minister,

Minister of State, Parliamentary Under Secretary). After the creation of a separate Department of Transport in September 1976, it still had seven Ministers at four levels. See A. Clark, 'Ministerial Supervision and the Size of the Department of the Environment', *Public Administration* Vol. 55 (1977) pp. 197–204.

7 *Report of the Tribunal appointed to inquire into certain issues in relation to the circumstances leading up to the cessation of trading by the Vehicle and General Company Ltd.*, H.C. 133 (1971–2).

8 See the Home Secretary's speech, *H.C. Debs*, Vol. 836 (1 May 1972) col. 159.

9 The controversy surrounding the publication of the diaries is outlined in H. Young, *The Crossman Affair* (London, 1976).

10 T. D. Kingdom, 'The Confidential Advisers of Ministers', *Public Administration* Vol. 44 (1966) p. 271.

11 The effect of British EEC entry upon the relationship between Ministers and civil servants is one of the areas identified by David Coombes as needing research. See D. Kavanagh and R. Rose (eds), *New Trends in British Politics* (London, 1977) Chap. 4.

12 This was followed up by a letter sent by the Head of the Home Civil Service to Permanent Secretaries in July 1977 informing them that, contrary to earlier practice, the working assumption should be that background material *would* be published unless Ministers decided otherwise. See *The Guardian*, 23 January 1978.

13 Fulton Report, Vol. 1, paras 277–80.

14 *Report of Departmental Committee on Section 2 of the Official Secrets Act 1911*, Cmnd. 5104 (1972).

15 *The Citizen and the Administration: the Redress of Grievances* (Whyatt Report) (London, 1961).

16 The Government's case is set out in *Area Excluded from Parliamentary Commissioner's Investigation*, Cmnd. 4661 (1971) pp. 2–3.

17 These changes in interpretation are discussed by Frank Stacey in *British Government 1966 to 1975* (London, 1975) pp. 185–6, and by Geoffrey Marshall in S. A. Walkland and M. Ryle (eds), *The Commons in the Seventies* (London, 1977) pp. 232–5.

18 *Seventh Report of the Parliamentary Commissioner for Administration 1974–75*, H.C. 680, p. 14.

19 *Second Report of the Parliamentary Commissioner for Administration 1977–78*, H.C. 157, p. 5.

20 Nor does the Commissioner believe that he needs the power to enforce implementation of his recommendations. See *The Guardian*, 8 February 1978.

21 *Fifth Report of the Parliamentary Commissioner for Administration 1975–76*, H.C. 496, pp. 194–7 and *Second Report from the Select*

Committee on the Parliamentary Commissioner for Administration 1976–77, H.C. 524, pp. xi–xiv.

22 Second Report of the Parliamentary Commissioner for Administration 1971–72, H.C. 116, p. 9.

23 See Our Fettered Ombudsman, Report by a committee of Justice (London, 1977) pp. 3–5. In his report for 1977–8, the Commissioner indicated that he would be willing to receive complaints direct from the public if Parliament so decided.

24 See Stacey, op. cit., p. 190.

25 H.C. Debs, Vol. 734 (18 October 1966) col. 61.

26 For details see Chaps 10 and 11 in A. H. Hanson and B. Crick (eds), The Commons in Transition (London, 1970).

27 First Report from the Select Committee on Procedure 1968–69, H.C. 410, 'Scrutiny of Public Expenditure and Administration'.

28 Select Committees of the House of Commons, Cmnd. 4507 (1970).

29 Eighth and Ninth Reports from the Committee of Public Accounts 1976–77, H.C. 531 and 532.

30 The work of the Expenditure Committee is discussed by Ann Robinson in Walkland and Ryle, op. cit., pp. 144–8.

31 J. P. Mackintosh, 'Failure of a Reform', New Society Vol. 12 (28 November 1968) p. 791.

32 Report from the Select Committee on Agriculture 1966–67, H.C. 378–XVII, 'British Agriculture, Fisheries and Food and the European Economic Community'. See also Special Report from the Select Committee on Agriculture 1968–69, H.C. 138, which is devoted to the practical difficulties experienced by the Committee and the issues of principle which they raise.

33 See, for example, the views of Harold Wilson in 'The Prime Minister on the Machinery of Government', The Listener Vol. LXXV (13 April 1967) p. 481.

34 In 1975 the Prime Minister refused to allow the Chancellor of the Duchy of Lancaster, Harold Lever, to give evidence to the Expenditure Committee on the Chrysler rescue plan on the grounds that, although he had had special responsibilities in this matter, he was not the Minister with departmental responsibility. In 1978 there was conflict between the Select Committee on Nationalised Industries and the Secretary of State for Industry and the Chairman of the British Steel Corporation about the disclosure of information.

35 The type of people appointed as advisers is outlined by Nevil Johnson in S. A. Walkland and M. Ryle, op. cit., pp. 184–5.

36 Fourth Report from the Expenditure Committee 1971–72, H.C. 172. The gradual elimination of private facilities in NHS hospitals was provided for in the Health Services Act, 1976.

37 Nevil Johnson in Walkland and Ryle, op. cit., pp. 195–6.
38 See, for example, the views of Michael Foot in *The State of the Nation: Parliament* (London, 1975) pp. 190–3.
39 Study of Parliament Group, *Specialist Committees in the British Parliament* (London, 1976) p. 26.
40 *Fourth Report of the Parliamentary Commissioner for Administration 1967–68*, H.C. 134, paras 12–15. The effect of the Parliamentary Commissioner on departments generally is discussed in R. Gregory and P. Hutchesson, *Our Parliamentary Ombudsman* (London, 1975) Chap. 10.
41 *H.C. Debs*, Vol. 891 (29 April 1975), cols 113–14.
42 T. D. Kingdom, op. cit., p. 272.
43 *Second Report from the Select Committee on the Parliamentary Commissioner for Administration 1967–68*, H.C. 350, pp. xi–xii.
44 *The Civil Service, Government Observations on the Eleventh Report of the Expenditure Committee 1976–77*, Cmnd. 7117 (1978).
45 A summary of the report was published in *Public Administration* Vol. 50 (1972) pp. 167–82. It is discussed by Maurice Wright in 'The Professional Conduct of Civil Servants', *Public Administration* Vol. 51 (1973) pp. 1–15.

PART TWO

Theory

VI
People
and organization

Organization theory

We have now outlined the main features of the British system of central administration as it is at present. Its evolution has been related to changes in the work it has been asked to do. Some parts of its task (for example some aspects of the parliamentary system of control) have hardly changed at all over the last century. Other parts have altered a great deal, and continue to alter at an increasing rate. The administrative system has to cope with many new problems in the fields of planning and management, while some of the old ones have become much more complex, particularly those of coordinating a growing area of government control and influence.

To meet these new demands, the administrative structure has been modified in a number of ways, with differing degrees of success. The attempted solutions can be grouped in terms of structure, process and personnel. By structural solutions are meant experiments with the grouping of government functions in departments and agencies and with the stratification of responsibilities between levels of administration. Examples of the first include the amalgamation of departments and the creation of new ones. Examples of the second include the changing relationships of the central departments (Treasury, Cabinet Office and Civil Service Department) to the rest of Whitehall, and the transfer of functions from conventional departments to *ad hoc* agencies. By process solutions are meant changes in the way government conducts its business, particularly in the areas of expenditure planning, policy review, target-setting for other agencies, and systems of accountability; some of the latter have been touched upon in the last chapter. Among personnel solutions are included the changes in recruitment, training and career structure which were discussed in Chapters III and IV.

Such issues are the subject-matter of organization theory, which since the early 1960s has been one of the fastest growing areas of applied social science. There is now a vast literature on organization.[1] Much of it is American, although British and European writers have made distinguished contributions. Much of it is concerned with industry, and care is needed in translating it to the public sector; but there is a good deal of work on public bureaucracies also. Some general discussion of organization theory is therefore a desirable preliminary to the examination in Part Three of specific problems in public administration.

Two conclusions can be anticipated here. One is that there are dangers in embarking on a piecemeal approach to administrative change; changes in any part of a complex system have unexpected and often unwanted consequences elsewhere. Administrative reform can at best achieve a better balance among imperfections: there are limits to what administration can do.[2] The other is that all failures should not be blamed on administrative deficiencies. No amount of restructuring will avoid the need for political decisions about the claims of increased personal consumption, expanding social services, industrial investment and defence on a limited national purse.

Classical theories of management

Two generations ago there was a wave of optimism that some of the problems of public administration would yield to scientific analysis. In 1941 the Select Committee on National Expenditure looked at the small beginnings of what are now the Management Services divisions of the CSD. Its report complained that the years between the wars had been marked by 'almost complete failure to foster the *systematic study of organization* as applied to government departments'[3] [our italics]. It suggested that O & M should be the supreme arm of Treasury control and that the remit of O & M officers should cover the distribution of functions at the top of the civil service hierarchy as well as the discharge of routine business at the bottom. A few years later the theme was taken up again by the Estimates Committee. It defined the purpose of O & M as 'to secure maximum efficiency in the operation of the government's executive machinery and, *by the expert application of scientific methods to organization*, to achieve economy in cost and labour' (our italics). It also suggested that more attention should be paid to the higher levels of administration: 'The part played by O & M techniques and knowledge must be that of planning the structure and machinery of government rather than that of attending to its plumbing and maintenance.'[4]

Members of the Select Committee were aware of the impact in the United States of the Brownlow Committee on Administrative Management. This expert, three-man committee had been appointed by President Roosevelt to examine the chaos of administrative agencies created to carry out the New Deal programme. The successful implementation of many of their recommendations was hailed as a victory for analytic reasoning in a field previously dominated by politics.[5] The Committee claimed to be applying universal principles.

> The foundations of effective management, in public affairs no less than in private, are well known. They have emerged universally wherever men have worked together for some common purpose ... Stated in simple terms, these canons of efficiency require the establishment of a responsible and effective chief executive as the centre of energy, direction and administrative management; the systematic organization of all activities in the hands of a qualified personnel under the direction of the chief executive; and to aid him in this, the establishment of appropriate managerial and staff agencies.[6]

In this it was echoing the founders of the two (rather ill-assorted) streams of what is now often termed the classical school of management theorists.

Frederick W. Taylor (1856–1915) and his followers adopted the title 'scientific management' for the critical approach to production methods which they developed and recommended. In essence their method consists of careful study and pre-planning of repetitive operations in order to find the 'one best way' of doing a job. Under names like work study, O & M, and production engineering, their techniques have provided a foundation for modern mass-production methods in the factory and in the office. Allied to the modern computer, they have developed into an impressive range of management tools for simulating and pre-programming expensive operations before taking final decisions. Critical path analysis, operational research, statistical decision theory and cost-benefit analysis all belong to the same family. They have been extensively used in public administration and need not be discussed in detail here.[7]

Taylor claimed, with some justification, that his methods were equally applicable in all spheres of life from government to the domestic kitchen, and that their general adoption would make great achievements possible.[8] This is true, and it has happened, where they are applicable (although not, as we shall see in a later section, without side-effects). But the field of application is limited to repetitive, or very expensive, operations. It may be sensible to invest some time and energy discovering the 'one best way' of travelling from London to Hong Kong via Warsaw; but it is hardly sensible to spend much time investigating the most economical route for a single journey from a government office in Curzon Street to one in Marsham Street. At high administrative level a fair proportion of problems fall into the second group. Or they involve questions of policy or structure in which efficiency tests are hard to find and are subordinated to political factors. Even at management level, efficiency is relative to a stated goal, and the real problem may be to define the goal. Here Taylor cannot help. As W. J. M. Mackenzie put it, Taylor's theory is 'not the science *of* management, but science *for* management, an ambiguity neatly concealed by the phrase "scientific management"'.[9]

The other stream of thought is associated with the name of Henri Fayol (1841–1925), a successful general manager of a French mining company. Fayol attributed his success to the application of 'principles of administration'. He believed that some such principles were valid in any field and that a body of administrative theory could be developed, partly from the reflections of successful administrators, and could be taught. After retiring at the age of 77, he reviewed the organization of the French post and telegraph service and took part in an enquiry on the tobacco monopoly, attributing their deficiencies to failure to apply sound administrative principles. He also founded an early Centre for Administrative Studies in Paris.[10]

Fayol's own principles were intuitive generalizations. They are concerned with the kind of formal structure that the head of a firm should develop as an instrument of his will. There are principles concerned with the need for specialization, stability in post (to which Fayol felt political leaders gave insufficient attention), unity of command, a hierarchical chain of command, and so on. As administrative proverbs they appeal to common sense if they are not examined too closely. They used to be popular with management consultants who found them clinically useful, in a somewhat refined form, as a check-list of possible organizational diseases. It was essentially Fayol's principles that guided the American Brownlow Committee. But they have no real coherence. Like most proverbs, they come in contradictory pairs (for example, centralization and initiative; specialization and unity) and often fail to fit the real situation.[11] Like Taylor's methods, they are concerned with means and give no guide to the choice of ends. Consequently they offer, at best, prescriptions for abstract problems of organizational engineering without taking account of the social and political problems faced by the members of real organizations. They still tend, however, to be trotted out by administrative reformers who imagine that the problems of managing a field of administration or a nationalized industry will respond to the application of whatever set of concepts is in good currency at the time.

Bureaucracy

While Taylor was writing in America and Fayol in France, the German sociologist Max Weber (1864–1920) was making a more lasting contribution to organization theory. His analysis of an 'ideal type' bureaucracy has been criticized and refined. But it remains the most-quoted starting point for the study of large organizations, particularly in the public sector.

The word 'bureaucracy' has many meanings.[12] Some are pejorative: sociologists sometimes define it as an organization that is too inflexible to learn from its own mistakes[13] (a viewpoint which evokes a warm response from the man in the street). To political scientists it is a system of government by 'bureaux' of officials. To Weber and other students of organization the word refers to the structure found in modern large organizations, whether they are government departments, business firms, armies or organized religions. It is 'a continuous organization of official functions bound by rules'.[14]

The members of a bureaucracy are career officials, who are selected, controlled and as far as possible promoted according to impersonal rules. They occupy positions in which they carry out prescribed functions. The authority which they exercise (on behalf of the head of the organization) belongs to their office, not to themselves. They are expected to approach their work impersonally, regardless of their own feelings. Senior positions are filled by promotion. The security of a salary and a life career protects them from any personal consequences of their decisions, so long as they have been taken in accordance with the rules.

Such a system has many advantages beyond the obvious ones of continuity and orderliness. The clients of large (and particularly public) organizations expect fair, and therefore uniform, treatment which can best be secured by a system of centralized authority implemented according to rules. In public administration a bureaucratic form of organization is closely associated with political accountability. A new Minister inherits an organized staff of officials ready to implement his will, with no personal commitment to the policies of his predecessor. Through them his personal charisma can be widely diffused. Weber thought that bureaucratic organization was the most rational means of deploying power in any setting.

The model implies that the person at the apex of the hierarchy is completely responsible for the organization and has its resources at his entire disposal, subject to any external constraints on his own authority. Since he cannot discharge this responsibility personally, he preserves certain key decisions to himself and, after deciding in broad terms how the organization will work, delegates limited discretion to his subordinates. They in turn reserve certain questions to themselves and delegate the rest, with slightly narrower terms of reference, and so on down the line. In a large organization like a government department, the model becomes intelligible only in terms of roles. It is inconceivable that a single person should decide consciously what to delegate and what to retain over the whole field of work. In practice, a new head would learn, fairly slowly, the delimitations of the role that had been evolved by his predecessors, while gradually modifying it to suit his own interests and abilities. In the meantime, junior staff have to keep their work moving and use their discretion in dealing with new problems. In many ways their staff work defines the problems that will later be considered higher up.

The hierarchical element in a bureaucracy supplies career rewards and sanctions, since an official's superiors can grant or withhold promotion. It also provides a chain of accountability. Does it therefore lead to efficiency? In theory, it is likely that senior officials will be more proficient than subordinates who have not yet earned promotion; the most knowledgeable members of the organization are also the most powerful. But this argument is sound only if the career structure is completely closed, if the relevant techniques are of a sort that can be learned only within the organization (as in, perhaps, the administration of a defined code of law) and if the work is not too specialized for a superior to be able to draw on his own experience in guiding his juniors. There may be some corners of older government departments where such conditions apply, but they are becoming rare, as more people with special skills are brought in to the administration and the work itself becomes more 'professionalized'. Senior posts may be filled by outsiders with no direct knowledge of the work at lower levels. Junior staff may have special qualifications or experience not shared by their nominal superiors. In such circumstances too much emphasis on supervision and control may lower the efficiency with which work is done. Most real hierarchies include fairly sharp discontinuities, with an abrupt change in character and oulook at a particular level. Posts below this level are concerned solely with the efficient performance of a defined block of work. Above it, interest shifts to the value of the activity and its relationship to others. The higher group cannot effectively supervise the lower, since it is concerned with a different type of problem.

A major weakness of the Weberian approach to organizations is its assumption that the proper task of subordinates lies in the impersonal application of general rules to particular circumstances. This is certainly a characteristic of many public services, including tax, customs, social security, and the immigration section of the Home Office. But even here there is an element of discretion at all levels.[15] In the industrial sector the need for general rules is often outweighed by the importance of giving local managers the opportunity to respond quickly and flexibly to new demands and commercial opportunities. In professionalized services, like the National Health Service and government research establishments, the most important operating conventions are established by doctors and scientists, not by the centralized sources of power and finance. In many organizations today, therefore, innovation and initiative in response to change are often fostered (or at least tolerated) at the expense of uniformity and discipline. Moreover, the higher civil service is more concerned with formulating and adapting rules than with implementing rules determined by others.

Another challenge to the robot-like demands of the ideal bureaucratic system comes from the belief that they are inconsistent with the needs of staff and with their right to have some say in what they do during the working day. This challenge takes many forms, from the conviction of many social scientists that some autonomy and opportunity for personal development must be granted if individuals are to make their full contribution to organizational objectives,[16] to the more cynical view that power to influence the implementation of policy has shifted from the nominal decision-makers to organized labour, even in the public sector. Nevertheless, it seems that some elements of bureaucracy are needed to maintain political accountability and to put into effect the intentions of politically legitimate decision-makers.

Human relations

Any organization needs some kind of control structure if it is not to fall apart. In a voluntary cooperative we find self-control by members who share common objectives. There are probably some elements of this in most organizations: even prisons, whose purpose is control through coercion, are in practice run partly by the prisoners themselves. In a professionalized organization, or one where hierarchical supervision is difficult or inappropriate, the most significant form of control may be through the initial selection of personnel, possibly followed by occasional performance reviews. Professional training and some forms of academic training inculcate values and approaches which enable the organization to rely to a large extent on self-control. This is pre-entry socialization. Training and experience on the job are forms of post-entry socialization. In any wage-paying organization, the reward system offers incentives which can sometimes be manipulated to encourage some forms of behaviour and discourage others. If, however, money is the only incentive (as envisaged by Taylor and to some extent by Weber), day-to-day control will be exercised by a hierarchical superior who gives detailed instructions and checks whether they have been carried out. The effects of this kind of control have been closely studied by management and social scientists, some of whom claim that it is inherently damaging to the individual and, in practice, counter-productive for the organization.[17]

Underlying these arguments is a belief that the demands made by bureaucratic organizations conflict with the human needs of their members. People need social and psychological rewards, like status and self-fulfilment, as well as a salary and economic security. Moreover, organizational standards differ from those of the outside world. In society at large, people are respected for their integrity, their self-reliance, their home-centredness and their ability to plan ahead on a fairly long time-scale. By contrast, a bureaucrat is expected as part of his work to carry out the instructions of others and to subordinate his own values and needs to those of the organization. His career is planned for him and he is often expected to accept abrupt changes in function and status without complaint when the organization requires it.

The first important recognition that failure to take account of these conflicts might affect performance on the job came about fifty years ago after a famous series of experiments in the Western Electric factory at Hawthorne, near Chicago.[18] Social psychologists began to think about factors affecting the satisfactions men obtained from work. They noted that many 'human needs' – for recognition and social esteem – were satisfied through the working group which interposed itself between the individual and the organization and conditioned his attitude to it. They suggested that managements should take account of these social aspects, and that management itself was essentially a social skill. It was thought that factors leading to high job-satisfaction – like a participative rather than authoritarian pattern of supervision – would lead to greater involvement in work and to higher output.

The original findings have proved to be naïve. Many exponents of a 'human relations' approach were excessively optimistic about the effect on productivity of involving workers more in their work. It has become clear that in some cultures workers are conditioned to expect substantial differences between their roles at home and work, and do not mind work that is intrinsically unsatisfying, so long as it is adequately paid. But meantime, the original theories have inspired a great deal of useful research about 'group dynamics', the effect of different leadership styles, motivation and attitudes to work. A fresh dimension has been added to the formal theories of organization discussed earlier, and much of the new material is based on empirical research.

The original work at Hawthorne was concerned with industrial assembly workers, and much of the subsequent research has been directed at this group. But it is probable that 'human relations' factors are more important at senior levels. American studies suggest that the needs for 'self-actualization', creativity and achievement are felt most keenly by managers and professional staff.[19] At these levels, basic material needs are not so pressing, but work as such occupies a more important part of life. Social and geographical mobility weaken the claims of other ties and, for people like senior civil servants, long hours of duty and commuting reduce the opportunities for social contacts outside the work place. In large organizations, where authority is centralized, postings are frequent, and it is seldom possible to take a decision without impinging on the discretion of colleagues. Even those near the top are likely to complain about the lack of autonomy and achievement.

In general, the 'human relations' approach has failed because research has shown that human beings are readier to adapt themselves to organizational roles than seems likely on *a priori* grounds. But this does not mean that they acquiesce in all the organization's demands. Explicitly or implicitly, they bargain with the organization. Working groups fix a price for accepting tighter controls and adopting better methods. The price may be too high to be met without modifying the original objectives and the result is a compromise between what the organization wants and what its members want. To take an example from higher levels in the professional civil service, it may not be possible to obtain the services of a prominent architect unless he is given a chance to do some building himself, nor to recruit scientists unless they are given facilities for research that is not strictly necessary. The human relations school forced organization theorists to recognize the importance of private and group objectives. But more recently interest has shifted away from the possibility of reconciling these goals with the needs of the organization to the process of bargaining through which modifications are made on both sides.[20]

The interest has been sharpened by a growth in the power of trade unions and in militancy at the shop-floor. It has become commonplace for clerical staff in, say, the Department of Health and Social Security to 'work to rule' or take other forms of industrial action to extract concessions from the management. While this has not yet been properly studied, it appears that militancy is most prevalent when large groups of staff work together in factory-type conditions. Solutions have been sought along the lines of worker-participation (already well developed in the civil service through the Whitley Council system). It has been suggested that in private industry the workforce should participate through worker-directors in policy decisions at the highest level.[21] Similar suggestions have been made in the public sector and applied in the nationalized industries.[22] But in the civil service and local government there is an obvious clash between industrial democracy and political democracy. It may be accepted that public servants have the same right as other workers to frustrate the implementation of political decisions, except on their terms. But, to take the argument to extremes, it is difficult to accept the possibility that representatives of the civil service clerical staff should take part in policy decisions at Cabinet committee level.

Modern organization theory

Most of the early theories were incomplete. Some treated administration as a technological system geared to efficiency; others regarded it as a social process, in which morale may be as important as the attainment of objectives; others, to be discussed in the next chapter, described it as a system for making decisions and formulating policy. First, however, we will examine some of the attempts which have been made both to modify and improve the original concepts and to integrate all the approaches into a general theory of organization.

Contingency theory

Weber's belief in the efficiency of bureaucratic patterns of organization has been subjected to exhaustive tests, both theoretical and empirical. So has Fayol's suggestion that there are universally valid principles of organization. For example, Pugh and his colleagues have demonstrated that the concept of a bureaucracy is not as simple as it looks: an organization may adopt some Weberian characteristics (centralized authority, formalized relationships, standardized decision-making on the basis of rules, etc.) but not others, so that the characteristics are not interdependent.[23] In an internationally famous study of the Scottish electronics industry, Burns and Stalker found that firms which were organized mechanistically on Weberian lines were effective in dealing with a stable environment, but were unable to react quickly enough to rapidly changing technologies or market conditions; such an environment seemed to call for more flexible 'organic' methods of working.[24] After studying a hundred Essex firms, Joan Woodward concluded that different production technologies (e.g. mass production compared with one-off production) called for different managerial structures and that some firms had made difficulties for themselves by trying to apply 'universal principles' in inappropriate circumstances.[25]

At a more theoretical level, Thompson and Tuden sought an explanation of the fact that some organizations were clearly not operating in a bureaucratic fashion.[26] Their conclusion was that a bureaucratic form of organization was appropriate only when there was consensus about what needed doing and about how to do it, so that the decisions to be taken were mainly computational. If the objective was clear but there was uncertainty about means, the best strategy was likely to emerge from the collective judgement of qualified experts (i.e. a more professionalized type of organization was required). If consensus about objectives was also lacking, the working of the organization would become permeated by politics and the rational neutrality on which bureaucracy depends would not exist.

Studies like these led naturally to the abandonment of the idea that there was 'one best way'; instead, it began to look as if the best structure for any organization was 'contingent' on the nature of its task, the technology used in pursuing it, and the predictability of the environment in which it was operating. This is not however an invitation to rely on experience and intuition, since management scientists claim to have established general relationships between contingencies and requisite structure which would not be obvious to practising managers. Indeed, some writers seem to imply that the relationship is so deterministic that managers would have no choice once the contingencies had been clarified. This is manifestly untrue. Choices are influenced by internal factors, like personalities, power-play and past history as well as by external contingencies. We are brought to the idea of organization as a complex system.

System theory

The system theorists abandon the classical view of the organization as a passive instrument serving ends determined for it from outside, and see it as a semi-autonomous system which develops goals of its own. One goal is the desire to survive: there are 'conservation' objectives as well as 'performance' objectives.[27] Schon uses the phrase 'dynamic conservatism' to describe the reaction of an organization to a proposed change which threatens its basic structure and operating assumptions.[28] Another goal is to maintain some kind of equilibrium between the functional requirements of the organization and the personal objectives of its members. For example, the introduction of a new technology, or the establishment of a new research department, involves strains and political threats to existing members of an organization. If they are not recognized, the general loss in morale and efficiency (particularly at the higher levels) may outweigh the advantages to be gained from the innovation.

The problem of relating organizations effectively and stably to the environments in which they operate is one of trying to balance the economic, technological and socio-psychological advantages. The hypothesis proposed is that to optimize any one of these elements does not necessarily result in a set of conditions optimal for the system as a whole. To strive for maximum technical advantage and economic reward might well create social and psychological havoc, which in turn jeopardizes economic goals. Similarly, to attempt to create high job satisfaction might adversely affect the gain to be had from technological efficiency and so on.[29]

New goals, and new rules, emerge within the organization in the process of bargaining with its members and adapting to environmental stress. Very often the goals are mutually inconsistent, in the sense that conflicts between objectives cannot be resolved by appealing to some overriding principle. It is not, therefore, realistic to assess organizations solely by their effectiveness in achieving particular goals. The real challenge is not to secure one goal at the expense of others but to achieve and maintain some kind of practicable balance among them. An administrative organization is a self-sustaining social system which has important metabolic and adaptive functions as well as goal-centred ones. Argyris, for example, defines an organization as 'an organic interrelatedness of parts' which has three 'core activities': (a) achieving particular objectives; (b) maintaining itself internally; (c) adapting to the external environment.[30]

The system is not completely autonomous. It interacts with other systems in the environment and constantly needs to adjust its relationship to them. Moreover, changes in any part of the system have repercussions in other parts. For example, changes in the control system may affect the organization's ability to recruit staff and ultimately its capacity to cope with its work.

The notion of a system is valuable, because it focuses attention on the interconnectedness of organizational activities and on the probability that partial changes may have undesired consequences. But the concept has limitations. It suggests that the organization is an entity, reacting in a complex but passive way to changes in the environment like the Arctic hare changing its coat as well as its habits in winter. Some writers have tried, indeed, to find a general systems model, whose properties of adaptation, self-maintenance and so on are common, not only to any conceivable organization, but also to any 'system' from an atom to a galaxy, embracing cells, biological organisms, telephone networks and whole societies on the way. This approach has produced some interesting analogies (e.g. the idea that organizational growth becomes 'cancerous' at the point where its powers of coordination begin to break down[31]). But analogy can be taken too far, and the idea that an organization is not very different from an animal can be misleading. Like contingency theory, it ignores the effect of internal politics and personalities on organizational behaviour and response.

A special difficulty in a conglomerate organization and in the public sector is in deciding what the boundaries of the 'system' are. Is the system a functional division of a large department? Or is it the department as a whole? The civil service? The central government structure? The whole public sector? It is simply not true, for example, that all units of central government exhibit strong survival instincts or dynamic resistance to change: witness the amalgamation and splitting-up of government departments in the 1960s and 1970s (although these probably did not have much effect on the constituent working units). For some purposes it may be more helpful to think of systems and sub-systems which display general system characteristics in varying degrees.

Concluding comments

In the summary form in which they have been stated above, these theories may appear somewhat arid. Unfortunately, too, some organization theorists (although not on the whole those cited in our endnotes) seem to find it impossible to escape from a particularly self-defeating form of impenetrable jargon. But the persistent or selective reader will find many ideas that increase his insight into the problems of British public administration. He is likely to be both impressed at the efforts that have been made to knit various researches and concepts into a single theory and at the same time disappointed at the results.

It may be helpful to distinguish between what Mouzelis calls 'conceptual framework' and 'content' theory.[32] The former is concerned with the conceptual tools of analysis; it provides a common framework through which empirical observations can be related to one another and 'constitutes a more or less useful guide which tells the researcher how to look at organizational reality and what to look for'. By contrast, 'content' theory is concerned with sets of hypotheses about particular problems of organization. Unless the framework concepts can be made reasonably unambiguous and applied on a fairly general scale it is difficult to see how there can be any meaningful discussion of organizations at all. But this does not mean that it is also possible to arrive at 'content' theories that are universally valid. There is no reason to suppose that a statement about the relationship between the control system and the efficiency of General Motors will also be true of a government department in the Sudan,[33] without regard to differences in purpose, technology or cultural setting.

It is probably fair to claim that framework theory has developed at least to the point at which there is a common language for describing problems that occur in very different sorts of organizations – like the relationship between hierarchical control and specialization, or the effect of professionalism on innovation. Developments in theory are also helping to link the study of organizational problems to general developments in the social sciences, particularly sociology, social psychology and political science, to the enrichment of both sides.

The position in content theory is less satisfactory. There is a vast literature of conflicting research results. The organization theorist has to be careful not to make general statements about leadership and inter-group conflict by extrapolating from the results of experiments among ten-year-old schoolboys. He cannot assume that clerical workers in Paris or Newcastle will respond to the same incentives in 1980 as telephone assemblers in Chicago in the 1920s. Too many generalizations have already been proved to hold only for a particular social group in a particular cultural and economic environment. Some well-entrenched theories are not as well supported as their proponents imply. For example, many of the 'laboratory' experiments on group behaviour and on problem-solving have been conducted in rather artificial conditions with students from one or other of half a dozen United States universities. In real organizations things might happen differently.

The concepts of administration are simply systematic ways of thinking about the organization of human work and purpose. As principles they remain abstract and as such they are useful tools of exposition and analysis. But these abstract principles take on operational meaning only when they are applied to concrete organizational situations at a particular time in a particular environment. And then the cloth of principles must be cut to fit the form and personality of the organization being examined.[34]

Notes

1 Several general introductions to organization theory are cited in the Guide to Further Reading. Works on specific topics are referenced at appropriate places in the text.
2 C. C. Hood, *The Limits of Administration* (London, 1976).
3 *Sixteenth Report from the Select Committee on National Expenditure 1940–41*, H.C. 120, 'Organization and Control of the Civil Service', para. 81.
4 *Fifth Report from the Select Committee on Estimates 1946–47*, H.C. 143, 'Organization and Methods and its effect on the Staffing of Government Departments', para. 49.
5 L. Urwick and E. F. L. Brech, *The Making of Scientific Management* (London, 1957) Vol. I.

6 *Report of the President's Committee on Administrative Management* (Washington, 1937) Introduction.

7 The application of modern techniques to British public administration is discussed in John Garrett, *The Management of Government* (Harmondsworth, 1972) and Maurice Spiers, *Techniques and Public Administration* (London, 1957).

8 F. W. Taylor, *Principles and Methods of Scientific Management* (New York, 1911) Introduction.

9 W. J. M. Mackenzie, 'Science in the Study of Administration', *The Manchester School* Vol. 20 (1952) p. 8.

10 Henri Fayol (tr. Storrs), *General and Industrial Management* (London, 1949).

11 H. A. Simon, *Administrative Behavior*, 2nd edn (New York, 1957) Chap. 2.

12 Martin Albrow, *Bureaucracy* (London, 1970).

13 Michel Crozier, *The Bureaucratic Phenomenon* (London, 1964) Chap. 8.

14 Max Weber (tr. A. M. Henderson and T. Parsons), *The Theory of Social and Economic Organization* (Glencoe, Ill., 1947) p. 330.

15 M. J. Hill, *The Sociology of Public Administration* (London, 1972).

16 John Child, *Organization: a guide to problems and practice* (London, 1977) Chap. 6.

17 e.g. C. Argyris, in a series of books of which *Personality and Organization* (New York, 1957) is the best known.

18 F. J. Roethlisberger and W. J. Dickson, *Management and the Worker* (Cambridge, Mass., 1939). The experiments and their implications are discussed more briefly by E. Mayo, *The Social Problems of an Industrial Civilization* (London, 1949).

19 The research is summarized in P. B. Applewhite, *Organizational Behavior* (Englewood Cliffs, N.J., 1965) Chap. 5.

20 R. M. Cyert and J. G. March, *A Behavioral Theory of the Firm* (Englewood Cliffs, N.J., 1963); also Crozier, *The Bureaucratic Phenomenon*, op. cit.

21 *Report of the Committee of Inquiry on Industrial Democracy*, Cmnd. 6706 (London, 1977).

22 For example, the Post Office Act, 1977, created a directing board for the Post Office Corporation which included 7 worker-directors, 7 management members and 5 independent members.

23 D. S. Pugh and D. J. Hickson, *Organizational Structure and its Context* (London, 1974); D. S. Pugh and C. R. Hinings, *Organizational Structure: extensions and replications* (London, 1976).

24 T. Burns and G. M. Stalker, *The Management of Innovation*, 2nd edn (London, 1966).

25 J. Woodward, *Industrial Organization: Theory and Practice* (London, 1965).

26 J. D. Thompson and A. Tuden, 'Strategies, Structures and Processes of Administrative Decision' in J. D. Thompson *et al.* (eds), *Comparative Studies in Administration* (Pittsburgh, 1959).

27 Simon, *Administrative Behavior*, op. cit., pp. 117–18.

28 D. A. Schon, *Beyond the Stable State* (London, 1971).

29 Tom Lupton, *Management and the Social Sciences*, 1st edn (London, 1966) p. 44.

30 C. Argyris, *Integrating the Individual and the Organization* (New York, 1964) p. 17.

31 Sir Geoffrey Vickers, *The Art of Judgment: A Study of Policy Making* (London, 1965) pp. 141–2.

32 N. P. Mouzelis, *Organization and Bureaucracy* (London, 1975) p. 178.

33 W. A. Robson, 'The Managing of Organizations', *Public Administration* Vol. 44 (1966) p. 276.

34 W. S. Sayre, 'Principles of Administration', *Hospitals* (Journal of American Hospital Association) (16 January 1956).

VII
Decisions

The most characteristic activity of a government department is reaching decisions; at senior levels, there may be no other output. 'Decisions' in the sense of grand strategic determinations of policy are, of course, infrequent and elusive. But decisions of another sort are being made all the time – whether to consult a committee, how to time a memorandum, what advice to give the Minister, how to deal with a particular case. There are equivalents to these at managerial levels in most organizations. Administration, indeed, is sometimes defined as a problem-solving and enabling process.

Theories about decisions can be divided into two groups. One is concerned with the way decisions ought to be made, the other with the way they are in fact made.

Normative theory

Normative decision theories are about the way a completely rational decision-maker would analyse a problem and arrive at the best possible solution, given the circumstances and the information at his disposal. The usual problem is to select the strategy which gives the greatest possible chance of maximizing a specified value, like profit. Often this means estimating probabilities. The calculations can become very complicated if the number of factors and the range of uncertainties are increased to approximate to a real-life situation. In games theory, the complication of playing against a calculating opponent is added. In the theory of teams, the object is to find the 'best' decision-rules for a number of players, none of whom has complete information. All these branches share an essentially computational approach to decision-making. There is assumed to be a highly structured problem-situation, in which all relevant information is known or knowable and the results of adopting any strategy can, perhaps with difficulty, be expressed mathematically.[1]

This approach has many uses. It can clarify the general logic of a problem and accustom decision-makers to look out for aspects that can be quantified. It was once a vogue subject in British civil service training.[2] Problems of this type can also be given to groups in 'laboratory' conditions to ascertain the effects of different incentives, working conditions and social factors on the speed and accuracy of their solutions.

But it also has distinct limitations. Real-life decisions are seldom like this. In the first place, the values to be realized are not usually set out clearly and distinctly. Sometimes implicit objectives emerge only in the process of aiming at something else. When they are clear, they often conflict. Consider the complex of considerations facing a civil servant who is asked for advice on the future of a statutory service, employing large numbers of people, which was established with popular support under the party now in opposition to meet a need that has apparently declined in importance in the meantime. If he were to approach this 'rationally' he would have to place relative weights on existing commitments to staff and clients, the financial requirements of some (probably unknown) other service and the risk of political embarrassment for the Minister if a popular service is abandoned. It is not just that it is difficult to establish these values – there is no unique way of combining them.

Secondly, it is not often in fact that the individual decision-maker is able to take a comprehensive view of a whole problem. In real life what at first sight appears to be a deliberate decision is apt to turn out to be the formal culmination of a slow process of commitment over a period of time, in which the range of possibilities has gradually been narrowed as different members of the organization contribute to it in their turn. Decisions can not often be attributed to one person, or even to a group of people consciously acting together at one time.

A third and most damaging limitation is that most organizations would be paralysed if even a small proportion of decisions had to await the outcome of such a process. Decisions often have to be taken in a hurry. Only the really important ones justify the expense and delay of setting up a computer programme to analyse them. An essential part of 'effective' decision-making is the use of incomplete data.

A rather different approach to normative theory is represented by the works of Yehezkel Dror.[3] Dror accepts the unreality of the pure rationality model, but nevertheless argues that it is essential to improve the quality of public decision-making. This requires improvement in decision-making institutions; we need policies about policy-making, for which Dror has coined the phrase 'meta-policymaking'. His books prescribe conditions for the analysis and comparison of one possible course of action with another, including political feasibility and cost as well as the more obvious costs and benefits. The necessary apparatus would include a capacity for research and forecasting as well as a unit staffed by policy analysts. One of the functions of such a unit would be to advise how far it was rational to pursue rationality: there is little point in investing resources in the examination of theoretical possibilities that are never likely to get off the ground in the prevailing climate of political opinion.

Descriptive theory

It is fruitful to turn from normative theories to theories which try to explain how decisions are actually reached in real-life situations.

> The role of decision-making in behavioral science is to describe how people make decisions under conditions of imperfect information – that is, where complete information as to the present state of affairs, possible courses of action, and consequences is not available. Decisions are influenced

by individual differences, social pressures, leadership differences, communication structures, etc. Social scientists are interested in how individuals and groups reach a decision; how much information is necessary, who influences the outcome the most, how disagreements are resolved, what procedures are used and how choices are made.[4]

Unfortunately, it is difficult to study the normal processes of decision-making. There are practical difficulties, including confidentiality, about observing senior people in their normal settings at all. It is also difficult to isolate a 'decision' from the incessant stream of consultations, committee discussions, authorizations and initialling of papers that makes up the normal day. Many experiments, therefore, have been made with college students – or with administrators when they are on courses, away from their normal work – and can be criticized as artificial. This in itself is not a ground for dismissing theories which appeal to common sense and experience, which provide insight into the way administrators' minds work, and which are not apparently contradicted by any research findings so far. But the *caveats* mentioned in the last chapter should be kept in mind.

The main framework concept behind most of these studies is the assumption that any decision is reached in stages, each of which can be analysed and examined separately. First is an awareness that the problem exists. A signal must be received which suggests that some action or policy change is needed. In a government department, the signal may come through political channels, or through the formal and informal machinery that links the department to the outside world, or perhaps from some internal source in the department, like a research and intelligence section which receives information suggesting that an existing policy is not working as well as it might. However the signal originates, it needs to be interpreted and related to other information so that the nature of the problem can be seen. When it has been structured in this way, there is an exploration stage. Possible courses of action or inaction are listed and a rough estimate is made of the probable consequences, desired and undesired, of each. This is followed by evaluation and by a provisional decision that one policy is preferable to the others. (In Whitehall terms, this is the point at which a 'departmental line' is taken.) There may follow a process of consultation in which the proposals are tested for acceptability (to interested parties and political groups) and feasibility (in the eyes of various sorts of expert), and finally, perhaps after modifications, brought to a higher level for authorization. This might be followed by communication of the decision reached, its implementation and, ultimately, review to check whether the consequences are as expected.

These ten or so stages have been set out as a logical sequence. In practice, they may not occur sequentially. The process of consultation may lead to a redefinition of the problem as well as to the consideration of fresh alternatives. Authorization may be conditional on further consultations. The implementation and review stages may never be completed. If they are, they may lead to a reappraisal of the original problem, thus converting a linear process into a cyclical one. A diagrammatic representation would have to include a series of possible feedback loops and dead ends.

Bounded rationality

If the problem is at all complex (as are most problems in public administration) the range of considerations which this process entails is beyond the scope of a single human mind. The only way it can be tackled at all is by factorization. Different aspects are handled by different people, each of whom is forced, by and large, to take the work of the others on trust. To take a crude example, civil servants who are considering the merits of a proposed increase in a service do not personally have to work out the 'opportunity costs' that would be incurred through spending money on it rather than in an infinity of other ways. They assume, if they think about it at all, that opportunity costs are somehow reflected in the amount of Treasury opposition that has to be overcome. It would be unreasonable to expect them to do more. Similarly, if a proposal entails the use of scarce manpower, they would seek advice about its availability from the appropriate department, which they would not question.

Responsibility for a decision can be divided horizontally and vertically. In a hierarchical system different contributions will be made at different levels. Typically, junior members will not question their seniors' definition of the ends to be served, while the latter will assume that the factual information reported by their juniors is correct. Typically, too, the most senior levels will be concerned with authorization – with the final check that a proposed course of action is consistent with a general system of values – rather than with working out detailed proposals. But they may also take the initiative by setting a broad agenda, or specifying general rules to which their subordinates have to work.

But the factors have to be brought together again. An administrative organization can be regarded as a system of communication which exists in order to link decision-makers and to reassemble information about aspects of a problem that have been settled separately. Its coherence is maintained by specifying rules to guide its members in their partial decisions and, by setting limits to the range of acceptable solutions that they may adopt. The limits appropriate to different levels in the hierarchy may be laid down precisely in so many words in terms of the financial or other commitments that an official has authority to incur. More often there is merely an understanding, to which the inexperienced officer may find it difficult to attach a precise meaning, that he ought to 'take his superiors with him' on questions of a certain character. The decision-rules say what criteria should influence the decision, what consultations should be undertaken and so on. Again, the rules may be unwritten but this does not necessarily make them less compelling or less rigid.

So far, this is simply a spelling-out, using different language, of the structure of a Weberian bureaucracy. Duties and responsibilities are allocated in order to allow finite human beings to contribute collectively to the rational solution of infinitely complex problems. Marshak, indeed, suggests that the student of an organization should ask, not for an organization chart, but for a rough description of 'who does what in response to what information'.[5]

But the rationality of the organization as a whole is limited by the capacity and motivation of its human members. In a typical decision situation, an official looks at a number of pieces of information, rejects some and selects others to be rearranged and passed on in the form of information, a recommendation or an instruction to somebody else. Both in what he takes into account and in what he does with it there is an unavoidable element of uncertainty. Even in the most routine cases, when his choice of action is supposed to be completely determined by circumstances, he may not react as expected. He may be insufficiently trained to understand what he has to do or he may mistakenly believe that there is some room for the exercise of his own judgement; this is a frequent cause of misunderstanding. In non-routine matters, where there is room for discretion, the number of factors an official thinks of and the weight he gives to them will significantly affect his performance as a decision-maker. They are influenced – and meant to be influenced – by his personal qualities and by his position within the organization. Rarely will he exercise choice over the complete range of possibilities that is logically open to him. The real situation, even after some aspects of it have been dealt with by others, is nearly always too complicated to be grasped. It cannot be tackled unless some of the detail is removed. 'Rational behavior involves substituting for the complex reality a model of reality that is sufficiently simple to be handled by problem-solving processes.'[6]

Selective perception

The first element of uncertainty is whether the existence of a problem will be recognized at all. If the problem is one that the organization is accustomed to handling there will be programmes for bringing it to the notice of the appropriate people – government departments have well-developed procedures for dealing with the Minister's correspondence, questions in Parliament, and so on. In other cases a good deal depends on the ability of someone in the organization to recognize it as a problem.

Different people will identify a problem in different ways. In an experiment at the Carnegie Institute of Technology some middle-management executives were asked to read a long factual account of a company and its current position and to say what aspect of it they thought should be attended to first. Eighty-three per cent of the sales executives saw the main problem as sales.

But only 29 per cent of the executives from other divisions saw it as sales, although both groups were working from identical material.[7] Training and experience help people to structure a problem situation by focusing on one or two main features of it. But the focus will be different for different people.

In administration it is sometimes a sign of immaturity and inexperience to accept complaints and suggestions at their face value. It is not difficult to imagine a penetrating parliamentary question which evokes quite different responses from three officials, one of whom has for some time been advocating a review of the policy under attack, while another is an expert at the political game and knows that the questioner is unlikely to know how well aimed his question is and a third is mainly anxious to keep the peace until he retires and hands over a tidy block of work to his successor. Each reaction might be predicted from social and psychological information about the official concerned.

People 'rationalize'. They try to structure their experience in ways that are consistent with their previous background, beliefs, prejudices and values. Features that do not fit in tend to be rejected. In an organizational setting an official's approach to a problem will be governed by his experience. He will have developed a repertory of programmes for handling different situations. If the problem looks superficially like ones he has already solved successfully he will be inclined to look for a solution along the same lines. In a large-scale organization experience takes on an extra dimension, since the collective experience of the whole organization over a period of time is, in theory, available to the individual decision-maker. Relevant facts may be ascertainable from the filing system or from colleagues working on similar problems. Problem-solving techniques may be available and some of these may have been elevated into decision-rules. Methods that have been developed for one purpose tend to be used for another. For example, consultative procedures in government departments tend to follow a set pattern, regardless of the subject-matter. Once an organization has settled down and developed a memory, precedents are available for many situations and much has to be treated as given that would be left to discretion in a more open situation. All this makes for economy of effort and is fairly commonplace. But there is inevitably a biasing effect on the way problems are perceived and structured. The policies that result may be less than optimal.

Moreover, if collective experience is to be useful, it must be accessible. In large organizations the arrangements for pooling information tend to become very complex. The staff may be unable to use them without special training. We can say that a person's potential contribution depends on: (a) his personal qualities and experience; and/or (b) the total relevant experience that is available in the organization as a whole combined with (c) procedures, channels of communication and filing systems (with the staff to operate them) to make the experience accessible and (d) his own knowledge of the procedures and readiness to use them. Character-istically, a professional will tend to be most at home with (a); a general administrator will tend to rely on (b) to (d). In both cases there is likely to be some distortion.

A different type of distortion appears when decisions are taken collectively by groups or committees. Groups do not necessarily use all the experience that their members possess. It has to be communicated and accepted by a majority as relevant. If most members of the group share certain attitudes, these are reinforced by 'resonance' and are difficult to dislodge. A group that has been successful in the past is particularly inclined to reject unfamiliar suggestions from new members. Even in a 'brainstorming' session, when the group is actively seeking new ideas, it is psychologically difficult for members to produce ideas that deviate markedly from the general consensus. Fewer creative ideas emerge in a homo-geneous group, in spite of the ease of communication. Face-to-face groups are inclined to accept the ideas of more senior members, if there are differences in status, or from the most talkative, regardless of their merit. In tackling constructive problems groups seldom surpass the performance of their best individual members: a greater range of creative solutions is likely to be produced by the members working independently for an equivalent number of man-hours. Groups can be more effective than individuals at analytic problems of an arithmetical or 'twenty questions' type, when effort can be saved by division of labour and through the mutual correction of errors. But even this is not true if much time is needed for intercommunication and coordination. The utility of group work as a device for achieving consensus, is, of course, another matter.

Search activity

The individual decision-maker has different types of considerations at his disposal. There are 'facts', or at least statements supplied by others which appear to describe a real situation. There are 'value-premises' indicating the objectives, sometimes conflicting and sometimes ambiguous, at which he should aim. And there are problem-solving techniques and 'decision-rules' to guide him in integrating and relating these other premises. Some of these will be in the front of his mind, immediately within his span of attention. Normally they will be a small sample, far short of what he needs to make anything approaching an objectively 'rational' decision. If he feels unable to reach an 'adequate' decision on this basis, he will have to search for additional material, in his own memory for personal experience, in his set of office instructions or regulations for decision-rules and procedures, in files and consultation with colleagues for information and advice. The search may be intensive or it may be superficial. The more it is extended, the more complete will be the decision-maker's model of the situation, and the closer will his actual decision approximate to a theoretically ideal one. (This assumes, however, that he structures his material logically when he has it. There is a point beyond which additional information impedes rather than assists effective decision-making. Wilkins describes an experiment in which probation officers were systematically supplied with items of information, in a sequence determined by them, bearing on a case where they had to make a provisional decision and say how confident they were about it. Different probation officers called for information (e.g. on home background, previous criminal records, etc.) in different sequences. Regardless of the sequence, the probation officers became more confident in their decisions as they received more information in the early stages; but long before all the factors had been taken into account they began to lose confidence and their decisions became erratic.)[8]

The question how widely search activity is likely to range is a motivational one, conditioned partly by the prevailing 'ethos' of the organization. An individual will not search beyond the point at which he is enabled to make a decision that appears satisfactory to him. If such a solution occurs to him right away, he will not spend time and energy looking for an 'ideal' one. In H. A. Simon's phrase, the administrator does not 'maximize', he 'satisfices'. If he does not feel that any of the obvious solutions is satisfactory, he will search for a better one, by calling more and more factors into his span of attention. The search will be sequential; only a few additional factors will be considered at a time and the search will be abandoned when he feels that he has found a reasonably satisfactory answer. His standard of 'satisfactoriness' will vary. If he does not find a satisfactory answer fairly quickly, he may continue searching, or he may lower his standards. Sometimes circumstances may compel him to decide on what he feels to be unsatisfactory evidence. In any case he is likely to stop long before all possible alternatives have been examined. This may be partly because of the way human beings reason. The character of a situation is quickly inferred from a few tentative observations and perhaps only the scientist feels a need to test exhaustively for the unexpected; for others, 'subjective rationality' is enough.

Search activity may be cut short by time pressure. The number of other problems clamouring for attention is a major factor influencing the quality of decisions. It is also affected by increasing difficulty. As the enquiry extends from familiar territory to more distant parts of the organization it is pursued with decreasing vigour unless it is known from experience that information of a given sort is normally available at a certain point. A participant in a highly complex system tends to be uncertain about how to deal with more remote parts of it and therefore to concentrate on the factors within his immediate range of vision. It is no disparagement of civil servants to say that they are often unaware of information that is relevant to their problems even when it is being collected as a matter of routine in another department. A study of the possible applications of census data or material from the General Household Survey might reveal many instances of this.

In two interesting studies of American federal administration, Downs[9] and Gawthrop[10] draw attention to the role of information as a political resource in the competition for power and jurisdiction between agencies; part of the cost of obtaining information from another agency may therefore be some surrender of autonomy in dealing with a problem. Self[11] has cast doubt on the self-seeking assumptions behind such analyses and has suggested that this phenomenon, if it exists, must be attributable to the fragmented nature of American administration. It remains true, however, that the cost of obtaining and assimilating information, relative to its potential value, increases with organizational distance.

Perhaps this can be summed up by saying that the depth to which it is felt 'reasonable' to take a problem will vary with its importance, the accessibility and adequacy of relevant data, the training and experience of the official dealing with it, and the number of other problems requiring his attention in the time available. These factors may not seem to apply in, say, a research and planning division since such divisions 'are deliberately constructed to enable the organization to continue search activity even when most of the organizations' members are quite satisfied'.[12] But this is simply to say that different conditions may be made to apply in different parts of the same organization.

Uncertainty absorption

Much of the information reaching an official will already have passed through a similar process at the hands of colleagues. In an organization of any size information may be used as a basis for decision many removes away from the point at which it enters the system. As it is transmitted it is progressively structured and simplified. One consequence may be that material which was initially highly ambiguous tends to become more and more precise; this is what March and Simon call 'uncertainty absorption'. Decision-making is impeded if there are inconsistencies in the information relating to the same situation. 'Official' figures are developed so that conflicting information can be ignored. 'The greater the need for co-ordination in the organization, the greater the use of legitimized facts.'[13] To selective perception and rationalization, we have to add uncertainty absorption as the third main source of distortion in the simplified picture of reality with which decision-makers work. An example is the way interest groups become committed to policies that may have originated in marginal choices by a bare majority of their members.

This is one reason why it is so difficult to say who 'makes' a decision; filtering at each stage successively reduces the range of possibilities that is available to be considered. Once proposals have been formulated the range begins to decline quite sharply. Ultimately, only one possibility may be presented for approval. There is also an important difference between formulating proposals and considering them. Experiments have confirmed the commonsense observation that once concrete suggestions have been put on paper (for example to a Minister or a committee) it is less likely that fresh ideas, independent of the set framework, will come to mind.[14] This means that great power is wielded by those at the point where the greatest amount of uncertainty is absorbed, since they can considerably influence the decisions that will finally be made by others. Such a position may be filled by an 'expert' who is nominally quite junior in the hierarchy or by an 'adviser' who can be appealed to on matters of difficulty that cannot be resolved by rational analysis.

In a study of the planning process in Britain, Levin has stressed the importance of commitment. Once a Minister, or his representative, has become committed to a particular solution on the basis of the material available to him at the time, it becomes much more difficult to introduce new factors into the discussion.[15] The management of uncertainty requires a degree of myopia.

Structural influences

The decision-maker emerges from this analysis as a sort of human computer, with limited storage capacity and a partially random input. Up to a point, he can be programmed. Organizations influence their members by structuring their environment, that is, by controlling the information supplied to them and, through training and other means, conditioning the way they react to it. The extreme case of a fully programmed decision, in which all the ingredients are supplied and also rules for dealing with them, is a clerk dealing with routine cases according to the rule-book. Programmes allow central but recurring problems to be handled as routine. Hence the paradox noted by Mackenzie and Grove that 'on the whole the least qualified members of the service must do one of the most difficult parts of the business, that of meeting the public as individuals'.[16]

Organizations also try to control the framework of experience which their members bring to problems. The main instruments are recruitment, training and career policies.

It is not always easy to predict what sort of personal experience will be most appropriate. One factor is the amount of experience that is already available in the organization's memory. Many problems which face civil servants involve the application of general administrative principles to a concrete situation. What bodies must be consulted? Should the Treasury be informed? Should the matter be cleared with the Cabinet? How should any decision be made public? A great deal of experience has been accumulated on such matters, so that new problems can often be handled effectively and economically as examples of a familiar type. Internal experience of precedents and procedures over a wide field may then be most useful. Hence the case for recruiting people of general ability and transferring them frequently from one post to another, assimilating 'organizational wisdom' and learning how to use it as they go.

No amount of mutual laundering, however, will create expertise that does not already exist. If the problem contains substantial new elements, additional experience may have to be imported by recruiting staff with special qualifications.

The relative emphasis on personal or 'organizational' experience implies different types of career structure. Personal experience can be kept at a high level by avoiding frequent changes of post. But long periods in specialized posts may not help officials to accumulate the general knowledge of the system that they need in order to exploit its resources of information. Specialist knowledge of a professional type is less relevant to problems which are too complex for the individual specialist to grasp.

Training has a number of functions. Training courses can supply a repertory of programmes for solving problems. By making people familiar with the organization's resources and its communication system, training can develop self-confidence and make them more ready to search fairly widely for relevant information. Sometimes training courses have a 'staff college' function. They provide an opportunity for colleagues to meet and develop a common outlook. This helps communication, since the usage of communication channels is affected by the ease with which they can be used and this in turn is influenced by the compatibility of the users. Generally speaking, decision-making becomes more predictable if participants share a common culture of beliefs, norms and aspirations. Training courses, therefore, often focus on certain values and beliefs about the system and its objectives in the hope that the trainee will make them part of his own frame of reference. One aim of this sort of training is to sensitize the official to certain aspects of problems and to guide his choice of priorities.

Perhaps the most effective instrument of orientation is departmentalization. If officials are grouped so that over their careers they are constantly exposed to the same kind of information and value-systems, and interact with others in the same position, all the findings about selective perception, role concept and group resonance point to the emergence of a characteristic departmental philosophy. That philosophy will, of course, reflect current conceptions of the administrator's role. If these include a strong sense of mission, and encouragement of innovation, they will be inculcated. But the socialization process can equally well transmit a passive, reactive style of administration. A criticism of civil service training in the 1970s was its failure to compensate for the British civil servant's lack of a sense of purpose.[17]

Priorities

Administrators have finite spans of attention. They also have finite amounts of time at their disposal. Can we say anything about the way they allocate their priorities? How do they decide to which problem, or to which aspect of a particular problem, they should pay most attention?

The administrator tends to give his attention first to tasks for which a programme exists ready to hand. In another laboratory experiment at Carnegie subjects were made responsible for managing an inventory control system. They had to pass on to clerical staff some routine information about inventory levels in various warehouses; at the same time they were responsible for adjusting the allocation of clerks to warehouses so that each group of clerks had a comparable workload; finally, they were to suggest changes in procedures. They were told that all three jobs were equally important and should receive equal attention. All the subjects spent considerably more than a third of their time on the routine part of their job even when the flow of information was kept light. As the amount of information was increased, the time they spent on planning was consistently reduced until virtually no planning was done at peak loads.[18] This is 'Gresham's Law' of planning – that daily routine drives out planning. Staff at all levels tend to get the easy jobs out of the way first and there is a risk that long-term ones never get done at all.

When activities are not programmed there is an apparently random element about the way priorities are determined among them. Similarly, if no technique for analysing a problem is ready to hand, decision time tends to be short and the outcome is likely to be influenced more by the order in which alternatives are presented than by any serious attempt to find a common yardstick. This seems to apply particularly to problems of allocating uncommitted resources. If some additional money suddenly becomes available, it will go to those who are quick off the mark. The beneficiaries are likely to be those whose strategic position in the communication system enables them to time their bids rather than those who have a good case on merit.[19]

An important part may be played by external cues. Fire precautions will receive more attention than normal if there has been a fire recently. Safety precautions will be tightened up after an air crash. There is likely to be a spate of instructions on even minor aspects of security (to an extent that may seriously interfere with normal performance until it is felt safe to ignore them) after a prominent espionage trial. Sometimes it is impossible to restore the previous balance because a system of priorities becomes institutionalized, for example by appointing a security inspector to report breaches of regulations. Similarly, an active training department may succeed in making a whole department training-minded, even if this entails a loss in productive time.

There are various ways in which the organization can influence the individual's choice of priorities. Through training and programming some kinds of jobs can be made easier to tackle. A common device is to provide a formula which enables easy computational problems to be substituted for difficult qualitative ones. This may entail giving excessive attention to aspects of a problem that can be measured. There are interesting examples in the formulae used to calculate the need for motorways, based on traffic densities to the exclusion of environmental and other factors.[20]

Priorities can be attracted for some questions by the use of deadlines: a letter from an MP has to be answered within a given number of days; a parliamentary question is given top priority because of the tight timetable for preparing a reply. Considerations thought to be important can be 'cued-in' to the administrator's frame of reference by constant reminders (like letters from MPs). They can be institutionalized by building pressures into the structure – for example in an advisory committee – and instituting procedures to ensure that they are brought into play. The tendency to give priority to the short term can be counter-balanced by creating a special unit which is concerned solely with long-term planning and innovation.

The problem of priorities is no less acute for the organization as a whole. It is seldom possible to attend to all its objectives simultaneously. They may be inconsistent – fresh commitments are acquired over time without always being related to existing ones. Separate units develop their own goals, which may be mutually incompatible. The goal of the training branch is to develop training schemes; the finance officer is concerned with economy; the establishment officer is interested in the efficient use of personnel; administrators in executive divisions are at various times concerned with all of these, as well as with carrying out the wishes of Parliament, placating pressure groups, sponsoring new legislation and furthering their own careers. In normal times an organization manages to survive with inconsistent goals by the simple expedient of failing to attend to more than a few of them at any one time.

Lord (then Sir Edward) Bridges unwittingly emphasized this point in an address which he gave to the Royal Institute of Public Administration at Exeter in November 1954. 'However complicated the facts may be – however much your junior may try to persuade you that there are seventeen arguments in favour of one course and fifteen in favour of the exact opposite, believe me, in four cases out of five there is *one* point and one only which is cardinal to the whole situation. When you have isolated that one point, and found the answer to it, all the other things will fall into place. And until you have done that, you have done nothing.'

Incrementalism

Attending to one point at a time may help to preserve the decision-maker's sanity. It may also reflect the needs of the situation. Many issues present themselves in a form, and at a time, when there is one aspect that calls for action, and fairly urgent action at that, while other considerations can wait. Instead of attempting, therefore, to undertake a comprehensive review of the possibilities and their implications, the practical administrator may feel impelled to deal with the impending crisis as quickly as possible, taking only one step at a time and not paying too much regard to the possible long-term consequences. If these prove intolerable, they can be dealt with in the same way when they arise, so that the step-by-step process is endlessly repeated. This is 'incremental' decision-making.

In 1959 Charles Lindblom started a fierce controversy by arguing, in a paper called 'The Science of "Muddling Through"', that incrementalism was in fact a sound strategy for public policy-making.[21] The argument rests on a pluralist view of society as a set of competing interests, among which the government tries to maintain a balance. The current point of balance will not fully satisfy any interest group, and government will be under constant pressure to alter it in favour of one or another. So long as the pressures cancel out, no action is necessary or desirable, since independent government action would probably make things worse. But occasionally the pressure from one quarter becomes irresistible. Government must then make the smallest possible con-

cession to meet it: over-reaction would merely cause more dissatisfaction elsewhere. Lindblom's opponents (including Dror,
whose 'meta-policymaking' approach has been mentioned earlier)
have pointed out that incrementalists are likely to overlook
interests, and needs for the future, that are not represented in the
existing power structure. Whatever its failings as a prescriptive
model, however, incrementalism probably offers a fair description
of the way most decisions are taken most of the time.[22]

Levels of decision-making

The important difference between the formulation and the authorization of policy has already been mentioned. There is a stage at
which the various components of a decision can be brought
together and integrated in a workable set of proposals. The proposals may have to be referred to higher authority for approval
but this is often a formality. Usually, the 'level of integration' is
kept as low as possible to ease the burden at the top and to increase
the speed of decision-making. Occasionally a deliberate attempt
is made to keep the options open by making it impossible for the
various strands to be woven together except at the top. Senior
members of the hierarchy may also be forced to review matters
of detail if they have to resolve conflicts among their subordinates.
This is one of the ways in which they keep in touch.

But those at the top have value-systems of their own which they
apply in giving judgement. Consequently a centralized system of
authority is one means of securing priority for these values. Junior
staff learn what considerations will rank as most important if their
work is reviewed. If, for example, the formal structure allows
conflicts to be resolved only at 'political' level (perhaps because
two departments have strong opposing interests in a question which
neither of them can settle independently) officials try to anticipate
their Minister's (or the Cabinet's) frame of reference when they
are deciding whether a particular point of view is worth pursuing
to the limit. In the late 1960s, when responsibility for economic
policy was divided between the Treasury and the Department of
Economic Affairs, some journalists alleged that the object was to
ensure that the Prime Minister's view prevailed on certain issues.

This would have been achieved even if no disputes were in fact referred to him, so long as those involved kept in mind how he would decide if he had to.

Up to this point, the words 'decision' and 'policy' have been used interchangeably, since the same analytic considerations can be applied to any process of deciding on a course of action. But it is convenient to find a meaning for 'policy' which distinguishes it from a decision, however important, on a particular case. We follow Friend in defining policy decisions as strategic choices which articulate a 'policy stance', which will contribute to the framework for specific decisions at the same or a lower level of administration.[23] A policy is a decision-rule which deals with substantive rather than procedural aspects of lower-level decision-making. One would expect to find a greater proportion of policy decisions at senior levels in a hierarchy, although some policy decisions are taken lower down and some decisions without policy implications reach the top. Attempts have been made to decentralize decision-making, without sacrificing central control and direction, by limiting the top echelons to the determination of broad strategies which set guidelines for more specific decisions lower down.[24] They tend to become impaled on the dilemma that if the policies are too specific they become too restrictive and lead to inappropriate action, while if they are too general they tend to lack impact.

Concluding comments

The theories discussed in this chapter are concerned with the supply of information, including information about other people's ideas, to the decision-maker, and the use he makes of it. The model of the organization as a communication system makes it possible to judge a procedure, an arrangement of functions, a recruitment policy or a training scheme by its contribution to good decision-making. If these are well devised, they will make it more likely that the 'relevant' considerations will be taken into account by the right people at the right time. Decision-making is not the whole of organizational life, but it is a very important part of the life of government departments. It is worth taking some trouble to see how it can be improved.

As in Chapter VI, there are no universal prescriptions. If the head of a department knows what kinds of decisions he wants, he can be shown how to design an organization to increase the chances of getting them. Often he will not know too clearly what he does want. He may be persuaded to say in broad terms what relative weights he places on particular elements in decision-making, like accuracy, speed, economy, flexibility, good co-ordination and various sorts of expertise. It is certain that he will not be able to get an organization in which all these elements are maximized. Compromises are unavoidable, because there are limits to what human minds can assimilate and because there are limits to what a communication system can handle. Moreover, there is no absolute standard of 'relevance'. The requirements change with time. What is relevant to 'good' Treasury decisions today may be relatively unimportant next year. But it is some help to see what is involved.

It is especially useful to have a model which interprets the general theories of the last chapter in terms of individual performance at decision-making. What emerges is the now familiar point that every conceivable arrangement carries costs as well as advantages. If decision-makers are trained and equipped to focus sharply on A, their vision of B inevitably becomes a little bit distorted. The cumulative distortions that result can to some extent be balanced within the overall organizational structure, but never completely, because of communication and coordination problems.

In aiming at the best balance, the organization's leaders cannot control the perceptions of other participants. But they can influence them through training, recruitment, the structure of authority, communication links and so forth. The mechanisms at work are largely cognitive. In a bureaucracy ignorance is usually a structural problem – the official does not know what he has not been told, or had a chance to learn, nor can he remember everything all the time. But motivational factors are important too. The bureaucrat can sometimes be induced to try a little harder, given reasonable conditions and a modicum of encouragement.

Notes

1 There is a vast literature on statistical approaches to decision-making. A useful starting point, which relates team theory to organization structure, is J. Marshak, 'Efficient and Viable Organizational Forms' in Mason Haire (ed.), *Modern Organization Theory* (New York, 1959).

2 'The primary objectives are to develop an understanding of the contribution to decision making in the public service of techniques based on mathematics, statistics and economics, together with an appreciation of the role of the present and the next generation of computers in this field of management.' HM Treasury, *Civil Service Training 1966–67* (London, 1968) para. 27.

3 Yehezkel Dror, *Public Policymaking Re-examined* (San Francisco, 1968).

4 P. B. Applewhite, *Organizational Behavior* (Englewood Cliffs, N.J., 1965) p. 54. The discussion in this chapter borrows heavily from the work of Cyert, March and Simon at the Carnegie Institute of Technology in Pittsburgh. The main sources are: H. A. Simon, *Administrative Behavior*, 2nd edn (New York, 1957); J. G. March and H. A. Simon, *Organizations* (New York, 1958); R. M. Cyert and J. G. March, *A Behavioral Theory of the Firm* (Englewood Cliffs, N.J., 1963).

5 Marshak, 'Efficient and Viable Organizational Forms', op. cit., p. 309.

6 J. G. March and H. A. Simon, *Organizations* (New York, 1958) p. 131.

7 D. C. Dearborn and H. A. Simon, 'Selective Perception: A Note on the Departmental Identification of Executives', *Sociometry* Vol. 21 (1958) pp. 140–4.

8 L. T. Wilkins, *Social Policy, Action and Research* (London, 1964) Appendix 4.

9 Anthony Downs, *Inside Bureaucracy* (Boston, 1967).

10 L. C. Gawthrop, *Bureaucratic Behavior in the Executive Branch* (New York, 1969).

11 Peter Self, *Administrative Theories and Politics*, 2nd edn (London, 1977).

12 Amitai Etzioni, *Modern Organizations* (Englewood Cliffs, N.J., 1964) p. 31.

13 March and Simon, *Organizations*, op. cit., p. 166.

14 Applewhite, *Organizational Behavior*, op. cit., p. 65.

15 P. H. Levin, *Government and the Planning Process* (London, 1976).

16 W. J. M. Mackenzie and J. W. Grove, *Central Administration in Britain* (London, 1957) p. 450.

17 R. A. W. Rhodes (ed.), *Training in the Civil Service* (London, 1977); particularly the contribution by Peter Self.
18 J. G. March, 'Business Decision Making', *Industrial Research* (Spring 1959).
19 Royston Greenwood, C. R. Hinings and Stewart Ranson, 'The Politics of the Budgetary Process in English Local Government', *Political Studies* Vol. xxv (1977) pp. 25–47.
20 *Report of the Advisory Committee on Trunk Road Assessment* (Leitch Report) (London, 1978).
21 C. E. Lindblom, 'The Science of "Muddling Through"', *Public Administration Review* Vol. 19 (1959) pp. 79–88; see also D. Braybrooke and C. E. Lindblom, *A Strategy of Decision* (New York, 1963).
22 R. G. S. Brown, *The Administrative Process as Incrementalism* (Milton Keynes, 1974).
23 John Friend, 'The Dynamics of Policy Change', *Long Range Planning* Vol. 10 (1977) pp. 40–7.
24 Bernard Taylor and David Hussey, *Realities of Planning* (London, 1977).

VIII
Decision-making in a political environment

In this chapter and in Chapter IX the analysis is taken further into the British political framework. Before applying concepts from Chapters VI and VII to public administration, it seems necessary to start by asking how great are the differences between public and other organizations. This leads to an examination of policy-making in a political setting and of the contributions made by different participants. Traditionally, one of the main issues in public administration has been taken to be the relationship between permanent officials and elected politicians. In order to understand this relationship, some discussion is needed of the place of lay judgement in policy-making.

Public and private administration

The hypotheses discussed in the previous two chapters have often been illustrated with an example from a government department. But perhaps this has been premature. It may be argued that the character of an organization is intimately related to its purpose. The purpose of a public department is very different from that of a business organization designed primarily to secure profit for its owners. It is not, therefore, realistic to extrapolate from one to the other. Blau and Scott argue that the characteristic problems facing an organization depend on whether its primary beneficiaries are its owners, its members, its clients or the public at large. The crucial problems of a business firm are thus concerned with efficiency and profit; those of a mutual-benefit association with internal democracy; those of a service organization with balancing the professional service ethic against administrative procedures; and those of a commonweal organization with the retention of political control. The differences, however, are only of degree: commonweal organizations have to face the problems of internal efficiency as well as of accountability.[1]

The alleged uniqueness of the public sector was a controversial topic for several years after the publication of the Fulton Report. Some argued that its only special characteristic was inefficiency, which could be cured by the introduction of business methods. Others claimed that these had very limited application. For example, Self argued that whereas business management was oriented towards market growth, the main problem in public administration was to restrain demands that could not all be met from a limited public purse. Similarly, since business management aimed to secure a maximum return on investment, there was scope for the application to it of 'specific but socially narrow tests of resource efficiency, which can be confined to the firm in question. The equivalent tests for government must refer ultimately to the whole of society, as politically articulated. Tests of resource efficiency therefore dissolve into a seamless web of the interacting benefits and costs of the whole set of public policies...'[2] Another point made by Self is that the coercive powers which are at the disposal of government call for special control arrangements as a safeguard against abuse.

The validity of distinctions like these rather depends on what is compared with what. Parts of the public sector, like the Stationery Office and the nationalized industries, have commercial objectives. Others, like the social security administration, advertise to encourage demand. Some private firms and consortia are so large and powerful that their activities attract special attention from the Monopolies Commission and the Price Commission. Others, like those in the aerospace industry, depend more on government contracts than on market forces. There is a large grey area of quasi-governmental and quasi-nongovernmental organizations.[3] In a mixed economy there is a tendency for large public and large private industries to become more alike. After reviewing the evidence, Dunsire concluded that differences within each sector were probably greater than those between them. From a distance, both would be seen to have much in common as compared with either business or public administration in a different culture.[4]

Nevertheless, the imputed characteristics of public administration become more in evidence as one moves closer to the political centre and the policy-making core of ministerial departments. And their flavour does affect the next layer out, and so on. A former head of the civil service claimed that its whole character stemmed from parliamentary control of legislation and finance.[5] Through the Minister, the work of civil servants is open to detailed criticism in Parliament. Parliament's servant, the Ombudsman, investigates complaints of maladministration and reports direct to a select committee. This affects the public administrative process by putting a premium on probity, impartiality, rectitude and fair and equitable treatment of individuals. It requires detailed record-keeping so that decisions can be justified retrospectively, and to enable precedents to be consulted. This applies as much to a social security office in Bootle as to the regulatory branches of a Whitehall department. There is little reward here for risk-taking or corner-cutting in the name of efficiency. Non-regulatory work, such as policy advice, takes place in the same atmosphere. Here there are even fewer tests of efficiency and effectiveness. There are pitfalls, notably a failure to consult another interested department, or insensitivity to the ever-shifting political climate. Success may therefore depend as much on avoiding the pitfalls as on the intrinsic quality of the advice.

After an exhaustive survey of the literature, Parker and Subramaniam came to the conclusion that the main difference between government and private activity was its 'allocative' and 'integrative' character. Society is made up of a great number of interlocking subsystems. A firm, a club or a family group is itself a system of members who carry out an economic or social function. They interact with other systems from which they obtain resources in return for providing goods or services. No system of this sort is self-sufficient: its continued existence depends on maintaining satisfactory relationships with the other systems in the environment (that is to say the higher-level system of which it is a subsystem). The relationships between subsystems are often regulated by the market. Alternatively they can be regulated by conscious political decisions. The characteristic function of government is to control or influence the distribution of resources among the subsystems of a society and to integrate their activities in the interests of the whole. Government departments and agencies provide the necessary apparatus. In addition, a government may itself take over direct control of some activities as an alternative to manipulating the market.

From this can be inferred the essential characteristics of public administration.

> The public administrator, by the very nature of Government's integrating function, must look at *all* the organizations in society and integrate different interests into something like a general interest. Different forms of polity may shift the stress given to different interests as well as affect the process of working out a general interest, but the need to *consider* every interest always remains a corollary to the need to integrate all sub-systems in society. The Government administrator must take account of the whole where the private administrator representing a single part can restrict his field of vision.[6]

Hence the exceptional problems of coordination which cause so much difficulty in the public sector. Hence too the centralization of decision-making and the prevalence of 'Treasury' methods of control: purely governmental bodies have to bargain for resources within a framework of what is supposed to be best for society as a whole. The emphasis on rationality, consistency and justifiability is extended to the internal operations of the departments themselves and also, to a lesser extent, to government-sponsored agencies, even when their activities are not primarily integrative or allocative but are directed to the production of goods and services. It explains the convention that the managers of nationalized industries accept ministerial suggestions even when they lack statutory as well as commercial force.

It is not, of course, possible for the individual public administrator to take such a comprehensive view. He has to be placed in a framework (another subsystem) which obliges him to take into account a limited number of 'integrating' factors in making his own, partial, decisions. The general interest is represented by the political environment in which he works. Parker and Subramaniam are not concerned with any particular type of political system. But clearly, in a democracy, the ultimate criteria for decisions about integration and allocation are supplied through the channels of political representation. The organizational problem is to make sure that the administrator pays attention to these criteria. This can be done by the elaborate machinery of structural devices and attention-directing cues that we call political accountability. The rather obvious conclusion follows that the public administrator must be sensitive to public opinion, as expressed through orthodox political channels, and that the traditional questions of the political scientist about the constitutional devices for maintaining political control over the administration are as important as ever.

The general interest

But the concept of 'control' is far too narrow for analysing the complex relationship that now exists between, say, the Home Office, the House of Commons and the Home Secretary. It suggests a division between policy (reserved for politicians) and administration (which can safely be handled by properly controlled officials) that hardly anybody now believes to be useful. High officials are not mere instruments of a political will. They have knowledge and values of their own which are applied not only in executing policy but in arranging for the policy to be changed. Their views on what should be done complement, rather than compete with, those of politicians. In developing the concept of 'control' in complex organizations, management theorists have drawn attention to three elements: a plan, strategy or less explicit framework for action; an information system which lets the controller know what is actually being done; a mechanism through which the controller can correct behaviour which is inconsistent with the framework. This is not a bad way of analysing much of what actually happens. Home Office officials are responsible for administering Acts of Parliament and for implementing government policies. The Home Secretary sees a sample of work and cases, and has the authority to correct what he sees as undesirable. Individually or collectively, MPs also see a sample of the Home Office's activity, and can make life unpleasant for the Home Secretary if they do not like what they see. But the model has only a limited application. Parliament has little effective power over a strong government. Its members are often more interested in changing policies than in seeing existing ones correctly implemented (unless there is a question of unfairness, perhaps in a constituency matter). Some civil servants see the control system as something that they have to live with, and see themselves primarily as servants of the state rather than of its representative institutions.

The relationship between Parliament and the executive can be analysed in a different way. The integrative and allocative functions of government imply a need for some procedure for bringing specialized activities before a court where they can be tested for consistency with the welfare of society as a whole. Very roughly, the perspective widens as the level rises. The National Coal Board may be concerned only with the most effective use of coal. The Department of Energy may try to relate coal to other fuels in its investment and pricing policies. The Cabinet will be more concerned with the overall effect of pricing and energy policies on the economy and on the standing of the government. Members of Parliament will be concerned, as individuals, with the impact of alternative policies in their constituencies and, collectively, with their effect on the outcome of the next election. There is a shift from the specific to the general, from the technical to the political, from fact to value.

This is not because Members of Parliament are wiser and better than Cabinet Ministers and the Chairman of the National Coal Board, but because the House of Commons is designed to reflect a broader range of opinion than the leadership of the ruling party, and so on back down the line. The problem is differently perceived at different points. Left to themselves, the coal experts might settle for a policy that was best from their industry's point of view, but not well related to the other needs of society. On the other hand, a policy based on general political preferences might be very unsound technologically. If coal has been brought under public control, the public expects the industry's activities to be co-ordinated with those of other public bodies and to be integrated in the general interest. But this does not mean that technical aspects are unimportant.

The example, of course, is an artificial one. Experts have their ideals and politicians have their sectional interests. But a more realistic illustration would obscure the logic of the situation. Professional experts, civil servants, Ministers, Members of Parliament, all contribute to the consideration of a policy. So may academic thinkers and research workers, members of pressure groups, and press and television journalists. Their contributions can be arranged along a spectrum, with experts and pressure groups near the specific-technical-fact end and politicians and journalists nearer the general-political-value end. It is helpful to see the system of accountability not as a hierarchical filter in which those at the top are superior people controlling those lower down, but as a set of procedures for ensuring that new policies are considered from various points of view along the spectrum. It suggests that meaningful organizational questions can be asked about: (a) the kind of contribution to be expected at different points; (b) the most effective way of dividing the labour; (c) the order in which contributions can best be combined to avoid wasted effort.

All this is another way of saying that Parliament is only one of several specialized channels through which ideas, information and pressures are legitimately applied to the development of public policy. It is at the 'general' end of the spectrum and therefore of distinctive importance in public administration. But on any specific issue, the contribution of Parliament may be very small and overshadowed by professional expertise, material from surveys, and so on. This can be spelled out in terms of what we know about decision-making to arrive at a model for analysis.

Initiation of change

In a well-established service, existing policies may be reviewed in the light of routine reports and statistics, provided that the information they contain is in a useful form and that it is somebody's job to study it. But routine feedback is more likely to suggest minor modifications than real changes in direction. More substantial innovation within the service itself implies a readiness to consider new ways of doing things – a more active search for alternatives than is normal when things are apparently going smoothly. It seems to need time for reflection and a sort of psychological emancipation that is often denied to members of busy hierarchies, watching their deadlines and conscious of the need to reach a consensus quickly. For this reason, special 'thinking' units are sometimes set up and freed from the pressures of day-to-day business. But there is then a problem of preventing the thinkers from getting out of touch and of bringing their ideas to the notice of those able to apply them.

In a service which employs professional staff, changes in policy may be suggested by those who provide the service. Professor Donnison and his colleagues have described how professional fieldworkers played the major part in the development of local social services.

> The providers of the service usually take this initiative . . . in an attempt to meet in a more appropriate or satisfying way the actual or potential demands they perceive. Thus their perceptions of the needs to be met and the standards of service they regard as fitting are crucial. These perceptions depend largely on the education and previous experience of the staff, and the climate of opinion they establish amongst themselves.[7]

Their case studies suggest that developments in services of this sort, which necessarily leave a good deal to the discretion of professional workers, are quite likely to be implemented before approval is sought from the authority nominally responsible for the service – possibly in order to secure additional resources. 'Formally approved "changes in policy" announced by the governing body may simply recognize and codify a process worked out

over several years by people at humbler levels.'[8] Their analysis
is probably equally applicable to national services whose development is stimulated by lobbying from professional groups like
teachers, doctors or admirals. Such pressures, coming from the
best-informed source, naturally reflect the commitments and
aspirations of the profession involved and are, in a very important
sense, sectional.[9] A similar role may be filled by academic
experts who have specialized in a particular field and are interested
in its development.

It sometimes happens that innovation comes mainly from
political levels. The Labour Government of 1945 offers the most
conspicuous examples in recent times of major acts of policy –
the decision to grant independence to India, the final shape of
the National Health Service, the creation of nationalized industries
– stemming from a decisive political initiative (although technological imperatives also came into play, for example in reports from
expert working parties on the problems of key industries). The
1974 Labour Government promised to achieve 'a fundamental and
irreversible transfer of power' to the working class and passed
a good deal of employment legislation which increased the rights
of trade unions; such measures would not have emerged spontaneously from the civil service machine. Really radical change
probably comes most easily from political levels – from a Minister
looking at problems with a fresh eye, from the election manifesto
of a new government, or from a pressure group whose case commands more political sympathy than administrative logic. Such
initiatives are unpredictable and may have a wanton element about
them. Radical change is costly. Procedural devices, and the need
to consult advisers, may prevent it being introduced too easily.

Simplification

If a new idea falls on fertile soil, it has to be made 'operational'
by translating it into workable proposals. The range of thinking
must first be widened and then narrowed again. The widening
process means placing the proposal in the context of existing
schemes and policies and searching as widely as possible for information about its repercussions. In the case of a public service,

since nearly all problems interlock and the immediate range of possible repercussions is therefore very wide, the theoretical limits to this search are set by the whole boundary of actual and possible public policy. In practice, a minimum field of consultation will be defined by formal instructions and departmental habits. It may be extended by the personal knowledge and interests of the staff directly concerned. The Treasury will normally be involved and perhaps an advisory committee or two.

When enough data has been collected it has to be structured. The range of considerations has to be narrowed down to one or two broad alternatives that can reasonably be put to other bodies and to the person who will take formal responsibility for the decision.

It is in this process of simplification that one finds what Donnison and Chapman have called the 'major junctions' in policy at which decisions are taken to select one route and exclude many others potentially available up to that point. Lord Bridges makes a similar point.

> The experience of anyone who has worked in Whitehall is that there is an early stage in any project when things are fluid; when, if you are in touch with those concerned and get hold of the facts, it is fairly easy to influence decisions. But after a scheme has been worked on for weeks and months, and has hardened into a particular shape, and come up for formal decisions, then it is often very difficult to do anything except either approve it or throw it overboard.[10]

Nothing that is done at this stage is irrevocable, since formulated proposals have to clear other hurdles before they become policy. But if they fail, they come back to the same crossroads to start on another route.

Clearly much depends on the people who are involved in the process at this stage. Their ideas about what is relevant will be influenced by personality, background and training. They will also be influenced, particularly in the amount of trouble they are prepared to take, by the atmosphere in which they work – how much credit is given for personal initiative, how much pressure there is to reach amicable compromises, and so on. In a government department, Ministers are unlikely to be involved in most matters at this stage, even if the policy originated with them, unless they have a strong personal interest in it, simply because of pressure on their time. In a department which employs them, professionally qualified officers and members of the Inspectorates will be involved very closely. A vital part, including 'procedural' decisions about whom to consult and what use to make of their advice, is played by generalist civil servants in the Administration Group.

The process of formulation becomes rather easy (perhaps dangerously so) if there are mechanical means of resolving uncertanties and ambiguities. Favourite devices include a majority recommendation by a committee, the report of an Inspector or Tribunal, the results of a cost-benefit analysis, a categorical opinion from an authoritative source, and precedent.

Securing consent

Before a final decision is sought on a new policy it nearly always has to be discussed with other interests that are going to be affected. This means that it will be put in the form of a proposal to a number of other government departments and consultative bodies in the hope or expectation that they will endorse it. One function of advisory bodies is to provide a touchstone for policies drafted in the appropriate Ministry. Most of the papers considered by the Central and Scottish Health Service Councils, for example, are prepared by professional staff in the Health Department, and presented by civil servants who attend Council meetings. Meetings tend to be short and agendas long. It is rare for a paper to be rejected, or even exhaustively discussed. But papers are prepared with possible reactions in mind. In other words, the known views of the interests represented on the Council have been taken into account at the 'simplification' stage, which will often have included a more open-ended discussion on a subcommittee or working party of the Council itself.

The habit of consultation is very strong in British administration; indeed the ease with which affected interests and relevant expertise can be co-opted into the decision process has largely compensated for lack of subject specialization in the permanent administrative machinery. The process of being consulted on a proposed policy, however, is not unlike that of being asked to authorize it. The policy is already there in draft. It may be difficult to discuss in detail and it is often possible only to confirm that it is not objectionable or to ask for it to be reconsidered. If objections are raised at this stage and the policy goes back for a remould, there is likely to be great pressure to salvage the effort already invested in it by reaching agreement on a compromise which may smother some of the disagreement. The effect may be to blunt the cutting edge of the policy, since conflicting interests can often best be accommodated by not making a policy too explicit. There are occasions when a policy has to be modified substantially after consultation – but this suggests that it has been formulated too hastily or, if it happens too often, that the administrative structure needs attention; the assumption would be that policies were being put together in an inappropriate way.

Authorization

In our system of government, no change of any substance can be made without the agreement of the responsible Minister and often of a Cabinet committee. A very large number of questions has to be considered by a small number of very busy people. Most of them can be considered only in terms of bare essentials. By the time a question has reached the Minister it is usually in a form in which it is really only possible to say 'yes' or 'no' and it is usually easier to say 'yes'. What the Minister does is decide for himself the general principles on which he will intervene personally in the stream of business flowing across his desk.[11] What he cannot do is to work out a new policy himself, partly because he has not the time, partly because he lacks the knowledge and partly because he cannot get involved in detail if he is to stand back and look at things politically. It is extremely difficult to do such a job well. None the less, individual Ministers differ greatly in personal style and in their pattern of activity: some see themselves primarily as policy-makers, others as managers, most perhaps as arbitrators.[12] A British Minister, of course, has some of his interventions chosen for him by the fluctuating interests of Parliament.

Parliament itself exercises something like a 'ministerial' function when it is considering draft legislation or major items of government business. The mechanics are different, if only because there are so many individual MPs, and the pattern is complicated by Parliament's other functions as a sounding board for individual grievances and as a court of appeal for dissatisfied pressure groups. It is always possible, when a proposal is presented for statutory authorization, for individual MPs to represent interests that were overlooked or overriden in earlier discussions. Parliament's role in legislation thus involves elements of consent as well as of authorization. In fact, as is well known, only a tiny proportion of the detailed matters coming formally before Parliament are even discussed, let alone seriously reviewed. But the possibility of challenge is more important than the fact. When this latent power *is* exercised, policies are criticized from a 'political' standpoint, that is, in terms calculated to appeal to public sympathy by reference either to the general welfare or to supposedly general principles like equity and good faith. Parliament links public departments to the political interests of the public at large, and parliamentary accountability obliges Ministers and their civil servants to keep in mind how their policies will look if they are challenged from that point of view. We shall see in the next chapter what kinds of factors seem to be significant in this context.

A system within a system

A government department is only part of a larger social and policy-making system with which it merges at the edges. The larger system includes Ministers, Parliament and the electorate, and it is conventional to speak of the department's relationship to them in terms of control: Parliament controls Ministers who in turn control their departments. But the department touches other parts of the larger system in its contacts with pressure groups (some of whom look to it as a sponsor), in its dealings with the public and in its arrangements for securing expert advice, to say nothing of its own recruitment needs. In order to avoid dislocating criticism and review it has to preserve some sort of equilibrium in all its relationships. The political relationship does not even supply the department's main contact with the external world. But it is qualitatively different from the others because it provides a higher court of appeal. Its total effect, although not necessarily felt in any particular instance, is to supply a general pressure towards integration and rationality, and it is the directly experienced strength of this pressure that distinguishes a government department from a private firm.

Formally, the department is designed to respond to pressures from the political subsystem, if they are forthcoming. And pressures are in fact being applied all the time, directed almost randomly through the Minister at different sections of its work. But it is misleading to describe the department as an instrument of its political head. He does not (like the head of Weber's bureaucracy) specify broad objectives which are progressively broken down into divisional and branch assignments, except on the rare occasions that involve major questions of party policy. No more does the Permanent Secretary. Any part of the department can best be described as a self-sustaining machine, organized generally on bureaucratic lines, which has the capacity to generate improvements within the broad policy directions given to it and will continue to do so until stopped. It continues in operation without much regard to a change of government. It has elaborate adaptive mechanisms through which information is processed and translated more or less automatically into requests for authority to modify the prevailing policies. Its methods of working are influenced by the pressures exerted on it by all its neighbours, not only the political environment. If any of these forces were to alter, or to be removed, the work of the department would also alter in character.

Organization theory and public administration

We can now look again at the question raised at the beginning of this chapter. How far are the theories of organization discussed in Chapters VI and VII relevant to the problems currently facing public administration in Britain?

Chapters VII was concerned with decisions. It touched on the limitations of human rationality and their consequences for individual and collective decisions. Since people have limited reasoning capacity, the way they perceive and analyse problems is biased by their previous experience and by their position in the communication system. Different people respond to different cues. Their response is always incomplete, whether they are politicians, professional advisers or potato merchants.

This framework seems likely to prove helpful in analysing the contributions of all those who take part in making public policy. Civil servants are influenced in their choice of priorities partly by the way they perceive the demands of the political system. But those demands are in turn governed by the way politicians interpret the material coming before them, and by their motivation to pursue one aspect of a question rather than another. Similar questions can be asked about the impact of pressure groups on government departments, and indeed about the way members of the public perceive issues and the effect on their voting behaviour. Altogether, the application of Simon's theoretical framework seems likely to provide sensitive instruments for analysing a wide range of political and administrative behaviour.

But the most important questions are about the way policies emerge from the *combination* of incomplete perspectives. We are led back to the questions about organizational design discussed in Chapter VI. Towards the end of that chapter, the main point of the discussion was seen to be the suitability of different types of organization for getting different sorts of work done. Relevant considerations included the readiness of organizational members to participate and the need to balance social, economic and operational factors in arriving at the best pattern of organization for a given purpose. These are the kind of questions we raise about the organization of individual departments or of the civil service as a whole.

When these structural theories are viewed from a wider perspective, it seems that they are really about relationships and about relating the structure of a department or agency to its function in the total system. What is a department (or the whole service) required to do? What resources are available to it and on what conditions? Which of its objectives are primary and which problems must it be able to tackle effectively? In the context of the department or the government as a whole, is a unit responsible primarily for carrying out specified tasks, or for maintaining the system, or for picking up signals about changes in the outside world? While there is a great deal of research to be done, some crude hypotheses about the requisite structures can be made. For example, some task-centred units are likely to benefit from a clear structure of command and control, others from a more collegiate structure: the administration of customs and excise calls for the former, the development of policies for the elderly requires the latter. Similarly, efficiency tests of performance may provide useful incentives in the Stationery Office but cannot be sensibly applied to a 'think tank' or a Minister's private office. A purchasing unit does not need the same kind of open network, to link it with research and pressure groups, as a unit whose main concern is with the adaptation of policy to changing circumstances. Most of this is obvious enough, although the wider implications do not seem to be so obvious to those who insist on treating the government system as a homogeneous entity. The immediate point is that organizational theories on this type of problem apply as much to the public as to the private sector.

Given what we have said about the political system, the central policy-making machinery has some special requirements. It is necessary to ensure, by a combination of specialization (to ensure expertise) and coordinating machinery (to bring different forms of expertise together) that policy is not settled on too narrow a base. The integrative-allocative function of government will not be achieved unless there is a place for 'lay' (not necessarily political) thinking, even on the most technical issues, before policy becomes concrete. The system has to ensure that technical considerations, for example in the design and construction of motorways, neither predominate nor are ignored. The exact balance will almost certainly be influenced by the structures within which decisions are made and by the statuses of the participants. It is also likely to be affected by the order in which the various perspectives are applied. Are policies initiated by experts and approved or vetoed by laymen (now including politicians)? Or is it, somehow, the other way round?

Organization theory has perhaps a more limited role here. There are altogether too many variables. But if the aims can be made more specific, organization theory can help to show how they might be achieved in a way that is compatible with the recruitment and retention of enough public servants of calibre to do the work (a factor sometimes ignored by hostile critics of the civil service) and with the limited cognitive capacity of all the human participants in the system. A department can be structured, and its members trained, so that more attention will be paid to one set of considerations than to others. For example, the relative weight given to political and technical factors in formulating policy is likely to be a factor, among other things, of the relative positions of general administrators and specialists in the hierarchy.

In an illuminating article Subramaniam contrasts the specialist and the generalist in terms of the relationship between fact and value in decision-making. He accepts Simon's analysis that every decision is a conclusion derived from a value proposition combined with several relevant facts. Any major decision involves (a) more than one value, (b) not each of which is clearly postulated, (c) several facts, it not being always clear what facts need to be assembled, (d) nor easy to assemble those needed. Subramaniam suggests that the specialist is particularly good at assembling the facts in his field (d). But he will be less alert to the explicit and implicit values involved in (a) and (b) and may consequently lack skill in identifying all the factual material that is relevant at (c). By contrast, the general administrator (or the politician) is sensitive to the scope and value implications of a decision but unable to explore factual areas without specialist help. The main weight of decision-taking can be placed either on the specialist or on the generalist, according to the relative importance and difficulty of value elements and factual elements in the decision.[13]

There are important choices to be made, not only in the extent to which administration is entrusted to specialists but also in the extent to which politicians are involved in detail, in the weight that is given to continuity, and in the economic, political and human costs that it is felt reasonable to incur in order to maximize some other value. We are a long way from the universal 'canons of efficiency' quoted from the Brownlow Report in Chapter VI. But the basic assumption in the Brownlow Report, that the method of analysis is the same for public departments and private organizations, holds up fairly well.

Differences in application have been over-emphasized in the past because the teaching of administration has been fragmented. Until recently the different fields of administration have tended to be taught separately in Britain to different groups of people and to stress different concepts. Courses in 'public administration' have been mainly about the history and legal powers of public authorities and have emphasized the problems of control and accountability. 'Social administration' has been concerned with the functions and aims of social service organizations and their success in terms of welfare output. 'Business administration' has been firmly rooted in the economics of profit, while 'industrial administration' has tended to stress efficiency and to use engineering principles. Only fairly recently can it be said that common concepts have begun to appear in all these fields. It is now reasonably likely that a university course under any of these titles would include some of the material discussed in the previous two chapters. As a result, some of the traditional differences have become less stark and have faded into shades of emphasis. For example, it is often suggested, rather crudely, that the accountability of a government department to Parliament is not very different from the accountability to shareholders of a board of directors. If behavioural rather than legal concepts are used to analyse each relationship, it becomes obvious that the analogy is misleading in some respects (because the 'sense-making' tendency of parliamentary intervention is more obtrusive and less consistent than the 'profit-mindedness' of shareholders) but helpful in others (for example, the conditioning effect of accountability on executive decisions).

The differences of emphasis are, of course, important. Even when a common 'organizational language' is employed, some of the basic questions of organizational choice in the public sector – accountability versus flexibility: centralization versus initiative – are very old friends to the political scientist. Some of the more acute points of controversy will be examined in Part Three, after further discussion in the next chapter of the significance of 'lay' control as an integrative and allocating factor in public administration.

Notes

1 P. M. Blau and W. R. Scott, *Formal Organizations* (London, 1963) pp. 42–57.
2 Peter Self, *Administrative Theories and Politics*, 2nd edn (London, 1977) p. 269.
3 D. C. Hague, W. J. M. Mackenzie and A. Barker (eds) *Public Policy and Private Interests: the institutions of compromise* (London, 1975).
4 Andrew Dunsire, *Administration: the word and the science* (London, 1973) Chap. 10.
5 Sir William Armstrong, *Professionals and Professionalism in the Civil Service* (London School of Economics, 1970).
6 R. S. Parker and V. Subramaniam, 'Public and Private Administration', *International Review of Administrative Sciences* Vol. 30 (1964) pp. 354–66. The quotation is from p. 365.
7 D. V. Donnison and V. Chapman, *Social Policy and Administration* (London, 1965) pp. 237–8.
8 ibid., p. 246.
9 See also Maurice Kogan, *Educational Policy-making: a study of interest groups and Parliament* (London, 1975).
10 Lord Bridges, 'Whitehall and Beyond', *The Listener* Vol. LXXI (25 June 1964) p. 1016.
11 J. E. Powell, 'Whitehall and Beyond', *The Listener* Vol. LXXI (26 March 1964) p. 505.
12 Bruce Headey, *British Cabinet Ministers: the roles of politicians in executive office* (London, 1974).
13 V. Subramaniam, 'Specialists in British and Australian Government Services: a Study in Contrast', *Public Administration* Vol. 41 (1963) pp. 357–73.

IX
The politician's
contribution

A distinguishing feature of public administration is the part played
in it by lay politicians. What kind of contribution do laymen make
to policy? How does it differ from the contributions of experts
and administrators? Is there any special significance in the order
in which it is combined with other elements in policy formulation? The discussion will be illuminated by an illustration.

The police widow's gratuity[1]

The case concerns a proposal to pay a gratuity to certain police
widows. In its original form the proposal provoked such opposition
in the House of Commons that it was withdrawn and a more
generous one substituted.

The story begins in 1961 when the Police Federation (representing the lower ranks of policemen) took the initiative by asking
for a change in the Police Pensions Regulations which would allow
a £4,000 gratuity to be paid to the widow of any policeman who
lost his life in the course of duty. A policeman's widow is normally
entitled to a pension, which is paid on a higher scale if her husband
died after a murderous assault (but not, for example, after an
accident incurred while patrolling a motorway in the fog). The

new gratuity was to be additional to the increased pension.

The claim was discussed, under the usual procedure, by a committee of the Police Council for Great Britain. This is a Whitley-type body which settles questions of police pay and conditions of service. It consists of a 'staff side' representing various grades of policemen and an 'official side', consisting of representatives of the local authorities, which employ the majority of policemen, in addition to representatives of the Home Office and the corresponding Scottish department. The local authority representatives on such a body are occasionally professional officers but more often elected councillors or (until 1974) aldermen with no technical knowledge. They may express general views from time to time, but on the whole they take their lead from the civil servants and from the secretary to the official side, who also acts as chief negotiator. The civil service members, in turn, are bound by general government policy on public expenditure, and it is well known that they look to the Treasury for guidance. This was the body that had to 'structure' the problem.

The official side was quick to reject the claim as it stood. It pointed out that it could lead to a flood of claims for the payment of gratuities to widows whose bereavement could be attributed to public employment. The repercussions would be excessively costly – one can see Treasury influence here in widening the frame of reference. It would, however, be prepared to consider the merits of a less generous scheme which could be limited to policemen.

The Police Federation then modified its figure to roughly £2,000 (two years' pay for a constable). It also agreed to exclude from the claim the widows of colleagues whose husbands had been killed on point duty or had lost their lives in rescuing people from drowning or from burning buildings, since special treatment for such cases could clearly run up against the objection about repercussions. It made a fresh proposal which was limited to three categories of widow: those whose husbands died as a result of a murderous assault; those who sustained fatal injuries while trying to effect an arrest (for example, by falling off a roof during a chase); and those who were killed while trying to prevent an escape (for example, through an accident to a pursuing vehicle).

The official side felt able to agree to a scheme covering the first category but not the other two. The problem had thus been simplified into a choice between the revised Federation proposal and the narrower one which was acceptable to the official side.

There followed nearly three years of stalemate in which all parties became increasingly embarrassed at the possibility that their continuing disagreement might deny a gratuity to the widow of a murdered policeman, since there would be no provision in the regulations to cover it. Changes in the police pensions code can be made only by amendment regulations which require the approval of both Houses of Parliament. By statute, amendments are proposed only after 'consultation' (which normally means agreement) with the Police Council. In this case the procedure for sanctioning and authorizing a change was largely (but not completely, since it contained no reference to the Treasury) defined in the statute.

The Home Secretary (then Mr Henry Brooke, later Lord Brooke of Cumnor) finally decided to seek parliamentary approval of regulations covering the point that *had* been agreed. Draft regulations appeared on the Order Paper of the House of Lords for 7 July 1964 and of the Commons for the following day. In the ordinary way they would have gone through, like hundreds of other regulations every year, without discussion and perhaps without even being read by more than a handful of members. Like most superannuation codes, police pensions regulations have become increasingly complicated over the years. Amending regulations are usually technical and difficult to understand, even with the help of the explanatory memorandum which is appended to all statutory instruments to explain their purpose and effect. At any rate, they seldom attract much parliamentary attention. Approval is often given formally, and few MPs are really aware of what has been done.

In this case, there was in fact a short debate in the House of Lords in which Liberal and Labour spokesmen both expressed doubt, on general social policy grounds, about treating some widows more generously than others with the same financial needs. The draft regulations were, however, approved.[2]

In the meantime, the Police Federation was directing a campaign at members of the lower House. Every MP received a broadsheet urging him to ask for the regulations to be withdrawn and replaced by more comprehensive ones. Since MPs receive many such appeals, it is unlikely that many of them studied it very carefully. But constituency pressures are another matter. On the day of the debate itself, each MP received a telegram from the local branches of the Federation in his constituency. They all read alike: 'Members of the —— Police Federation ask you to oppose Police Pensions (Amendment) No. 2 Regulations 1964. Proposals provide for officers who die after an attack but not for officers who are killed while attempting to make an arrest.'

It is worth describing in some detail the course of the debate on the Home Secretary's motion to approve the draft regulations.[3] His opening speech was interrupted by five Opposition MPs who flatly condemned the proposals as inadequate, without offering any arguments. After Mr Brooke sat down, Mr James Callaghan, declaring his interest at that time as consultant to the Police Federation, gave a reasoned exposition of the Federation point of view and criticized the Home Office for acting unilaterally. He was interrupted by two Conservative MPs who complained about being 'bombarded' by telegrams without being given time to find out about the problem and understand it. In the rest of the short debate there were four Conservative and three Opposition speakers. On the whole they made conventional points expressing sympathy for widows and hoping that the Home Secretary was not being niggardly. There was, however, a deeper undercurrent. Sir Spencer Summers (Conservative) said that this was 'one of the rather rare occasions when backbenchers bring an influence to bear on the front bench'. Mr Robert Mellish (Labour) said: 'Let the House of Commons prove itself just once in a while.' Finally, the Home Secretary said: 'I might not yield to the Opposition; but I will certainly yield to the House.' He promised to ask the Police Council if it would agree to widen the category of widows to whom the special gratuity would be paid.

The official side evidently agreed without difficulty (although the Federation Secretary later complained rather ungraciously that the Home Secretary had violated a constitutional principle by not consulting the staff side too!). A few days later, fresh draft regulations were presented which gave the police all they had asked for (and indeed rather more, since they extended the higher pension as well as the gratuity to widows in the two additional categories).[4] They led to some mutual congratulation in Parliament but no real discussion on the merits of the issue.

This case is interesting because it was argued throughout in terms of principle. There was no question of party discipline and the financial effects were unimportant: the additional cost of accepting the modified Federation proposal was estimated at a maximum of £20,000 a year. The question was a fairly simple one of deciding at what point a generally accepted principle, that the needs of widowhood should normally be met through universal comprehensive schemes, should yield to the moral claim of a policeman's widow for selective treatment. The main protagonists were the Police Federation, pressing the sectional case, and the Treasury officials behind the scenes who, as experts in this branch of social policy, represented the general community interest and stimulated the official side's resistance. (It is not always appreciated that the Treasury, now succeeded in some respects by the Civil Service Department, is the main source of expertise in many matters like this. The Treasury is usually thought to be concerned only with saving money; in this case it appears as the 'sense-maker' which opposes sectional interests that cannot be reconciled with a general system of values running through a whole field of policy.) The Home Office officials seem to have acted mainly as intermediaries. The interesting question is the role of the lay participants, since it is on this kind of 'value' issue that lay judgement might be supposed to come into its own.

The official side of the Police Council included a majority of local authority laymen (who, as employers, also had a minor interest in economy). They seem to have been content, as laymen often are on such bodies, to acquiesce in what the administrators proposed to them (that is to say, in the Treasury point of view until the Home Secretary himself abandoned it). They had the voting strength to reject the official line. But this strength, normally latent, remained so on this occasion.

The other lay body involved was Parliament. The Members of both Houses were invited to acquiesce in a minor piece of policy determined by the executive. The Lords did so. In the normal way the Commons would also have approved the draft regulations without difficulty even when the Home Secretary had drawn their attention to the value questions involved. This time the broadsheets and telegrams triggered off some of the latent forces. But when the interests of MPs were aroused, they did not go on to discuss the value questions in detail. Nobody said: 'The issues here are so and so; they are pretty finely balanced, but on the whole x is preferable for these reasons.' The points raised were apparently much more gross – 'political' rather than analytic. What they conveyed was, approximately: 'Hold on! There must be something wrong or the Police Federation would not be going to all this trouble. Take it away and think again.' When the Home Secretary came back, having rethought, nothing tripped the wire and perhaps only those immediately involved were fully aware of what had been done.

This is a minor case and it is untypical in many ways. The Home Secretary could have forced his original proposals through the House had he so wished. Although he referred to 'the feeling of the House', only thirteen members spoke apart from himself. What seems to have happened is that the Federation's lobbying coincided with a particular mood among backbenchers, possibly anxious to demonstrate their independence, and struck a particular chord in representatives of both parties and perhaps in Mr Brooke himself. Mr Humphry Berkeley singled out this incident as one that gave backbenchers an unusual lift to the spirits, soon to be deflated by a succession of three-line whips.[5]

Laymen in politics

But it suggests some general hypotheses about the way lay 'control' works when it is not overshadowed by power factors and by party discipline. Although the MPs successfully resisted a government proposal, it was not on substantive grounds. They did not consciously oppose general to sectional values on the particular issue. There was a broad assumption that this unpopular job would be done anyway within the government machine – as indeed had been the case. The lay members were apparently concerned with a more abstract point – whether the job of formulating balanced proposals had been well done, with proper attention to the usual patterns of consultation and procedure. They were afraid that the balance of consideration had become distorted and produced a result that was not self-evidently acceptable. This is essentially a 'constitutional' approach.

Sometimes, no doubt, lay politicians do have to apply their judgement and experience in settling difficult questions on their merits after considering all the available information. One tends to think of nineteenth-century government in these terms. It may be that some small local authorities still work in this way. Royal Commissions, usually with a lay chairman and at least a majority of lay members, are set up for this very purpose. But such bodies are the exception and even in these cases members do not work in a vacuum. They are exposed to pressures of various sorts and have to take a minimum of factual material into consideration. As the volume of political and technical factors increases, their ability to handle it comprehensively declines. There is usually far too much material for them to digest. Members split into sub-groups, or define their paramount concerns in such a way as to reduce much of the information to irrelevance. Schon claims that this method of dealing with the overload problem is essentially extra-rational: 'the politics of the group process are inseparable from the cognitive process'.[6]

For a Member of Parliament the difficulty is correspondingly greater because of the number and complexity of questions competing for his attention. He cannot hope to become involved in more than a fraction of them, nor to inform himself completely about those that do attract his notice. What sort of strategy can he work out to cope with such a responsibility? Three principles seem to apply fairly generally:

1 *Latency*. Since in practice he can intervene so little, he can maximize his influence by stressing what he might do rather than what he actually does. He will press for procedures that give him the *opportunity* of intervening – like regulations requiring an affirmative resolution and statutes that have to be renewed annually – and will resist any encroachment by the executive on the rights and privileges of Parliament. He is encouraged

by journalists and possibly by constituents who expect him to defend his ability to defend their interests. So far as he is successful, the effect is to keep the possibility of review constantly in the minds of administrators and departmental Ministers.

2 *Sensitivity to pressure.* He will not (or not very often) actively seek out matters to investigate. He has no need to. Party whips are looking for speakers and trying to man committees. Various interest and cause groups are seeking his alliance. Constituents are pressing him to take up various issues on their behalf. His problem is to choose to which pressures he will respond. Since he is a politician, and depends for success on his ability to retain support, he tends to take up issues that look most likely to command popular support, at least in his own constituency. A miners' MP is likely to be fairly deaf to the clean air lobby. Part of his job as a politician is precisely to identify the relevant political issues. If he mistakes his role, or misjudges his support (like some Members who have followed their consciences or defied the party whip on what they saw as a moral issue), he may be disowned by his constituency association before the next election. The effect here is to give him an integrative and mediating role, closely connected with the grievance-settling function of Parliament, which can counteract departmental tendencies to work from too sectional or too cosy a frame of reference.

3 *Non-competition with experts.* Conscious of his own ignorance, he will not try to dispute with experts on their own ground. He is more likely to press for the appointment of additional specialists when he suspects that there is some deficiency in the way decisions are reached. Occasionally, he may feel that a specialist has exceeded his competence – for example if the results of expert advice are producing unpalatable results in his own constituency – but this is rare. He is, however, ready to exploit a difference of opinion between experts. He will then make jurisdictional points – suggesting that a particular school of thought ought to be represented in the advisory system, or that more weight ought to be given to the views of a particular pressure group. His incentive is again political. There is no political kudos in challenging the views professed by an estab-

lished group of experts – whether they be doctors, economists or what have you – so long as they are generally held within the specialism. But reputations can be made by espousing the interests of emergent new groups whose strength is currently under-represented in the machinery of government. The effect of intervening in this way is obviously 'allocative', and also partly integrative, since jurisdictional settlements can recognize new movements and alter the general direction of development. But it can leave an entrenched body of opinion without challenge even when (as perhaps in both medicine and economics) it embodies or obscures important value elements. In this context, 'expert' implies membership of a recognized discipline or profession. Administrators are not experts in this sense and do not enjoy the same immunity.

MPs are not the only laymen in central government. Ministers are still politicians, although they experience pressures in a slightly different way when they attain office. Civil service administrators are also trained to anticipate and respond to such impulses. After a time in the machine, even professional advisers tend to become attuned to political realities, although less so than the administrators. There is a gradual shading from the completely lay to the almost completely specialized. In one sense this is a continuum of responsibility and political accountability. In another sense it is a continuum of different approaches to a particular issue – from precise but narrow specialism to the intermittent and sometimes badly aimed evaluations of the complete generalist.

Price has described the pattern, as it applies in the United States, in terms of the medieval relationship among estates. He distinguishes four estates – the scientific, the professional, the administrative, and the political – which form 'a spectrum from truth to power'. At one extreme the scientist (including the social scientist) is remote from actual power and not on the whole interested in practical applications of his work. Professionals – doctors, engineers and so on – use the work of scientists to achieve particular purposes for which they are accountable. In doing so, they have to find compromises between what is technically possible and what is politically and economically acceptable.

It would be possible to eliminate nearly all cases of any particular epidemic disease, or nearly all transportation casualties, or for that matter nearly all professional crime, if we were willing to pay the price, in money or freedom or both. How far we go in any given case depends in part on scientific and technical considerations and in part on the opinion of the average citizen. But it depends, too, on the degree to which scientific and professional people are permitted to act on their own and the degree to which they are subject to administrative and political control.[7]

Administrators are more concerned with the general purposes of the State and with the organization and management of power. They have their own forms of expertise, but in terms of policy they are too close to their political superiors to have even the limited autonomy of the professionals.

Politicians are at the other extreme from the scientists.

The men who exercise legislative or executive power may make use of the skills of administrators and engineers and scientists, but in the end they make their most important decisions on the basis of value judgements or hunch or compromise or power interests. There can be no common discipline or body of established principles to guide them, for their business is to deal with problems in which either the inadequacy of scientific and professional data, or the conflict of expert opinion, makes it necessary or possible to come to decisions that are based on judgement and must be sustained by persuasion or authority.[8]

The balance between truth and freedom is maintained by checks and balances among the estates.

This analysis is valuable (bearing in mind that the elected Congressman has a more direct influence on policy than the elected Member of Parliament; he is also subject to less party discipline but more external pressure). But it would be misleading to try to draw rigid dividing lines between the respective contributions of the professional and the generalist, or between the roles of the permanent official and the elected politician. Too many people move easily from one side of the line to the other – from professional to amateur status as it were. The careerist and the politician have their own clearcut brands of loyalty and commitment, but the differences are not reflected sharply in the way they approach policy, certainly not in any sharp distinction between 'fact' and 'value' or between 'administrative' and 'political' frameworks. After studying county government in Cheshire, Lee found the similarity between the chief county officials and the key elected representatives so great that he grouped them together as 'a kind of ministerialist party'.[9]

Since the date of Lee's study, local government has become more overtly political. Both in central and local government, however, the elected representative plays a number of roles: ideological partisan; policy-maker; specialist; party hack; mouth-piece for a pressure group; constituency grievance-chaser; watch-dog of the constitution; protagonist of good administration. Few individuals will play all these roles: some will be happier exchanging war-cries on the floor of the House than discussing financial procedures with senior civil servants in an upstairs committee room, and vice versa. (Two American observers classified British MPs as 'enthusiasts' or 'bureaucrats'.[10]) There are also great differences in interests, background and ability.[11] The kind of analysis attempted in this chapter therefore has elements of caricature.

Stronger lay control

It is natural for MPs to complain that they lack the opportunities, the information and the expert assistance to make their 'control' of the executive more effective. This is an expression of the 'latency' principle discussed earlier. There is persistent support, within Parliament as well as from outside, for specialist committees and other devices through which the MP can inform himself about the work for which Ministers are theoretically accountable to him. Some recent developments have been described in Chapter v. But MPs have not shown themselves over-zealous to use their oppor-tunities when they have had them. Many important debates are sparsely attended and not many members in fact seem prepared to put a great deal of work into something like the Expenditure Committee.

There are also administrative implications. Given the current attitudes of most MPs, a successful attempt to involve some of them more deeply in technical and administrative details is likely to have several effects on the development of policy. The first is that the few Members who do play an active part (particularly as chairmen of subcommittees) can acquire a great deal of influence. Because of the 'latency' principle, any parliamentary recommendation carries some weight in government departments. A comment in a select committee report is less weighty than a decision reached by the full House under party discipline. But it is studied carefully, and many changes in policy can be traced to, say, a recommendation from the Expenditure Committee. The reports themselves are seldom debated in the full House. Since the number of members on each committee is small, and few of these play a large part in the proceedings, the views of a single person may pass virtually unchallenged as the embodiment of parliamentary thinking on a particular matter.

On major issues, of course, this cannot happen, because major decisions have been processed in the Cabinet machine and perhaps brought before Parliament as a whole for ratification. (Committees are supposed to avoid 'policy' issues of this sort.) And even on minor questions a committee that chooses to review settled policy is likely to find a department defensive and inclined to appeal to a higher political court. But when it engages in discussion with departmental witnesses on an embryonic issue where policy is still fluid, the views embodied in its report can be very influential, simply because they appear in a parliamentary document. (The influence of Dr Jeremy Bray on official thinking about the structure of the civil service and the organization of government statistical services in the mid-1960s was attributable very largely to his chairmanship of the subcommittees which prepared Estimates Committee reports on these subjects.)

When a committee takes expert evidence, the effect is even stronger, because (at least in some circumstances) more attention is paid to the views of a witness who has gained the ear of a parliamentary committee than he might have received in the normal processes of departmental consultation. It may be unfair to cite the influence of three academic witnesses on the 1964–5 Select Committee on Procedure whose fourth Report recommended the establishment of specialist committees, since this was an exclusively parliamentary matter. But even in this case it is fair to claim that the outcome might have been different if different witnesses had been consulted or if the distribution of presentational skills had been different. Quite apart from the principle that the layman does not directly criticize the expert, it is, of course, difficult for a parliamentary committee, or its chairman, to assess the whole balance of considerations on a particular matter. A committee has to select the evidence on which it will base its recommendations and its selection is bound to be influenced by the personal views of its expert advisers. It has become more common to provide committees with a permanent adviser (often a distinguished academic expert) to guide them through an enquiry. There is sometimes a remarkable similarity between the background discussion paper prepared by the adviser at the start of the enquiry and the committee report that comes out at the end.

Independent assessments can be a useful addition to the regular machinery for preparing policy. The personal contributions of individual MPs may be (and in many of the instances that come to mind undoubtedly have been) of considerable value. But this has been because the MP is a knowledgeable and intelligent person. The fact that he is a member of a representative assembly does not seem to be relevant. Similarly, public discussion of government policies and processes is aided by bringing 'counter-experts' into the review machinery to help parliamentarians put official evidence into context. But this may merely provide an amplifier for the expert's views, especially with a weak committee.

A second effect of greater specialization by MPs may be to *weaken* the most useful part that laymen can play in the process. The special value of parliamentary review lies in the MP's place in the communication system which links departments to various publics. It cannot be delegated to a few members who happen to be knowledgeable and interested in a particular subject. Indeed, too much knowledge may be a disqualification. Special knowledge tends to imply a commitment, and committed laymen become relatively less sensitive to other pressures. To retain a balance, they may need to be made accountable to other laymen who are neither knowledgeable nor involved. Since Parliament cannot handle all the business with which it is charged, it is inevitable that some of its work should be delegated to committees, and in practice to the small number of active members on each committee. The older, non-specialized, committees probably approach their task of reviewing proposals and procedures in much the same spirit as Parliament as a whole. But it seems that the newer, specialized committees will not serve the same purpose. It may be necessary for their reports to be discussed by uncommitted laymen as critically as the older sort of committee discussed the work of departments. And pressures on parliamentary time (as well as the reluctance of relatively inactive backbenchers to criticize their more active colleagues) make it unlikely that this will be done. Of similar but earlier developments in the American system, Price comments on the risk that Congress 'will surrender its powers to its own committees, and that they will become too obsessed with new technological toys to deal with broader issues of policy'.[12]

The balance of contributions

The intermittent, amateur character of the present parliamentary system seems remarkably appropriate in the light of what is *distinctive* about politicians' contribution to policy. It is already the function of Ministers and general administrative civil servants to undertake a continuous and relatively knowledgeable review of the demands made by technical experts and special interest groups in order to relate them to other pressures and commitments. It is their business to take as broad a view as they can, to assemble as much information as possible about conflicting technical views on a problem and to formulate policies that have a reasonable chance of being acceptable to the special interests concerned and to the public at large. Their job is to achieve a kind of balancing act among facts, pressures and assumptions. Part of the job of politicians outside the government is to make sure that they do. If the policies that emerge from this process are repeatedly found to be unacceptable, the process is clearly deficient and perhaps the structure needs revision. But Ministers and civil servants, in their respective ways, are still in the best position to put matters right. It is not functional for those at a more general level in the system to try to do it for them. Granted that politicians are not supermen, the opportunist, random, way in which the attention of MPs is directed to particular subjects may well offer the most effective means for injecting their pressure for rationality – for consistency and integration – into the policy-making system.

A further point of importance here is the order in which different contributions can most effectively be combined. At what point can pressures for integration most effectively be related to technical aspects of policy? We have noted the difficulty of modifying policies once they have been formulated. There is constant pressure to involve lay interests at an earlier stage so that they (the public, MPs, Ministers, general administrators) can influence the direction of technical thinking. The desire for open government, the participatory democracy movement, and the warnings that Ministers should not allow themselves to be misled by their civil servants, have a variety of sources and motivations; but they all indicate lay distrust of the expert.

This question will exercise us from several points of view in Part Three. One or two preliminary points can be made briefly. A political decision tends to be more difficult to alter than a technical one. Since it is supposed to be based on *all* relevant considerations it is hard to admit later that an important point has been overlooked; the only real court of appeal is the still less expert one of public opinion. Experts, too, are at risk if they make technical judgements without taking political factors into account. But it is very difficult to make defensible political decisions without taking account of such technical information as is available. The model outlined in the last chapter is in fact functionally correct in normal circumstances: it is best for the focus to move sequentially from the technical to the general. If the 'integrative' and 'allocative' elements in public administration are to be attended to by finite human minds, it must normally be near the end of the process rather than the beginning, unless it is the process itself that is being scrutinized.

Civil servants have a number of perfectly respectable reasons for wanting to keep Ministers 'out of their hair' until the right moment. Ministers are concerned with their reputations, and are interested in action. On the other hand, they find it difficult to change their minds in public without embarrassment. Sir Edward Playfair has described how when he was at the Treasury he had, after intricate manœuvring, nearly reached a solution to a minor but long-standing problem when the then Prime Minister heard about it and started asking questions, with the result that everybody else fell back into inflexible bargaining positions.[13] Ministers feel the same about exposing their preliminary ideas to Parliament before they have been firmed up. For example, there are currently some advocates of a parliamentary taxation committee, which would discuss with the Chancellor of the Exchequer and Treasury officials the background to a forthcoming budget and the options available. The assumption seems to be that such a discussion could take place in the calm atmosphere of, say, the Public Accounts Committee. But the annual budget is central both to the management of the economy and to the allocative function. Advance discussion on such a committee would be highly political and would make it more difficult for a Chancellor to frame the final budget with proper regard to economic factors. Post-budget discussion (including the possibility of amendments to the Finance Bill) is another matter.

There is one other point to be made at this stage. It concerns the salience of political (and especially parliamentary) considerations in the minds of those who make and execute public policy. Much could be said about the changing status of the House of Commons in relation to the executive, the corporate bodies representing trade unions and employers, the EEC Commission in Brussels, and the prospects of devolution within the United Kingdom. The fact remains that parliamentary business takes up much of the time of Ministers and senior civil servants. There is inevitably a tendency to approach other matters from the standpoint of how they will look in Parliament. There is nothing wrong with this at all, unless it leads to window-dressing. But if Parliament and its committees probe deeper and earlier into the processes of administration, political pressures will be felt more strongly in areas where they may be less appropriate. This obviously applies to work which is mainly technical or professionalized: 'political interference' has unfortunate connotations here. It also applies to policies with a long time-scale, extending beyond the elected life of a government or Parliament. One attempted solution to the problem, as we shall see, has been to remove large areas of the public sector from direct parliamentary scrutiny and thus try to protect them from short-term political pressures. In terms of our analysis, less opportunity for parliamentary intervention allows more weight to be given to efficiency in a technical sense; but it also means that integrative and allocative pressures, concerned with side effects and the wider public interest, will have less impact.

Politics and organizational choice

Our model, which gives politicians a primarily appellate and mediating role, assumes that, in Britain at least, society has many purposes which are often in conflict. Within the framework of the social services, for example, the objectives of the health and teaching professions cannot ultimately be reduced to a common denominator. Even the various branches of medicine are competing for resources and prestige rather than mutually supportive in the pursuit of a common goal. The task of administrators and politicians is primarily one of integrating competing elements and allocating resources to them. An Act of Parliament or an annual budget represents a compromise among the conflicting interests of, for example, doctors, patients and taxpayers. The special function of elected politicians is to symbolize a 'general good' which can be opposed to more sectional goods. But in the last resort this is only a device to provide a focus for the allocative and integrative activities: in reality the 'general good' has no meaning apart from the sum of sectional interests. It is useful only so long as it is left inexplicit.

The model, however, will work only if there is mutual trust and a broad consensus about existing institutions and the values they represent. Even when these are present, changes will be taking place in public feeling about specific questions, like abortion legislation or the incidence of taxes. The reactive role ascribed to politicians in the model needs to be modified in at least one respect. As public representatives, they have an important role in putting issues on the agenda. Party organization, in particular, provides a convenient means of articulating new objectives (at least for those whom the parties think they represent) and is a major source of political initiatives which then have to be translated into workable policies by the government machine (see Chapter VIII, pp. 205–7. But if broad consensus is lacking, or there is a loss of confidence in public institutions (as seems in many Western countries to occur as the outcome of public disenchantment with the ability of governments to live up to their promises[14]) politicians have to play a more prominent role, involving themselves in matters of detail on controversial subjects like comprehensive secondary education and selectivity in the social services, where feelings run high but factual evidence is absent or ambiguous. In the final breakdown, people lose faith both in professional altruism and in the ability or will of politicians to protect their interests. Every man becomes his own expert and his own advocate. Some observers feel that such a trend lies behind the participative democracy movement in contemporary Britain.[15]

We are again faced with the problem of balance. If we know what we want to achieve we can devise an organization suitable for the purpose. A public administration system has to meet three sets of criteria. Particular services have to be administered with regard to internal efficiency and technical adequacy. There has to be provision at the centre for coordination and integration of policy. Depending on the political system and climate, the administrative process must include safeguards for the individual citizen and be conducted with sufficient openness to promote public confidence. These criteria tend to pull in different directions. The participation question falls just outside the scope of this book; one of us has explored its implications elsewhere.[16] In Part Three we shall examine a number of specific questions about central government administration in the light of the other two criteria.

Notes

1 Details of the incident can be traced in issues of the *Police Review* and *News Summary* (official journal of the Local Authorities' Conditions of Service Advisory Board) between 1961 and 1964, and in parliamentary papers.
2 *H.L. Debs*, Vol. 259 (7 July 1964) cols 931–8.
3 *H.C. Debs*, Vol. 698 (8 July 1964) cols 543–77.
4 *Police Pensions (Amendment) (No. 3) Regulations, 1964*, approved in the Commons on 27 July 1964, *H.C. Debs*, Vol. 699, cols 1176–86 and in the Lords on 28 July 1964, *H.L. Debs*, Vol. 260, cols 967–70.
5 Humphry Berkeley, *The Power of the Prime Minister* (London, 1968, pp. 18–19.
6 D. A. Schon, *Beyond the Stable State* (London, 1971) pp. 215–16.
7 D. K. Price, *The Scientific Estate* (Cambridge, Mass., 1965) p. 124.
8 ibid., p. 134.
9 J. M. Lee, *Social Leaders and Public Persons* (Oxford, 1963) p. 214.
10 J. P. Roche and S. Sachs, 'The Bureaucrat and the Enthusiast' in R. Rose (ed.), *Policy-making in Britain* (London, 1969).
11 P. G. Richards, *The Backbenchers* (London, 1972).
12 Price, *The Scientific Estate*, op. cit., p. 81.
13 Sir Edward Playfair, 'Minister or Civil Servant?', *Public Administration* Vol. 43 (1965) p. 268.
14 Organization for Economic Co-operation and Development, *Policies for Innovation in the Service Sector* (Paris, 1977) Chap. 5, 'Client–Supplier Relationships'.
15 L. J. Sharpe, 'Instrumental Participation and Urban Government' in J. A. G. Griffith (ed.), *From Policy to Administration: essays in honour of William A. Robson* (London, 1976).
16 R. G. S. Brown, *The Management of Welfare* (London, 1975) Chap. 9, 'Accountability and the Public'.

PART THREE

Problems

X
Planning

Introduction

In this final Part of the book, we look at some characteristic problem areas in public administration in the light of (a) the tasks, the civil service apparatus and the political framework described in Part One; (b) some of the theoretical concepts set out in Part Two. The present chapter is concerned with planning. It looks briefly at three recent innovations in British central government; the development of procedures for planning public expenditure; the growth of planning systems within departments; the (very incomplete) development of a planning approach over a whole field of policy. The second half of the chapter is concerned, more analytically, with the implications of planning for the politico-administrative structure.

The word 'planning' has had many meanings. For a period after the Second World War it had ideological overtones: the 'planned economies' of the communist countries were associated with controls and restrictions on individual freedom. By the 1960s, however, the word had been rehabilitated by the evident success of economic planning in France. Britain had a 'National Plan' in 1965. Although it was soon abandoned, the concept of planning was not. New techniques of planning, and new planning units, continue to proliferate. Planning, with its sophisticated derivatives of policy analysis and future-search, has taken over from management as the staple ingredient of administrative training.

The commonsense use of the word explains its significance. To plan is to look ahead and try to foresee the consequences of actions and trends in events instead of taking a series of *ad hoc*, uncoordinated decisions. There are perhaps still a few who argue that when governments do this they make so many mistakes that they had better not have tried: oft-quoted examples include a disastrous attempt to restrict entry to medical schools in the 1950s and miscalculations of the investment requirements of nationalized industries.[1] Any estimate of future probabilities is subject to error. It is also true that if some techniques of planning, particularly those that rely on a limited range of variables, are applied rigidly they may lead to stereotyped and inappropriate behaviour; we should use planning 'models', like horoscopes, with discretion. It may also be true that certain styles of planning lead to a concentration of power in the hands of the planners, and that governmental planning carries certain risks, both technocratic and autocratic. But that is a matter of how planning is conducted. In some sense or other, planning is here to stay in all advanced countries.

The main reason is the increasing cost of unplanned developments in a complex society where rising expectations are not matched by increases in resources. The most significant boost to planning in Britain was the 1961 report of the Plowden Committee, which pointed out that piecemeal decision-making was leading to uncontrolled growth in public expenditure that could, in total, have consequences that nobody intended.[2] All the elements of planning are explicit or implicit in the Plowden recommendations:

(a) widening the time-scale of decision-making – decisions about new schools or new staff appointments should be made, not on the basis of whether they can be afforded this year, but with regard to the continuing commitment next year and the years beyond;

(a) comprehensiveness – questions which are interrelated should be looked at together in order to develop policies which are coherent instead of inconsistent and competing;

(c) prioritization – since all things are not possible (and the true

cost of doing anything is the 'opportunity cost' of not doing
something else) there should be some rational basis for deciding
which are more important.

Planning can encompass the economy as a whole, the public
sector, or a particular service or group of services. Some examples
will be examined shortly. Plans can serve a variety of purposes.
They can be presented merely as a basis for discussion, so that
those pressing for a particular development (or their opponents)
will at least be made aware of the wider implications. They can
be used as a basis of decision, if those in power have preference
for one set of outcomes and feel able to impose it on others. Between
these extremes we find 'indicative' planning, which is intended
to establish a framework of assumptions (for example about growth
in the economy) to remove some of the uncertainty surrounding
more specific decisions about industrial investment and the expansion of public services. We also find plans whose main purpose
is political – to strengthen the case for a development by demonstrating its feasibility and longer-term benefits.

Among the components of plans are assumptions about causal
relationships (increased numbers of school-leavers will lead to a
greater demand for higher education). Plans which are used to
make or influence decisions contain value-judgements about a
hierarchy of ends and means (the cost of expanding higher education is justified because it is desirable to maintain the current level
of opportunities for school-leavers or – a less fashionable argument
– because graduates contribute disproportionately to national
wealth). Many plans include some assessment of the machinery
for putting them into effect. But the essence of planning is that
it helps to make decisions more rational by bringing together information about changing circumstances, such as changes in the birth
rate, and information about the probable consequences and inter-
relationships of alternative policies for relevant sectors like primary
schools and the pram industry. However it is used, the key to
a planning approach is the availability of information and its
insertion into the decision-making process.

There is one more introductory point. Planning can be a neutral
analytic tool, helpful in approaching the classic political problems

of prioritization and resource allocation. But there is another sense in which planning can be highly innovative. The process is the same: more information assists decision-making. But by uncovering new information the planners may hit upon new problems, or new ways of dealing with old ones. Almost certainly such information will be threatening and unwelcome to established interests, especially if it suggests radical changes in existing services, administrative structures and professional jurisdiction. Innovative planners may therefore become advocates of change rather than mere analysts who assist the existing decision-makers to operate more effectively. This difference is very important in understanding the potentialities and limitations of planning in the British administrative process.

Public expenditure planning

Since 1963, at first intermittently and then annually, the government has published a White Paper (i.e. a statement of policy intentions) on Public Expenditure. This is a direct outcome of the Plowden recommendations. Although its style, content and even title have varied, the purpose of the White Paper has remained the same.[3] The whole of public expenditure, normally for five years ahead, is projected under fifteen or so 'programmes' like defence, housing, roads and transport, health and personal social services. Reasons are given for projected increases or decreases in individual programmes (for example, the cost of implementing new policies, or of responding to demographic changes). There is a general statement about the government's spending plan as a whole. The exercise of preparing this instrument of public expenditure planning is known as PESC,[4] from the initials of the Public Expenditure Survey Committee of senior officials who coordinate it and present a preliminary report to Ministers.

Matters seldom turn out exactly as predicted in the White Paper. But it performs a number of important planning functions. First, it shows government intentions about total public spending, including the expenditure of local authorities and nationalized industries as well as of central government. For the latter, the expenditure forecast for the year immediately ahead provides the expenditure side of the Spring budget. The White Paper may or may not relate public spending to anticipated changes in the economy: one ill-fated attempt to do so was the 1965 White Paper (the 'National Plan'), whose demonstration that improvements in public services could be financed out of economic growth was sadly optimistic.[5] Second, it shows government priorities between programmes, with supporting figures showing past and future trends. Third, it shows the estimated financial implications of policies being pursued within individual programmes. This provides a starting point for reviews of particular policy areas by the House of Commons Expenditure Committee. The Commons also debates the White Paper as a whole (although few MPs take part in either review procedure).

PESC is therefore a major exercise in macro-planning. There are great technical difficulties about the actual figures, which need not concern us here. More important are the fierce battles over priorities between programmes which precede publication. Since most programmes are the domain of a powerful Cabinet Minister, political reputations are at stake. Final decisions are sometimes taken at a special Cabinet meeting at Chequers, the Prime Minister's country residence. Civil servants, of course, play a part in earlier negotiations with the Treasury, and the Treasury sets the rules for the actual presentation of the document. The exercise is one for which the basic Whitehall structure, with Treasury and Cabinet arbitrating among powerful functional departments (see Chapter XI), is well suited. The planning components simply make explicit the nature and implications of resource-allocative decisions that would have had to be taken anyway. That it is difficult to make the PESC decisions stick is, again, another matter.

Departmental planning systems

Other planning developments in the late 1960s and early 1970s took place within departments. Some resembled PESC on a smaller scale, analysing needs and allocating resources within a PESC programme for which the department was responsible; examples were to be found in the Ministry of Defence, the Department of Education and Science and, later, the Department of Health and Social Security. These resource-allocating systems naturally involved senior officials representing the main policy divisions of the department, and frequently Ministers as well. The staff work, however, was usually carried out by a designated planning branch or division. In other departments, planning units were set up to look in depth at specific areas, like technological developments in agriculture, alternative ways of providing an employment service, and the economic impact of direct taxation. Such units were generally detached from the main body of departmental work: some were almost indistinguishable from research units. Their impact on ongoing activities was very variable; the employment service study led directly to the setting up of the Employment Services Agency and to the separation of job-finding functions from the policing of unemployment benefit payments, but other studies of this sort seem to have had little effect. At the opposite extreme, the Foreign and Commonwealth Office, whose ability to foresee problems had been criticized (not for the first or the last time) by another Plowden Committee in 1964,[6] had set up a 'planning staff' whose main function seemed to be to act as staff assistants to the Permanent Secretary. In a survey completed early in 1972, from which these examples are taken, Fry found that ten departments had planning units of one sort or another.[7]

The planning system in DES was subsequently described in some detail by the Permanent Secretary of the Department and in a fairly critical report from OECD. At that time it operated at three levels. A policy steering group, chaired by the Permanent Secretary and including the most senior specialist and administrative officials, determined the total planning programme in consultation with Ministers, and later reviewed the outcome before submitting it, if appropriate, to Ministers. Below that committee several policy groups, usually chaired by a Deputy Secretary and including 'a mixture of under-secretaries in charge of operational branches and specialists such as HM Inspectors, statisticians, economists, architects, quantity surveyors and cost accountants', were responsible for planning specific programmes. Finally, the planning unit itself was responsible for preparing material for the steering committee and policy groups, in close cooperation with the operational divisions and specialists, and for coordinating the planning effort.[8]

The scope of the DES planning system was the whole educational system, from nursery schools to postgraduate education. Its purpose was to provide a framework for resource allocation over a period of about ten years, taking into account such factors as changes in the birth rate and ministerial wishes (e.g. Mrs Thatcher's desire to improve nursery education and to do something about poor primary school buildings). One of its first outputs was the 1972 White Paper, *Education: a framework for expansion*, which set out a ten-year programme for increased expenditure in five directions.[9] Clearly, the role of planners in such a system is mainly to coordinate and arbitrate among competing demands. The OECD report found some aspects of the system impressive, but criticized its closed, reactive style, its apparent complacency about the existing educational pattern, and its failure to recognize that wider social changes affected and were affected by the educational system: examples of the latter were lack of recognition that the anti-authoritarianism of youth had implications for the education of sixteen- to eighteen-year-olds or that the increasing obsolescence of skills had implications for continuing education and re-training.[10]

A somewhat similar system operates on the health side of the Department of Health and Social Security. A planning unit studies the financial implications of policies proposed by the operational divisions, collates them, assesses priorities, and submits to senior officials and Ministers proposals for spending the sums allocated to the department under the PESC programme for health and personal social services. The operational divisions produce new ideas. For example, the service development group concerned with services for the elderly and the handicapped includes an administrator, a doctor, a nurse and a social worker. As well as dealing with parliamentary business, the group tries to keep in touch with developments in its field. It is represented at conferences and seminars. Its members carry out field visits and try to assimilate the output from the department's extensive research programme.[11] Both its policies for the elderly and the handicapped and its position in the pecking order are evident in statements of DHSS priorities within the health and personal social services.[12]

In these examples, planning is concerned with the best way of cutting up the cake. New ideas do not come from the planners. Indeed, the DHSS service development groups would probably claim that they were the real planners, as far as regular parliamentary and ministerial business allowed them time. In another sense, planning is about policy effectiveness. Let us turn to a contrasting example, the Criminal Policy Planning Unit in the Home Office, where the roles are reversed.

This unit was set up in 1974, in a structure superficially similar to that in the DES. There is a top-level steering committee, a working committee (of which the special political adviser to the Home Secretary became a member in 1977) chaired by the Deputy Secretary in charge of the crime and probation departments, and then the planning unit itself. The latter consisted at one stage of four administrators and a research officer, with supporting staff, and part-time assistance from a statistician, an economist, a systems analyst, a prison governor, a senior policeman and a probation inspector. Like the DES unit, it can draw on the main types of professional and analytic expertise that are available within the Home Office. The unit's terms of reference are to coordinate and develop policy in the criminal field. But it is not concerned with resource allocation and does not therefore have any leverage over the operational divisions concerned with police, prisons, probation, criminal law and the administration of criminal justice. Its purpose is to explore policy options in a depth and on a time scale that is not possible for operating divisions working under the pressure of parliamentary business. One of its early studies was of factors affecting the size of the prison population. The head of the unit at the time claimed that this task could not have been tackled as thoroughly by any other means and that its accomplishment helped to establish the unit in the eyes of the Home Office.[13] There is, of course, a risk that such a unit will fail to make an impact; even top-level steering committees can fall into disuse. Its members therefore have to keep proving themselves and to present their creative contributions with some regard to organizational politics.

Although similar in title, departmental planning units differ in ways that reflect the purpose, traditions and style of the department. The Home Office unit was grafted on to the everyday administration of the rag-bag of functions relating to crime with which the Office has to deal. In the DES and DHSS, planning is largely concerned with priorities and resource allocation. In the Ministry of Defence, forward planning and policy analysis is a central task of the top decision-makers. In the Board of Customs and Excise, one of the main functions of the planning unit is to make contingency plans for tax changes in the annual budget.

Central policy review

Early in the 1970s an attempt was made to set up machinery through which the effectiveness of government policies and programmes would be brought under periodic and systematic review. The incoming Conservative Government brought teams of businessmen into the Civil Service Department to establish a system of programme analysis and review (PAR) 'to provide Ministers with an opportunity to identify and discuss alternative policy options which can then be explored in greater depth before final decisions are taken on the expenditure programmes'.[14] A small central policy review staff (CPRS) was attached to the Cabinet Office to help Ministers to take better collective policy decisions

> by assisting them to work out the implications of their basic strategy in terms of policies in specific areas, to establish the relative priorities to be given to the different sectors of their programme as a whole, to identify those areas in which new choices can be exercised and to ensure that the underlying implications of alternative courses of action are fully analysed and considered.[15]

The function of the CPRS is to provide an independent source of advice for Ministers collectively. It is the nearest approximation within the British government machine to a policy analysis unit which can range beyond departmental boundaries. The unit is small (currently 16 people) and, given the strength of the departmental tradition in Whitehall, its position is delicate.[16] Many observers were surprised that it survived the change of government in 1974, since it was so closely linked to Conservative concepts of the way government should function.

Members of the CPRS divide their time between very quick exercises, such as drawing Ministers' attention to the wider implications of a departmental proposal coming before Cabinet, and studies in depth of questions which do not seem to receive sufficient attention from the normal departmental and interdepartmental machinery. Some of the latter have been published and have aroused fierce controversy. Not for publication were the six-monthly reviews of general government strategy which were prepared for Ministers in the 1971–4 period.

The main function of the CPRS is to widen the framework of ideas, either in time scale or in comprehensiveness. For example, a great deal of analysis and discussion about the various strands of social policy led to the publication in 1975 of a short report which suggested regular meetings of social service Ministers and a programme of specific studies.[17] Two of the latter had been completed and published by 1977. One dealt with long-term population forecasts and explored the implications for health, education and other services.[18] The other examined relationships between central and local government: it made a case for greater consistency in the administrative procedures of the relevant central government departments and for more flexibility across departmental boundaries.[19] Both reports provide reference points for more specific changes, either in policy or in administration, which might or might not have happened anyway. Either report could have been produced through the normal departmental machinery, or by interdepartmental working parties. But the CPRS had a more direct interest in such wide-ranging analysis. Without commitment to existing policies (and, be it said, without the daunting responsibility for implementing change) the team was free to challenge the assumptions behind them.

But the coordination of social policy is a relatively safe area for planners. A CPRS report which suggested that Britain's overseas services were over-elaborate in relation to our economic interests and changing position in the world provoked understandable hostility from threatened interests, from the British Broadcasting

Corporation to retired ambassadors.[20] Whatever the merits of the
report, they had little chance of being considered dispassionately.
This shows the importance of the politics of planning. New ideas
are not universally welcome. They need to be fitted into the
political framework – to find a constituency. Planners who stick
their necks out without political backing are liable to suffer the
penalty.

The idea behind PAR was to complement the PESC exercise
by exploring the effectiveness of current departmental programmes
and opening up consideration of different means of achieving a
given policy objective. Each PAR would be conducted by a team
from the relevant department or departments along with the
Treasury and the CPRS. The report would go to a special Cabinet
committee. Some placed great hopes on the concept.[21] Although
PAR reports are secret, it is known that some have been successfully implemented. But in the form envisaged PAR depends on
the willingness of the spending department to cooperate with the
CPRS and the Treasury, and can be seen as a threat to its autonomy.
PAR needs strong political backing from the centre, which may be
easier to find at a time when the government is less besieged
by the kind of short-term crises that characterized the 1970s.
Informed observers feel that PAR never really took off.[22] But there
have been PAR-type exercises within departments; some have been
touched upon in the discussion of departmental planning units.

The reader should not therefore assume that the majority of
decisions are informed by a planning approach in its various forms.
If evidence were needed, political diaries show all too clearly how
often major decisions are taken on the basis of short-term
expediency. Nevertheless, the capacity to plan improved very substantially during the 1970s. We turn now to some general
factors affecting the development and use of planning capacity.

Planning in government

The Fulton Committee had criticized the civil service for not
making clear provision for long-term policy planning as distinct
from short-term administrative and political management. Since
the latter tended to take priority, the former tended to

be neglected.[23] The Committee argued that every department should have a planning and research unit for each major field of policy, on lines which will be discussed later in the chapter.

This criticism was not new. Fifty years earlier, the Haldane Committee was complaining that 'adequate provision has not been made in the past for the organised acquisition of facts and information, and for the systematic application of thought, as preliminary to the settlement of policy and its subsequent administration'. The Haldane Committee made a number of proposals for improving this situation. It proposed the development of government-sponsored research, the extended use of advisory committees, a separation of planning responsibilities from day-to-day administration, and encouragement for all senior officials to spend more of their time on 'enquiry, research and reflection'.[24] With the exception of the last, these ideas have passed into current orthodoxy.

There are three main questions. First there is the problem of ensuring that the material most relevant to a policy decision – information about facts, political opinions, future possibilities – is available. Then there is the problem of sifting this information and presenting the essential factors in manageable form to the group who are concerned with the final decision. Third there is the problem of ensuring that they are not prevented by other pre-occupations from evaluating and using the material.

Sources of data

There are four main sources from which the raw material for new policy can come: (1) the conventional political system; (2) the system of non-parliamentary pressures and consultative machinery within which departments operate; (3) internal feedback from the operation of existing policies; (4) research and intelligence. The categories overlap and some channels convey material of more than one type. Thus advisory committees may convey information or pressures or both.

1 The part played by the political system has already been discussed in Chapters v and viii. Criticisms of existing policies and proposals for new ones are continuously reaching Ministers from individual MPs through letters, questions and debates,

from backbench committees, and from the political party machine. Many of these ideas originate with sectional groups outside politics, but they acquire a new significance when they are taken up through political channels. During the minority government period in the late 1970s, parliamentary committees were unusually active in reviewing areas of policy and making suggestions. Examples include a report on preventive medicine from the 1976–7 Expenditure Committee and reports on the British Steel Corporation from the Select Committee on Nationalised Industries in the following year.

2 Advisory committees have been popular in British government. The Haldane Committee felt that every department should have an advisory committee 'so constituted as to make available the knowledge and experience of all sections of the community affected by the activities of the Department'.[25] Every major department has some sort of advisory committee structure and a high proportion of policy decisions is taken after a reference to such a body.[26] The element common to all advisory committees (whatever their title or status) is that they provide a channel through which information and ideas can be fed into the government machine from outside. There is, however, an important difference in function between committees composed mainly of experts and those which represent interested parties. Some advisory bodies made up of professional representatives (at least in the social services field) are frankly political rather than expert. They meet to consider papers prepared by civil servants and their real function is perhaps to tell the Minister what their constitutents will or will not stand. A recent trend is for committees of enquiry to commission research, which is published alongside the main report. It is not clear whether the availability of research simply sets limits to the range of bargaining among interested parties that goes on in such committees or whether it can provide a basis for a real shift in their understanding.

3 A possible function of the professional committee is to channel information about the way a policy is working out in the field. In practice, the institutionalized pressures at work on such a body tend to distort any feedback. Internal statistics may provide

a better indication of the need for adjustments within the framework of existing policy. Sir Geoffrey Vickers describes the 'cybernetic' collection of information that can lead automatically to a correction in course. For instance, chief education officers use information about a changing child population as a basis for continual modification in school building and maintenance programmes.[27] Similarly, the Treasury has channels for supplying information about the state of the economy as a matter of routine to those responsible for economic policy decisions. Another, perhaps more effective, source of information about a service is the number of complaints it generates – that is to say the amount of attention it receives from politicians in their capacity is grievance-settlers. These channels are augmented by the activities of the various complaints commissioners, inspectorates and institutionalized consumer bodies. But radical change is not likely to be prompted by information about the operation of existing policies.

4   The Haldane Committee thought that 'a Minister in charge of an administrative Department must have at his disposal, and under his control, an organization sufficient to provide him with a general survey of existing knowledge on any subject within his sphere'.[28] This may have been less utopian in 1918 than it is today; the world of knowledge is no longer so manageable.

From an abysmal start (the then Ministry of Health did not appoint its first statistician until 1955, after parliamentary criticism) departmental research and intelligence services have grown very rapidly. Many of the planning units described earlier have as part of their remit the responsiblity for keeping abreast of new ideas in their field. But in general they work alongside, and draw upon, separate branches concerned with research and statistics. These branches carry out research themselves, or commission it from independent researchers. By 1977, the DHSS was spending £20 m. on health research (most of it commissioned) and £0.3 m. on social security research. Other departments had similar programmes.

The Central Statistical Office, which is attached to the Cabinet Office and therefore at the disposal of all Ministers, publishes regular statistical series, including since 1970 the popular *Social Trends*. Its constituent Office of Population Censuses and Surveys monitors social developments and carries out special studies on behalf of individual departments. Similar work in the economic field has been longer established. The relevant government departments are represented on the research councils, which otherwise consist mainly of academics, allocating government money on academic criteria to fund independent research in universities and elsewhere; the scale of such research has expanded considerably since the establishment of the Social Science Research Council, the Science Research Council and the Natural Environment Research Council in 1965.

Indeed, the situation at one time threatened to get out of hand. In 1971 the head of the CPRS, Lord Rothschild, produced a report suggesting that government departments should fund only research which was relevant to their operational needs and whose results they could use: for each sponsored piece of research there should be a specific 'customer' in the relevant department. Other research should be left to the research councils.[29] After some controversy these recommendations were in essence put into practice. There was, for example, some redrawing of the boundaries between the programmes of the DHSS and the Medical Research Council. The service development groups in the DHSS commission research on, for example, the care of the elderly, if it promises to have policy implications. Help is given in putting their problems into researchable form by research liaison groups which include academics, thus helping to bridge the gap between the worlds of thought and action. The intentions are good, and there have been some successes; but the system cannot help the suspicious administrator who many have had unhappy experience of researchers in the past, or the busy one who has no time to conceptualize his work in problem terms.

Assimilation

The real problem is how to assimilate all this material in decision-making. It is easy to spot gaps in information. But on any major question of social or economic policy the amount of information already available somewhere in the system is formidable. The problem is how to bring it to bear, in time, on actual decisions that are being taken at or near ministerial level. If research and expert advice are to be useful they must be assimilated by those making policy decisions and carrying them out. This is not easy and there are grounds for pessimism about the ability of the policy-making system to cope.

We need to be clear about the nature of the difficulty. It is not a question of giving the Minister or any other single decision-maker all the information needed to reach a rational decision. No individual could cope with the complexity involved. Indeed, it is likely that his decisions would become wilder as the material grew beyond his handling capacity. We need a structure which allows major problems to be factorized – in departments, or sections of departments – and then, after processing, brought together again at ministerial or Cabinet level.

We are only slowly learning the necessary techniques. The Haldane solution of finding an administrator of quality and giving him more time to think is at best incomplete and at worst a blind alley. First, no amount of thinking in a padded room will do the job: the information theoretically relevant to any major decision is so vast that it has to be sifted several times before the range of considerations has been reduced to a scale on which the individual can take it in – he must be part of an efficient communication system. Second, there is no real evidence that administrators with additional time at their disposal would spend it by increasing their range of decision-premises. The evidence reviewed in Chapter VII suggests the opposite – that given a choice between short-term and long-term pressures the administrator will give priority to meeting short-term ones, perhaps more adequately, even if the total pressure is reduced.

Political demands take priority because the departmental structure, with a politician at the apex, secures priority to whatever interests or concerns the head of the department, and because senior civil servants are trained in habits of loyalty from their earliest days in the Minister's private office, around which a great deal of the top level work in the department revolves. This would not matter if the demands reflected through this system truly reflected a balanced assessment of priorities. We have argued in Chapter VIII that in the last resort the acceptability of a policy to a representative lay assembly is not a bad test of its consistency with widely held community values. But a lay assembly cannot plan. Planning (as Professor Beer pointed out in 1957)[30] is essentially an administrative activity; even Ministers are temperamentally unsuited to it. Because of the mechanics of lay intervention – its latency, eccentricity and subservience to professionalism – MPs are well equipped for assessing and criticizing developed policy proposals – or for initiating the consideration of new ideas – but badly equipped for making coherent and workable suggestions for new policy. In organizational terms, to rely for initiative on the political system may be to put the power of decision in a blind spot, where authority is not matched by knowledge and attention tends to be unstable.

The imbalance described above could in theory be rectified in a number of ways, but not all of them are viable in practice:

1 The quality of parliamentary intervention could be improved, by providing more information to MPs and providing opportunities to gain experience through service on specialized committees. In the work of select committees dealing with expenditure and specialist subjects, there are signs that a fruitful relationship could develop between departments and a small group of interested MPs. But in general politics is not like that. Cross-party committee reports do not receive much attention in the main body of the House, and can be brushed aside by a Minister who finds them inconvenient: early in 1978 Labour members of the Select Committee on Nationalised Industries found themselves obliged to vote against an Opposition motion welcoming their report. Some parliamentarians argue that all committees should be constructed on party lines and should concern themselves only with partisan issues.[31] The very substantial work of preparing material for such committees does not, therefore, always lead to a constructive debate.

2 The distraction caused by parliamentary interest in trivia could be reduced by limiting parliamentary rights to question

Ministers and to raise individual cases. But the tendency is to strengthen parliamentary powers, through the establishment of specialist committees and the office of the Parliamentary Commissioner, in order to protect individual rights. The Minister and his immediate advisers cannot dissociate themselves from the performance of their department as revealed in the reports of such bodies. Nor, in a country with our political traditions, does it seem likely that a Minister would wish to refuse to investigate cases raised with him privately by MPs. The question of 'hiving-off' is discussed more fully in Chapter XII.

3 Those responsible for planning could be separated from those responsible for day-to-day administration and thus shielded from the direct impact of parliamentary influence. This was the Haldane solution: the Committee drew attention to the 'proved impracticability of devoting the necessary time to thinking out organization and preparation for action in the mere interstices of the time required for the transaction of business' and said that responsibility for 'enquiry and thinking' should be placed 'in the hands of persons definitely charged with it'.[32] It was also the Fulton solution. But if specialist planning branches are too divorced from the regular political work of the Minister and the department, it becomes difficult to ensure that they are not ignored in a crisis and thus fail to confront political pressures with others at crucial moments.

4 Purely political influences can be counteracted by institutionalizing other pressures, orientated to long-term planning, in the top structure of the department. It is not enough, as we have seen, to have facilities for research and intelligence. The difficulty is to ensure that they are obtruded on the attention of top decision-makers at a time when these people may also be under political pressure to give priority to inadequate, short-term solutions. The answer may be to give sufficient status in the department to a special unit, or a specialist adviser (see Chapter XIII), whose whole function is to proffer advice about longer-term considerations at a level where it can hardly be ignored.

The Fulton proposals

The Fulton Committee proposed that a planning unit headed by a Senior Policy Adviser should be set up in each department to look after major long-term policy planning. The unit was envisaged as fairly small.

> Its main task should be to identify and study the problems and needs of the future and the possible means to meet them; it should also be its function to see that day-to-day policy decisions are taken with as full a recognition as possible of their likely implications for the future. The planning unit should not carry any responsibility for the day-to-day operations of the department. [It should be] equipped to assemble and analyse the information needed for its planning work.[33]

The Fulton concept seems to have been influenced partly by the view of its management consultancy group that there would be merit in making an organizational distinction between the management of existing policies and the forward planning role of examining and evaluating new policy options. Partly, also, it seems to have been motivated by a desire to reduce the Minister's dependence on his Permanent Secretary. The Permanent Secretary appears in the report as a rather dull stick-in-the-mud who cannot be discarded because of his part in securing continuity and financial accountability but who needs to be prevented from fielding the bright new ideas of the young whiz-kids in the planning units. This is a rather unrealistic picture and it is, of course, impracticable to separate the Permanent Secretary's overall responsibility for expenditure from the evaluation, in expenditure terms, of short- or medium-term policy options. The idea of a separate Senior Policy Adviser, as a rival to the Permanent Secretary, never got of the ground. The departmental planning units described in an earlier section are firmly under the latter's control.

Whatever the motives for it, however, the proposal was based on a realistic understanding of the difficulty of combining long-term thinking with meeting immediate deadlines. As we have seen, planning units have in fact been developed. By taking some of the ablest staff away from day-to-day pressures (at some inevitable cost to the adequacy with which the department meets these pressures) the units institutionalize a commitment to forward thinking and appraisal. But three questions were not tackled by the Fulton Committee. First, it was not clear whether the units were intended to be centres of creative thought or to provide bridges between the creative ideas of others and the executive activities of the department: this has important implications for staffing. Second, it was not clear how the unit should be related to the rest of the department and how any friction could be accommodated. Finally, it was not clear how far planning should become politicized.

Creativity or innovation?

A hierarchical decision-making and career structure tends to encourage consensus and conformity at the expense of creativity. One of its functions is to integrate centrifugal tendencies.[34] For normal operational purposes, the ability to compromise is an important virtue. Conversely it is difficult to accept conflict as legitimate. A really creative idea is likely to disrupt the smooth flow of business and therefore leads to friction. Those who are primarily concerned with resolving disputes will usually find it easier to turn down an unorthodox idea than to approve it. It is easy, too, to get into the habit of regarding time spent in discussion and research as wasted except when directly related to the achievement of immediate goals. This tendency will be accentuated in a production-orientated organization whose administrators are assessed against norms of output.

Consequently, proposals for radical change are most likely to come from staff who are insulated from the normal pressure to get on with the job and are put into a special environment where unorthodoxy is not only tolerated but approved. It seems essential that those involved should not be too inhibited by the consciousness of infinite ramification. They should be a bit irresponsible. In such an environment differences of status and rank are likely to be relatively unimportant compared with the ability to produce exciting new ideas. These new conditions are most likely to be achieved if the thinking unit looks outward rather than inward (possibly by employing mobile professionals whose loyalties are wider than a single organization) and is detached from the main organization. Dubin suggests that contacts between a research and development unit and the main organization should be reduced to a single highly selective channel.[35]

But the ideas that emerge from such an anarchic group of licensed rebels have to be assessed realistically before being put into practice. If consensus, coordination and commitment are inhibiting to the production of new ideas they are essential for their evaluation and implementation. Hence there is room for another sort of thinking unit, made up of people who have a foot on both sides as a bridge (or buffer) between ideas and the authority to accept them. Their task calls for open-mindedness, imagination and communication skills, but not necessarily for originality. Theirs is the task carried out by managers in Burns and Stalker's 'organic' firms, specializing in communication and in cooperative adjustment to change,[36] whereas the main qualities needed in the research unit proper are perhaps stubborn independence and refusal to abandon a line of thought too readily.

Various committees have seen a particular need for bridge-building partnerships between specialists and administrators in this context. Thus the Trend Committee on Civil Science argued the need for scientists to be closely associated with policy-makers in research-using departments.[37] The Heyworth Committee on Social Studies was even more explicit on the subject of social scientists, and deserves quotation at length.

Anyone engaged in administration in central or local government, or in the institutions of the welfare state, or in education, or in commerce and industry, is engaged in fields which social scientists study. Whether he knows it or not, he is using methods and techniques to help him deal with his work and solve problems that a social scientist would recognize. Rules that he uses may well be years out of date. Of course, much administration is concerned with day-to-day business, but unless an attempt is made to identify long-term problems or penetrate behind the curtain of everyday decisions, the decisions taken will be based on wrong or inadequate data. That is why research in the social sciences is important to the administrator . . .

There are two needs. The first is for administrators and managers to be familiar with the scope and value of the social sciences, not only as direct aids to administration, but also as disciplines which are able to limit the uncertainties within which decisions have to be taken, and to evaluate their outcome. But these steps will not be enough to ensure the fullest value is obtained from research in the social sciences. Problems in government or industry do not usually present themselves to administrators in a fashion which at once shows how they could be clarified by research in the social sciences. The second need, therefore, is for social scientists to work at points where problems first emerge and to help identify and deal with them. In order to carry out this intermediary function, social scientists would need to have a foot in both camps: on the one hand they would work closely with administrators as members of the functional team; they would also need to maintain professional contacts with each other and with the outside world.[38]

The Heyworth arguments are clearly sound. The research worker needs to be kept away from the day-to-day pressures of administration or he will not produce any research. The administrator is no longer in a position to attempt long-term thinking, but he must be able to deploy long-term thinking in his daily business. The full-time expert is also, these days, too close to the machine to attempt much long-term work. It is unrealistic to expect one man to carry the weight of human knowledge on any subject, but he should be sufficiently aware of what is going on in his field to know where to go for more detailed advice when it is needed. He must also be reasonably knowledgeable at a superficial level in order to provide advice off-the-cuff in a crisis. So we need a sort of interpretative process which shades into executive administration at one end and into pure research (including departmental research units) at the other.

In a sense the planning unit is a natural development from the diarchy (or 'joint hierarchy') of administrator and expert adviser that has existed for a long time in, for example, the Health Departments, where many administrators are paired with medical officers who have left clinical practice to become experts in a branch of administrative medicine. Sometimes a committee will have a medical secretary as well as an administrative one. The administrator provides a link with the main policy-making and executive system while the doctor is at the operational end of a chain of increasingly specialized professional expertise that may well end in a university laboratory, perhaps linking serum research to public health policy. In this sort of partnership the professional provides continuity and many of the ideas, the administrator deals with political crises, and a one-to-one relationship works fairly well within limits.

But a sound public health policy these days is likely to require more than medical expertise. It may well involve cost-benefit analysis, social research and demographic forecasting. The single medical adviser needs to be replaced by a team of doctors, sociologists, economists, statisticians, demographers, each at the terminal point of a chain of fundamental and applied knowledge. An executive administrator can no longer rely on such a team to speak with one voice to tell him what needs to be done. The team needs a coordinator, a sense-maker, someone to find common ground among the different disciplines, to bring its ideas into focus and to subject them to the appraisal of an uncommitted layman. Such a component cannot be supplied by the administrator who is busy with day-to-day crises; it calls for someone like the specialized and knowledgeable administrator who emerges from other Fulton proposals.

Relationship with executive divisions

The planning unit's functions cannot be dissociated from the main administrative direction of the department. If short-term decisions pre-empt the future, there is not much point in planning at all. Similarly, if the planners (as distinct from the researchers) are too isolated from the problems facing the department in its day-to-day work their ideas may lack immediate utility. Excessive detachment may be prevented by putting a reasonable leavening of career administrators in the planning units.

The most natural way of keeping planners in touch is by giving them a vetting function and a seat on committees where decisions are being taken. (This mechanism again fits the 'planning group of directors' concept better than the 'ideas and research' concept.) There is a nice problem of balance: if they are too close to the machine, they may be forced to neglect long-term work; if they are too detached from it they will not be able to influence pragmatic short-term decisions. Badly handled, the institution of planning units could lead to divided responsibility for regular operations, with the planners arguing for decisions to be postponed to await research while the managers want to get on with the job. In such circumstances, the units would probably end up as fifth wheels.

In practice, the relationship of planning to mainstream activities has varied from department to department. In some, like those concerned with the regulation of industry, it could be argued that the whole function of the department *was* planning, and that it was meaningless to separate the two; but this is too facile a view, and does not accurately reflect what supervisory departments actually do. In others, planning is so close to policy-making that the same senior people are concerned with both. In others again, planning is seen as experimental and closely allied to research; its relationship to policy divisions is at best semi-detached. Much the same could be said of the CPRS.

Planning and politics

Planning cannot, of course, be divorced from politics. The ultimate choice among options is a political choice, not to be avoided by greater use of research and statistics. But the analysis of options preparatory to political choice also involves political as well as administrative elements, except in the rare cases where planners are concerned only with the examination of alternative means, themselves valuationally neutral, of achieving a clearly defined political objective. Normally, the choice of lines to pursue, the weighting given to advantages and disadvantages that emerge

and the final selection of a limited number of viable choices all
involve value assumptions that are political in nature. The recent
vogue for cost-benefit analysis tended to overlook the qualitative
judgements that have to be made if 'chalk and cheese' comparisons are to be made at all. There has been a tendency for
planners to make inexplicit assumptions about the priority of
economic factors, that can be measured, over social factors that
can not. Samuel Brittan pointed out in 1964 that considerable
technical knowledge may be required to ascertain what the real
political choices are. He argued the case for a new class of adviser,
politically committed as well as an expert in his field, who can
examine the whole framework of assumptions on which policy is
based and open up the options for Ministers.[39] Many of Brittan's
ideas were widely shared and were put into effect by governments
of both complexions after 1964.

The lesson seems to be that planning units could usefully include
political appointees to challenge the existing framework and open
up new lines of thinking, but that these must not be powerful
enough to usurp by suppression the Minister's function of making
a final decision among carefully considered alternatives. But this
demands considerable restraint both on the part of the adviser
and on the part of the Minister who appointed him, especially
if the latter is anxious to see the speedy implementation of his
favourite schemes. In some cases, e.g. that of the Home Office,
political advisers have sat in on planning committees. Other
advisers may have been more concerned with a Minister's relationship with his party organization than with long-term strategies.

The politicization of planning carries an inevitable risk that long-
term plans, with effects beyond the life of the current government, will be influenced by a Minister's desire to gain a tactical
advantage in the House of Commons through leaks, promises and
assurances. But this danger is already present and is probably
inseparable from any system of parliamentary government.

Conclusions

In the 1960s those working in public administration were faced
with new problems of perception, assimilation, evaluation and

integration. The public expected the government to extend its activities and to coordinate them more purposefully in the interests of economic planning. The knowledge explosion was at the same time adding to the number of factors that had to be taken into account in any important decision. The new demands had to be met initially within the existing framework of political and governmental institutions – Treasury methods of financial control, detailed ministerial responsibility to Parliament and central co-ordination of policy through the Cabinet.

On the one hand, the government machine became more accessible to new skills and knowledge through the appointment of new specialists, the establishment of internal research and development units and substantial programmes of sponsored research. The proliferation of committees brought many able people and fresh points of view into the business of government. On the other hand all of this material had to be assimilated, brought into some sort of balance and related to the current framework of political assumptions and the economic resources currently available. There was more need for expertise at the periphery, but there was also more need for coordination and integration at the centre.

The traditional administrative pattern was partly a help and partly a hindrance. The system worked well as a sensitive and loyal instrument in the hands of a government that knew what it wanted done, as efficiently and with as little trouble as possible. General administrators, arranged hierarchically under a Minister, provided a ready channel for the transmission of political impulses. But if political initiative was lacking or (in the face of increasing complexity) uncertain, the interlocking ramifications of the administrative machine tended to stifle initiative and innovation. A weakness of the traditional Parliament-Minister-civil service structure was the low priority it secured for appraisal and for the application to policy of the fruits of research and intelligence. It is necessary to devise a structure which encourages research and ensures that the resulting data are properly weighed in the consideration of new policies.

Research suggests that radical rethinking is easiest for staff who are insulated from the ordinary routines, who have a low commitment to the traditional way of doing things and who work in an atmosphere where unorthodoxy is highly valued. It is also likely that innovation occurs most spontaneously in units which are reasonably isolated and in which hierarchical discipline is not oppressive. These requirements are incompatible with those of a conventional executive system, designed to foster loyalty, predictability and coordination. There is therefore a place for the commissioned research project, the departmental research unit, and the detached type of planning unit.

But, in a broader sense, planning needs to be integrated with the ongoing work of the department. We are talking here about a planning style, which extends time horizons, looks at policy areas in the round, and explores a wider range of options. The exact arrangements for relating planning to the core of a department's activities must be subject to a good deal of trial and error. Some departments (the DES is one example) have come under severe criticism. There will be failures in planning, for which there may be technical as well as structural reasons. But there has been considerable progress (not only in Britain) in the 1960s and 1970s. Further development depends largely on the needs and constraints of the political system which the planners serve.

Notes

1 D. Burn, J. R. Seale and A. R. N. Ratcliff, *Lessons from Central Forecasting* (Institute of Economic Affairs, London, 1965).
2 *Control of Public Expenditure*, Cmnd. 1432 (1961).
3 The first Public Expenditure White Paper, Cmnd. 2235 (1963) was entitled *Public Expenditure in 1963–64 and 1967–68*; the most recent, Cmnd. 7049 (1978), is called *The Government's Expenditure Plans: 1978–79 to 1981–82*.
4 For the history of PESC, see Christopher Pollitt, 'The Public Expenditure Survey 1961–72', *Public Administration* Vol. 55 (1977) pp. 127–42. For a contemporary analysis of unresolved difficulties, see Maurice Wright, 'Public Expenditure in Britain: the crisis of control', ibid., pp. 143–69.
5 *The National Plan*, Cmnd. 2764 (1965).
6 *Report of the Committee on Representational Services Overseas*, Cmnd. 2276 (1964).
7 G. K. Fry, 'Policy-Planning Units in British Central Government Departments', *Public Administration* Vol. 50 (1972) pp. 139–55.

8 Sir William Pile, 'Corporate Planning for Education in the DES', *Public Administration* Vol. 52 (1974) pp. 27–40.

9 *Education: a framework for expansion*, Cmnd. 5174 (1972).

10 Organisation for Economic Co-operation and Development, *Educational Development Strategy in England and Wales* (Paris, 1975) Part 2.

11 'Inside the DHSS', *Health and Social Service Journal* Vol. 87 (1977) pp. 1312–20.

12 Department of Health and Social Security, *Priorities for Health and Personal Social Services in England* (London, 1976); also DHSS, *The Way Forward* (London, 1977).

13 C. J. Train, 'The Development of Criminal Policy Planning in the Home Office', *Public Administration* Vol. 55 (1977) pp. 373–84.

14 *The Reorganisation of Central Government*, Cmnd. 4506 (1970) para. 51.

15 ibid., para. 47.

16 Christopher Pollitt, 'The Central Policy Review Staff, 1970–74', *Public Administration* Vol. 52 (1974) pp. 375–92.

17 Central Policy Review Staff, *A Joint Framework for Social Policies* (London, 1975). See also W. J. L. Plowden, 'Developing a Joint Approach to Social Policy' in K. Jones (ed.), *The Yearbook of Social Policy in Britain 1976* (London, 1977).

18 Central Policy Review Staff, *Population and Social Services* (London, 1976).

19 Central Policy Review Staff, *Relationships between Central Government and Local Authorities* (London, 1977).

20 Central Policy Review Staff, *Review of Overseas Representation* (London, 1977).

21 Sir Richard Clarke, *New Trends in Government*, Civil Service College Studies No. 1 (London, 1971).

22 Christopher Pollitt, 'The Public Expenditure Survey 1961–72', *Public Administration* Vol. 55 (1977) pp. 139–40.

23 *Report of the Committee on the Civil Service*, Cmnd. 3638 (1968) Vol. 1, para. 172.

24 *Report of the Machinery of Government Committee*, Cd. 9230 (1918) p. 6.

25 ibid., p. 11.

26 For a full account of the development of the advisory committee system, see R. V. Vernon and N. Mansergh, *Advisory Bodies: a Study of their Uses in Relation to Central Government 1919–39* (London, 1940); K. C. Wheare, *Government by Committee* (Oxford, 1955); PEP, *Advisory Committees in British Government* (London, 1960); Gerald Rhodes, *Committees of Inquiry* (London, 1975).

27 Sir Geoffrey Vickers, *The Art of Judgment: a study of policymaking* (London, 1965) Chap. 1 and *passim*.
28 *Report of the Machinery of Government Committee*, op. cit., p. 32.
29 *A Framework for Government Research and Development*, Cmnd. 4814 (1971).
30 S. H. Beer, *Treasury Control*, 2nd edn (Oxford, 1957).
31 National Executive Committee, Labour Party, *Reform of the House of Commons* (London, 1978).
32 *Report of the Machinery of Government Committee*, op. cit., p. 6.
33 *Report of the Committee on the Civil Service*, op. cit., pp. 57–8.
34 V. A. Thompson, 'Bureaucracy and Innovation', *Administrative Science Quarterly* Vol. 10 (1965–6) p. 1.
35 R. Dubin, 'The Stability of Human Organizations' in Mason Haire (ed.), *Modern Organization Theory* (New York, 1959) pp. 246–7.
36 T. Burns and G. M. Stalker, *The Management of Innovation* (London, 1966) (see our discussion in Chapter VI, pp. 166–7).
37 *Report of the Committee on Civil Science*, Cmnd. 2171 (1963) paras 44, 97–8, 118–19.
38 *Report of the Committee on Social Studies*, Cmnd. 2660 (1965) paras 19, 123.
39 Samuel Brittan, *The Treasury under the Tories 1951–64* (London, 1964) Chap. 10.

XI
The machinery
of government

Introduction

This chapter is about the 'macro-structure' of government. It is concerned with the distribution of functions among Ministers and departments. From one point of view, government is a seamless web. From another, it is a collection of things that government does, from supervising the economy to checking the liquidity of insurance companies and from investing millions in the car industry to deciding whether an individual is fit to be a teacher or to practise medicine under the National Health Service. The business of government is differentiated into a number of specialized tasks. These have to be integrated again so that ultimately there is a single channel of control and accountability through Cabinet and Parliament. In the middle we have blocks of tasks, assigned to departmental divisions and agencies, the departments themselves, generally headed by Cabinet Ministers, and the central coordinating departments, like the Treasury, which keep a watchful eye over the whole machine. The structural questions are familiar to management theorists: how many tiers should an organization have? how large a span can be controlled by one man? what groups of functions make most sense? The dogmatic answers of the past have been replaced by cautious suggestions that solutions are 'contingent' on the type of tasks, the stability of the environment and so forth; many contemporary theorists doubt whether clear answers can be found even along these lines. In public administration, the requirements of public accountability and control have direct and indirect effects (e.g. the politicization of questions that would otherwise be organizational) which complicate the matter still further.

The first half of the chapter deals with changes, mainly over the last decade, and the reasons advanced for them. The second half attempts to find general principles.

Departmental structure

Table 11.1 below lists the main ministerial departments at the start of the 1977–8 parliamentary session, with comparable information for five and ten years earlier. A noticeable omission is the Cabinet Office, which serves Ministers collectively. For simplicity, small departments like the Lord Chancellor's have been left out. So have non-ministerial departments, like the Board of Inland Revenue, which are headed by officials, although ultimately answerable to a Minister (in this case the Chancellor of the Exchequer). But all the main regulatory and promotional activities of the modern state are represented.

Table 11.1
Principal government departments, 1967, 1972 and 1977

1967–8	*Departments existing at the start of session* 1972–3	1977–8	*Name in full*
(a)	*Headed by a Cabinet Minister*		
Treas.	Treas.	Treas.	Treasury
—	CSD	CSD	Civil Service Department
DEA	—	—	Department of Economic Affairs
MOD	MOD	MOD	Ministry of Defence
HO	HO	HO	Home Office
DES	DES	DES	Department of Education and Science

1967–8	1972–3	1977–8	Name in full
MAFF	MAFF	MAFF	Ministry of Agriculture Fisheries and Food
SO	SO	SO	Scottish Office
WO	WO	WO	Welsh Office
—	NIO	NIO	Northern Ireland Office
FO	FCO	FCO	Foreign (and Commonwealth) Office
CO	—	—	Commonwealth Office
MHLG	—	—	Ministry of Housing and Local Government
—	DOE	DOE	Department of the Environment
MOT	—	DTp	Ministry/Department of Transport
MOL	DE	DE	Ministry of Labour/Department of Employment
BOT	—	DOT	Board/Department of Trade
MOP	—	DEn	Ministry of Power/Department of Energy
—	DTI	—	Department of Trade and Industry
MinTech	—	—	Ministry of Technology
—	—	DOI	Department of Industry
—	—	DPCP	Department of Prices and Consumer Protection
—	DHSS	DHSS	Department of Health and Social Security

(b)   *Headed by a Minister not in Cabinet*

ODM	—	ODM	Ministry of Overseas Development
MPBW	—	—	Ministry of Public Building and Works
M/Health	—	—	Ministry of Health
MSS	—	—	Ministry of Social Security
PO	MPT	—	Post Office/Ministry of Posts and Telecommunications

(Derived from the published list of Ministers at the start of each parliamentary session.)

There are marked differences between the columns. The number of separate departments thought necessary to administer a similar spread of functions was much smaller in 1972 than in 1967, but had begun to increase again by 1977. In 1967 several important departments did not qualify for a Minister of Cabinet rank; by 1972 (with the exception of Posts and Telecommunications, later absorbed into the DTI) they had all been merged into larger departments with a Cabinet Minister at the head. (The list of 'Cabinet' departments is not a safe guide to the size of the Cabinet. A Cabinet includes Ministers without departmental responsibilities and sometimes more than one Minister from a large department. The 1967 Cabinet had 21 members, the 1972 Cabinet 18 and the 1977 Cabinet 24.) Some departments have been renamed; some appear to have moved temporarily off the map, like Transport; others, like Technology and Economic Affairs, look as if they have disappeared altogether.

In fact, most changes have involved regrouping rather than gains and losses in the functions of government. Even the DEA, which made a brief appearance from 1964 to 1969, took most of its functions from previously existing departments, notably the Treasury, to which they were returned on or before its demise. During the whole period, government steadily acquired new functions, with only slight checks when the Conservative and Labour victors of 1970 and 1974 paused to dismantle some of the work of their predecessors. The Conservatives, it is true, had a proclaimed philosophy of less and better (i.e. more streamlined) government. But the process of merging departments started with Labour in the 1960s and the process of dismantling them started with the Conservatives before 1974.

Even the big changes were little more than skin-deep. For example, the 1977 DOE is remarkably similar to the 1967 Ministry of Housing and Local Government, having experienced a broken marriage with Transport (and, to compound the infidelity, with Public Building and Works, which later regained some independence as the Property Services Agency) in the meantime. As a final example, the Ministry of Overseas Development emerged apparently unscathed in June 1974 from the Foreign and Commonwealth Office, with which it had been merged in October 1970; in the interim it had operated as a distinctive wing, called the Overseas Development Administration, under its own Minister exercising powers delegated from the Foreign Secretary. Other 1967 departments survived as 'functional wings' within the new large departments after the mergers, which made it easy to extricate them later.

The 1977 departments, however, were not exact replicas of their 1967 predecessors. Some amalgamations, like that of the Foreign and Commonwealth Offices, had stuck. Moreover, government functions had changed and so had ministerial portfolios. There were endless minor reallocations, which did not leave unaffected the departments which escaped the merger round, like the DES, the Home Office and even the Cabinet Office.[1]

Superficially, the amount of administrative change and experiment over the ten years (and beyond) is impressive but worrying. Although it is possible to admire the adaptability of the civil service, most of the changes cannot have made much difference to its continuing work within departments, or it would have been impossible to accomplish them. On the other hand, the changes must have been intended to achieve something, or they would not have been attempted. Why were the official sign-painters kept so busy during this period?

Times of change

Questions about the machinery of government seem to attract public interest only at times when governments are taking on new kinds of responsibilities that cannot be absorbed along familiar lines and there is a period of experiment before they are fully digested. Three such periods can be identified in the present century. The first was prompted by the great increase in government activities, including new social services and the temporary control of industry, about the time of the First World War. The Ministry of Labour (1916), the Department of Scientific and Industrial Research (1915), and the original Ministry of Health, which looked after local government and the Poor Law as well as the Health Insurance Scheme (1919), date from this time.

The relevant controversies can be traced in the famous Haldane Report.[2]

The second period was immediately after the Second World War. First the Coalition and then the Labour Government accepted responsibility for full employment, for new and expanded health and insurance schemes, for large sections of the transport and fuel industries and, with the help of the local authorities, for new schemes of housing, welfare and town and country planning. It is now known that an opportunity to review and streamline the whole machinery of government, with support from Sir John Anderson and Sir Edward Bridges, was narrowly missed in the immediate post-war period.[3] Controversy about the most appropriate machinery for government supervision and control of nationalized industries stimulated a considerable academic literature.[4] An authoritative study of changes in central government organization which was originally commissioned by the Royal Institute of Public Administration during this period has become a standard textbook.[5] The main departmental innovations dating from this time were the Ministries of Housing and Local Government (1950), National Insurance (1946), and Fuel and Power (1942).

The third period of administrative innovation is still with us. It began in 1962 with important changes in the machinery for financial and economic planning: the Treasury was reorganized to give more weight to forward planning of public expenditure, and the National Economic Development Council was established as a joint government-industry-union organization to seek agreement on ways of improving the United Kingdom's economic performance. The process was accelerated after the Labour victory in October 1964. The long-term economic planning functions of the Treasury were transferred to a new Department of Economic Affairs, which set about the preparation of a national five-year plan and the establishment of economic planning councils and boards to encourage regional development (previously a function of the Board of Trade). To symbolize the new government's commitment to scientific progress, a new Ministry of Technology was set up to promote applied science; pure science and responsibility for the universities remained with the DES, in which they had been combined with the functions of the old Ministry of Education shortly before the election.

Throughout the years 1962–77 there was almost continuous change and experiment. For example, the DEA had originally been made responsible for prices, incomes policy and productivity. By April 1968 these functions had been transferred to the Ministry of Labour (renamed, for a period, the Department of Employment and Productivity). Ten years later, successor policies were being administered by the Department of Prices and Consumer Protection, by the Treasury (or the Civil Service Department for the public sector) and (again with exceptions in the public sector) by the Department of Industry. By the time DEA and MinTech disappeared from the administrative map in 1969 and 1970, neither bore much resemblance to the eponymous departments established in 1964. Within the economic and industrial field, similar changes were taking place in the penumbra of Whitehall, as new bodies to stimulate investment and to regulate prices, incomes and industrial relations were successively established, abolished and replaced.

The moving spirit behind these changes was the desire to arrest Britain's economic decline through an (unsuccessful) attempt to create an enabling institutional structure. Civil service reform was, in part, a chapter in the same story. There were at least two subsidiary themes. One was the desire to simplify and rationalize the machinery of administration, especially in relation to social and environmental services. Both will shortly be discussed in more detail; and it should be noted that local government and the National Health Service were also reorganized during this period. The other theme was administrative devolution. Scotland had a long history of separate administration in law, local government and social services.[6] The tendency during this period was to transfer additional powers, especially in relation to industrial development, from London to Edinburgh under the Secretary of State for Scotland. Wales too had begun to receive special treatment, mainly through out-stations in Cardiff of London-based departments. The Welsh Office as such was not established until 1964, mainly out of existing administrative units; thereafter it enjoyed a slow but steady accretion of functions. Towards the end

of our period, after a Royal Commission and a great deal of incon-
clusive discussion, plans were well advanced for political assemblies
to take responsibility for the devolved functions in both countries.[7]
Ironically, the collapse of the domestic Northern Ireland Parliament due to civil strife made it necessary for a United Kingdom
Minister to take responsibility for the affairs of the province.

The restlessness of the period can be tentatively analysed under
three headings. As in most such attempts at categorization, they
tend to overlap.

Changing circumstances

Ministerial portfolios and titles reflect what is politically important.
Until the collapse of the Stormont government, Northern Ireland
was not of great importance in United Kingdom politics: such
regulation as was necessary could be done from an odd corner
of the Home Office. By 1972, civil disorder had created a political
vacuum which necessitated the appointment of a Secretary of State
with a supporting Northern Ireland Office. Similarly, the oil crisis
of 1973–4, accompanied by a miners' strike and a compulsory
three-day week to conserve energy in industry, gave energy policy
sufficient importance to deserve the full-time attention of a
Secretary of State, where it had previously been a part-time concern of a second-level Minister. Conversely, the loss of imperial
status made it unnecessary to maintain a separate Commonwealth
Office beyond 1968; that Office had itself swallowed the once-
proud Colonial Office two years earlier. A more comforting case
is the absorption of the biological research unit at Porton Down,
originally set up as a secret establishment for studying germ
warfare, into the Public Health Laboratory Service under the
DHSS early in 1978.

On the broader economic front, the rise and fall of the DEA
reflected an initial belief that planning would produce economic
growth. This gave way to more specific concern first with low
productivity and poor industrial relations, seen, in the creation
of the Department of Employment and Productivity in 1968, and
later with the combination of rampant inflation and high unemployment in the face of a worldwide recession, which was

associated with a number of complex changes in departmental responsibilities.

Political symbolism

Whether the changes in ministerial responsibility made much difference to the way work was done down the line is almost impossible to say. There seems to have been an air of excitement in the early DEA and MinTech which one would not expect to find in the Treasury. Some of this might be attributed to the high proportion of specialist and imported staff (many of whom, however, did not stay long). Another factor could be the novelty of the task, backed by a Minister with a narrow field of responsibility: similar enthusiasm could be detected in the early days of the Civil Service Department, or even in the staid Treasury (out of which the CSD was largely carved) and the DHSS when large changes were being planned – in public expenditure planning or NHS organization – and there were many opportunities to influence events. The following (1968) parliamentary interchange hardly does justice to the complexity of the machinery of government question.[8]

MR BRUCE-GARDYNE   Now that the DEA has lost the prices and incomes policy, what other purpose does it serve, apart from providing the member for Stepney with a car, office, and a fat salary?

MR WILSON   The short answer is that he has an extremely important portfolio that ensures by the co-ordination of the industrial administration that the real resources are available to meet the requirements of the Chancellor's policy, both as regards producitivity, exports and import replacement. It is an important function that could not be left in the Treasury.

MR THORPE   Why is it that jobs discharged by the DEA cannot be discharged by the Treasury?

MR WILSON   The Treasury has an extremely full time job to do with not only the general financial policy, budgetary policy, expenditure and international liquidity policy. We have found over past years when the Treasury was also responsible for industrial co-ordination that the work was not done and was always sacrificed to purely financial considerations.

What cannot be denied is that the creation of new departments (even if their basic responsibilities are unchanged) under Ministers with exciting new titles reflects the the need of a government to be seen to be doing something. When the Bill to establish the Ministry of Technology was presented in the House of Lords, its sponsor (Lord Snow) admitted that its practical objectives could be met in other ways but said that it was desirable to mark the Government's commitment to technological progress by creating a new department with a Cabinet Minister at its head.[9] Similarly, concern about youth and vandalism led to the designation of a second-tier Minister in the DOE as Minister of State for Sport and Recreation in 1974; after two dry summers he acquired additional responsibility for water resources (a capacity in which he soon became redundant, since it apparently rained wherever he gave a speech). MPs and pressure groups frequently call for new Ministers to take charge of particular subjects; sometimes it is possible to concede a point by giving an existing Minister a new title, or by appointing a new junior Minister to an existing department, without necessarily supplying supporting staff or legislating for new functions.

Many of the important changes, however, are probably influenced by a different kind of political need – the need to accommodate the political ambitions of powerful individuals. The proliferation of 'Secretaries of State' where there had previously been 'Ministers' (and consequently the change from 'Ministry' to 'Department' on departmental notepaper) may also have something to do with patronage requirements.

The search for a panacea

A more charitable interpretation of the constant changes is that they were experimental approaches to the Holy Grail of administration – the 'one best way' of distributing groups of tasks. There was certainly a feeling in the early 1960s that something was wrong with the concentration in the Treasury of responsibilities for economic planning, fiscal policy, control of public expenditure and central management of the civil service: hence the DEA and later the CSD. There was general dissatisfaction with British economic performance and a general belief that the key might lie in the institutional structure. But until 1970 there was no sign of an overriding philosophy. Changes were made piecemeal, often apparently at the personal instigation of the Prime Minister.[10] There was no sign of a new Haldane Report. Indeed, Mr Wilson told the Commons that a general review of the machinery of government (which had been recommended by the Fulton Committee) 'was and is a continuing process' which it was impossible to refer to an outside body for study.[11]

However, the incoming Conservative Government of 1970 was committed to a comprehensive programme of administrative modernization. It had prepared itself carefully before coming into office and a general approach had been adumbrated in political writings.[12] It was given flesh and reality in an impressive White Paper on *The Reorganisation of Central Government*.[13] Like the Haldane Report fifty years earlier, this claimed to present a coherent philosophy of government which, when applied, would stand the test of time.

A new Haldane?

Although in practice some of the ideas in the White Paper were to enjoy a fairly brief life, they were greeted with enthusiasm by advocates of administrative reform. The White Paper also provided a rationale for many of the changes that were made in 1970–2. It is therefore worth pausing to examine some of them in detail. Their main practical consequences were (a) consolidation of an already existing trend to combine small departments into 'giants'; (b) adoption of the 'functional principle' as a basis for departmental grouping; (c) attempts to develop a more coherent approach to policy-making by strengthening the central coordinating departments.

(a) *Giant departments*

Although several new departments were created in 1964, the underlying trend in the 1960s was to reduce the number of separate departments. By the end of 1970, five 'giants' had emerged from a series of mergers, and it looked for a time as if the giant department would become the characteristic model for the future. The Ministry of Defence had gradually been absorbing the historic armed service departments over a long period. The Foreign Office absorbed the Commonwealth Office in 1968 and the Ministry of Overseas Development two years later. The Department of Health and Social Security was formed in 1968 by amalgamating the Ministries of Health and Social Security. Two new giants, the Department of the Environment and the Department of Trade and Industry, were formed in 1970.

The 1970 White Paper claimed that the grouping of functions together in large departments would have a number of advantages: it would allow conflicts (e.g. between transport and environmental needs) to be explored and resolved within departments rather than between them; it would facilitate the development of a single strategy over a wide field of policy; it would make it possible to obtain the benefits of scale in management and analytic resources. Such a large block of work could not effectively be supervised by one Minister, and additional Ministers, not of Cabinet rank, were therefore appointed to take responsibility for blocks of work (e.g. housing and construction), delegated from the Secretary of State who remained in overall command. Administratively, the departments were organized in functional wings, under Second and Third Permanent Secretaries. The idea of having more than one Minister and Permanent Secretary was not new: the Treasury had been organized in 'sides' since 1956, with a number of Ministers (one of whom sometimes had a Cabinet post) in support of the Chancellor of the Exchequer.

In an authoritative commentary on the White Paper, Sir Richard Clarke suggested that the smaller the number of departments the better for public sector management and policy-making. For example, it would be much easier to control a PESC programme (see Chapter x, pp. 240–1) which consisted of six large departmental programmes rather than one containing fifteen (the 1978 number) or twenty. Another advantage was that it would require fewer Ministers of Cabinet rank and therefore allow a smaller

Cabinet. The internal management problems of large departments were considerable but soluble. The ultimate limit on size was set by the amount of work that a Secretary of State could handle in his multiple role as departmental supremo, member of Cabinet, public representative and political figure. To make his task manageable, second-tier Ministers would have to work with him as a team, and their authority would have to be accepted by MPs and others.[14] The doctrine of individual ministerial responsibility to Parliament would need to be adapted accordingly. Earlier experiments, in which Cabinet Ministers had been appointed as coordinators or 'overlords' over non-Cabinet Ministers, had failed precisely because of uncertainties about responsibilities.

The advantages of large departments, therefore, were that they facilitated the integration of policy across the whole field of government, that they enabled narrower policy issues to be settled within the departments themselves, and that they carried administrative advantages of scale. Why then did they begin to break up so quickly?

The concept was perhaps too ambitious. The various wings (which, after all, were merely old departments or parts of departments being shuffled around) did not always work well together. There are obvious difficulties about creating a sense of common purpose in a department with 91 Under Secretaries and above (DTI, 1971; compare 20 in the DES). But the main factor was a shift in political priorities. Within a few years, interest had shifted from global strategies to the need to concentrate political resources on specific problems. The first casualty was the DTI, from which a Department of Energy was amputated after the oil crisis in 1973. A Department of Prices and Consumer Protection, to deal with the prices side of the government's anti-inflation policies, followed in 1974. These functions were too important to be left to a second-tier Minister, or to be lost in a giant department covering a huge field of activities. After 1974 the further dismemberment of the DTI and the DOE seems to have been influenced partly by the preferences and patronage requirements of the Prime Minister.[15] The two original giants (MOD and FCO) remain, as does the DHSS, whose history will be discussed later in the chapter.

Significantly, however, the new departments formed out of the
DTI and the original DOE retained common management services,
so that the administrative advantages of size were not lost. (These
elements of a common structure would make it easier to contem-
plate further reshuffles if they became politically necessary.)
Moreover, there are still traces of policy integration: Transport
and Environment were made jointly responsible for some aspects
of the roads programme. Coordination through interdepartmental
committees and the Cabinet machinery, of course, continues
as ever.

(b) *The functional principle*

The White Paper stated, as a broad principle, that the organizational structure should reflect the government's strategic policy
objectives. (Elsewhere it implied that the structure would help to
condition the formulation of overall strategy, which could mean
that any structure was self-justifying.) 'Government departments
should be organised by reference to the task to be done or the
objective to be attained ... The basic argument for this functional
approach is that the purpose of organisation is to serve policy.
And policy issues which are linked should be grouped together
in organisational terms.'[16]
  This is almost pure Haldane. And it raises the same questions.
What is a 'function'? Is it something like education? Or is it something like social services? If so, what are social services? If they
include the provision of municipal baths should these therefore
be linked with libraries and health centres? Should employment
services be coupled with industrial development, or with social
security, or with further education? The answers depend on one's
perspective, and every change of government or circumstances
brings the possibility of new perspectives on functional groupings.
In fact, there was not much attempt by the authors of the White
Paper to think the concept through. All the local government
functions of the former Ministry of Housing and Local Government (including municipal baths) became 'environmental' services;
libraries stayed with the DES and health centres with the DHSS.
  If, for all practical purposes, a 'function' is a service, or a group

of services, contrasting bases of organization might be the geographical area or client group (children, war pensioners, etc.). In fact, one of the functions of government departments is to provide a point of access to the political system for organized groups. For all their grumbles, the farmers and the teachers would not readily acquiesce in the fragmentation of 'their' sponsoring departments of agriculture and education. As for geography, the White Paper saw no inconsistency in retaining separate departments in Scotland and Wales. Even in England, many of the larger departments like Health and Industry have internal divisions which deal exclusively with the application of policy to the standard regions. At the time of writing, further devolution to geographical areas is very much in the air.

It looks, therefore, as if the 'functional principle' was little more than a rationalization of the case for giant departments in terms of the perspectives with which the Conservative Party came to office in 1970. This is not to dismiss the argument about grouping tasks in some rational manner, to which we shall return.

(c) *The centre*

Above the 'primary' departments, providing services or regulating some aspect of our lives, stands the central apparatus of the state. This includes the Treasury, the Civil Service Department, the Cabinet Office, which serves Ministers as a whole, and the Prime Minister's personal office. These central organs play a vital part in holding together the almost baronial Whitehall departments.[17] During the 1960s efforts were made to improve the balance between the primary and central departments. The role of the Treasury in controlling public expenditure was redefined. Its responsibility for the manning and cost of the civil service was transferred to the Civil Service Department after the Fulton Report. Improvements were made in the statistical and information services attached to the Cabinet Office, to which the National Economic Development Office also reported. For a brief period before the establishment of the Department of the Environment, the Cabinet Office coordinated the activities of the transport and local government departments, with Mr Crosland as Secretary of

State for Local Government and Regional Planning. There was much discussion about the role (and presidential implications) of the Prime Minister's office.

The 1970 White Paper promised to improve the 'capability at the centre for assessment of policies and projects in relation to strategic objectives'.[18] The key measures were the establishment of a central policy review staff (CPRS) and provision for the review, against overall objectives, of the contents of departmental expenditure programmes (PAR). These have already been discussed in detail in Chapter x.

Opposition speakers criticized these proposals as a recipe for friction, mess and muddle.[19] Sir Richard Clarke's lectures drew attention to the possibility of tension between the strong new giant departments and the enhanced centre.[20] In fact, as we have seen, the CPRS succeeded in establishing a role for itself, and it is understood that some useful PAR-type exercises have been carried out. But there has been nothing like the comprehensive review of the whole field of government promised in the White Paper. Its authors soon had to turn their attention to more immediate problems and went out of office in 1974.

These arrangements for integrating the total government task are perhaps less politically vulnerable than the 'functional' concept discussed earlier. There are, of course, value judgements implicit in any process of simplifying complex problems to make them amenable to strategic choice. But the greatest political threat to the new central capacity is that a particular Prime Minister may not be sufficiently interested to give it enough support. There are, however, some interesting administrative questions. Apart from centre–periphery relationships, there is the possibility of overlap and 'underlap' among the three central departments. All are concerned in some way with efficiency, with policy choices and with public expenditure. On the other hand, there was some initial uncertainty about where responsibility lay for pay policy in the public sector. Again, the authoritative source is Sir Richard Clarke, who suggested that it would be more logical to realign Treasury and CSD functions into a National Economy and Finance Department, concerned with taxation, economic and financial policy, and a Central Management Department which would cover all the central review and control functions of the Treasury, CSD and CPRS.[21] The suggestion was not taken up. But in 1977 the House of Commons Expenditure Committee highlighted the weakness of separating control of expenditure from the control of the civil service and recommended that the CSD functions which concerned civil service efficiency and manpower should be transferred to the Treasury. The Government decided to leave things as they were.[22]

Integrating social welfare administration

It may be helpful to turn from these general issues to some specific cases. First, we examine changes over time in the institutional arrangements for administering the services which by 1974 had come under the umbrella of the giant DHSS.

In July 1948 three of the main post-war welfare services came into operation. The National Insurance scheme was designed to provide universal subsistence benefits as a right in return for compulsory weekly contributions. National assistance was intended to provide relief, without contribution conditions but subject to a means test, mainly for those whose incomes failed before they had qualified for insurance benefits. The National Health Service was, with minor exceptions, free to the user but financed partly from a weekly contribution collected along with insurance payments. Family allowances, payable without means test or insurance conditions, had already been operating since 1946.

The Beveridge Report recommended that family allowances, national insurance and national assistance should be administered by a new Ministry of Social Security, which might also take over war pensions, employment services and the regulation of voluntary insurance schemes.[23] In fact, Britain acquired a Ministry of National Insurance which was initially made responsible only for family allowances and the National Insurance scheme. It was amalgamated with the Ministry of (War) Pensions in 1955, when both schemes had settled down and it was thought that a merger would produce economies. The supervision of private insurance companies and friendly societies remained with the Board of Trade (and its successors) and the Registrar of Friendly Societies.

To administer the assistance scheme, an independent National Assistance Board was set up on the model of the earlier Unemployment Assistance Board. Although the Minister of National Insurance handled the Board's parliamentary business, he was not answerable for its actions in individual cases. It was felt at the time that assistance and insurance were different sorts of services and were best administered in watertight compartments. The main problems of the insurance scheme were maintaining contribution records and checking claims for benefit against entitlement in the light of a complicated code of regulations. The National Assistance Board also had its scales of entitlement; but in addition it had to administer a means test humanely to applicants who were often in need of other social services; its staff became increasingly involved in 'first-aid' social work and referral. The Board and the Ministry both took their responsibilities to the public seriously. They developed impressive and highly specialized training arrangements for their staff, who worked with little overlap from different local offices. On the Insurance side, also, a great deal of effort was spent on streamlining office methods, with consequent savings on administrative overheads.

By the 1960s, however, the original financial distinction between the two schemes had collapsed. An attempt was made to keep the insurance fund in balance, but benefit rates had been increased to keep up with the declining value of money and the amounts paid out were not actuarially supported by what the recipients had paid in. Even so, the rates did not always cover subsistence needs: many of the elderly and unemployed needed to look to the National Assistance Board to supplement their insurance benefits. Those who were entitled to supplementation did not always seek it. A survey disclosed that a fifth refrained from applying because they wished to remain independent, while another three-tenths were prevented by ignorance or misconceptions.[24] The Government decided that an administrative merger between the two schemes would make for simplification and eliminate stigma. Early in 1966 Mr (later Lord) Houghton announced the Government's intention to create a new Ministry 'in which the old distinction between national insurance and national assistance officers will disappear and the name National Assistance will disappear for ever'.[25] Six months later the necessary legislation had been passed: the Minister of Pensions and National Insurance became the Minister of Social Security; the National Assistance Board was wound up and a Supplementary Benefits Commission set up to assist the Minister to run equivalent services; a number of minor changes were made in forms and nomenclature; and the process of integrating the two services was begun.

The primary object of the merger, therefore, was to present a better image to potential clients. (It was not only that. The Estimates Committee had criticized the cost as well as the inconvenience of parallel chains of local and regional offices for different government services, and had been assured that the question was under review.[26] Ministers also claimed that the change would make it easier to coordinate policy over the whole field; but it is hard to see how this could follow from a measure that did not alter political responsibility.) It is difficult to judge its success. There were half a million new claims for non-contributory benefits, but these could have been due to an intensive publicity campaign that was launched at the same time. A complete amalgamation of the two services on the ground proved impossible. Although there was some administrative integration at national and regional level, and local offices were brought together wherever possible, the client still has to deal with different groups of officers, with different training and different areas of expertise.[27] None of the subsequent improvements in the services seem to be attributable to the administrative realignment.

The offices involved in this reshuffle provided basically 'cash' services. The main 'care' service, the National Health Service, was given to the Ministry of Health, and became its main responsibility after the transfer of housing and local government to another department in 1951. The Ministry also supervised local authorities' welfare functions for the old and the handicapped. The social care of deprived children, however, was supervised by the Home Office. School welfare, the school health service, and school milk and meals came under the Ministry of Education. The Ministry of Labour was involved in welfare services connected with unemployment, including vocational guidance, the settlement of disabled persons and the administration of unemployment benefit on behalf of the Ministry of National Insurance.

One of the main objectives in the 1940s had been to get away from the all-purpose Poor Law and appoint separate agencies on Haldane lines for separate services. It was not long, however, before the disadvantages of specialization began to appear. Special arrangements had to be made to coordinate services for multi-problem families. Charges were made for some 'care' services, with exemptions for persons with low incomes, and eventually the theoretical distinction between exemption from payment and a cash grant was seen to be unrealistic. When prescription charges were reintroduced on a selective basis in 1968, the division of responsibilities between the Ministries of Health and Social Security is thought to have increased the difficulty of settling the basis for remission. Early in 1968 one of the leading members of the Cabinet, Mr Richard Crossman, was asked to amalgamate the two Ministries. The DHSS came into existence later in the year, and Mr Crossman became its first head, with the title of Secretary of State for Social Services.

This merger had already been advocated by the Conservative Opposition, in the belief that it would assist a move from universal to selective social services; it was also thought that administrative savings would follow and that an integrated research programme would show the desirability of new approaches throughout the social services.[28] In fact, nothing of the sort has happened. Within the DHSS, apart from a common Secretary of State and some common management services, health and social security are administered in separate wings, each with is own Permanent Secretary, its own headquarters building and its own PESC programme. The two operations have virtually nothing in common.[29] The Secretary of State has tended to concentrate on the side that commands more of his personal interest, leaving the other (except in a political crisis) to a second-tier Minister who may himself have a seat in Cabinet. Unless the National Health Service were to be financed through social security contributions instead of mainly through general taxation (and perhaps not even then) there is no obvious logic in association.

Indeed, if an idea that was popular in the 1960s had come to fruition, there would have been a strong case for a very different kind of reshuffle. Families who receive social security benefits may also pay income tax. In some circumstances an increase in nominal income can be disadvantageous because of the simultaneous loss of benefits (or exemption from charges) and liability to taxation – this creates the so called 'poverty trap'. One way of avoiding this would be to combine all financial transactions between the individual and the state into one system, in which taxes could be either positive or 'negative' (paid out, not paid in). Technical difficulties caused the idea to be abandoned, although the exercise led to a closer integration of taxation and social security policy, especially for children's allowances. Complete integration would sooner or later have required the amalgamation of social security with the Board of Inland Revenue.

The Secretary of State's title was intended to give him a slightly wider remit than his Department's. But this may involve trespassing on the territory of other Ministers. The DHSS took over responsibility for the school health service from the DES in 1974, and acquired child care services from the Home Office in 1971. In both cases, a realignment of responsibilities in Whitehall was a necessary concomitant of the restructuring of health and personal social services in the field. There had, however, been some tension between the Social Services Secretary and the Home Secretary over the Children's Service.[30] Moreover, occupational health, which some reformers would have liked to see more closely integrated with the main NHS, remains firmly embedded in the tripartite (government–union–employer) machinery for regulating conditions of employment.

Within its field of operation, however, the concentration in the DHSS of responsibility for the health and personal (i.e. social work and welfare) social services has enabled it to develop integrated policies for the care of the sick, the elderly, the deprived child and so on, not only across a large range of services but also in relation to each other. This has been facilitated by the form of internal organization, in which multi-professional service development teams act as focal points for the main client groups, that was adopted in the mid-1970s. But the enabling conditions for policy integration existed as soon as the separate functions were brought together under a Minister who could see connections among the different items of business flowing across his desk.

Tasks and their coordination

In the DHSS case, most of the significant issues concerned policy-making at the top: the question was what range of functions could sensibly be brought together under a Minister and his supporting team of senior civil servants. There was also some concern for administrative economy, simplicity and perhaps 'elegance'. But the administration of a function can be broken down into a large number of tasks, like checking claims for social security; and, as we have seen, that particular task was not much affected either by the amalgamation of insurance and assistance schemes or by the combination of social security with health administration in Whitehall.

Let us take a different example. In the DES, groups of administrators are concerned with the negotiation of salaries, pensions and conditions of service for teachers. Similar groups in the Home Office and the DHSS are engaged on almost identical problems affecting policemen, firemen, doctors and nurses. In their day-to-day work they are applying common principles about consultation, national incomes policy and public service conditions of employment. Their knowledge and techniques have far more in common with one another, and with the divisions in the Civil Service Department that supervise these things, than with those of colleagues in their own departments. They are, of course, applying departmental policy as well – the problem of providing incentives to aid recruitment in difficult areas, for example, is viewed differently in the three departments. But they specialize in remuneration rather than in education or health. Other divisions in the same department will similarly be applying interdepartmental techniques to building programmes, the control of revenue expenditure, routine servicing for technical committees, and the application of cost-benefit analysis to operational problems.

Nevertheless, the work they are doing is only a means to the provision of an education service employing staff of a certain quality, deployed over schools of certain types, bearing certain ratios to the numbers of children in each area. It is under the control of a Minister and senior staff who are concerned with the service as a whole and will have its broad objectives in mind in reviewing problems that come up (for example after parliamentary challenge) from the remuneration division. The staff in the division will have acquired a fair amount of personal experience of the problems facing other parts of the department. Through constant exposure they will also have picked up some of the department's characteristic ethos. Departments develop inbred habits and attitudes, both internally and in relation to outside bodies. They differ, for example, in their attitudes to professional expertise. They have characteristic patterns of consultation and of delegation. Whatever the pattern is, it tends to become entrenched in a social system, with its own norms and pressures, to which newcomers have to conform if they are going to fit in smoothly.

The Haldane Committee concluded in 1918 that departments should be organized on a basis of the service provided (for example health or education). Its argument was couched in administrative terms.

> ... the acquisition of knowledge ... and the development of specialized capacity ... are obviously most likely to be secured when the officers of a Department are continuously engaged in the study of questions which all relate to a single service and when the efforts of the Department are definitely concentrated upon the development and improvement of the particular service which the Department exists to supervise.[31]

If this was true in 1918, it is certainly not obviously true today. Services interact, and even the definition of a service is likely to change. Provision for deprived children was for two decades regarded as a 'service' and administered by the Home Office in a way that perhaps encouraged a liberal approach, within the same office, to juvenile delinquency; it is now part of 'personal social services' under the DHSS. Overseas aid was moved into the FCO by the Conservatives (who regard it as an adjunct of foreign policy) and moved out again by Labour (who do not). Moreover, there are now broad public policies concerned with employment, inflation and economic priorities which run across particular services: the export of drugs and medical equipment, especially to the oil countries, has become an increasingly important task within the DHSS, although both export policy and the relevant techniques might be thought more appropriate to the Department of Trade or the commercial section of the FCO.

It is particularly when we come to technical tasks that a service-based departmental structure seems less relevant. The skills and knowledge (and perhaps even the framework of assumptions) required to apply public policy to teachers' pensions may be quite different from those required to administer educational policy. Some subordinate tasks, like supplying DES officials with offices and furniture, and handling the Department's publications, are in fact entrusted to separate bodies – the Property Services Agency and Her Majesty's Stationery Office. It is quite possible that job analysis would show that work on teachers' pensions could be carried out more efficiently by officials who had no direct connection with education, perhaps in a Public Sector Pensions Board (whose functions, somewhat curiously, are partly carried out by the Board of Inland Revenue as a result of the complicated tax relief provisions relating to the pension schemes). Similar arguments could be made about the supervision of building schemes, manpower studies and many other aspects of the education 'service'. In practice, it is highly unlikely that any of these functions would be taken out of the DES, if only because it is convenient for Chief Education Officers and the local authority associations concerned with education to deal with a single 'sponsor' department across the whole range of their business. This need not, of course, preclude the establishment within the DES of a pensions 'bureau', staffed by specialists and linked laterally with similar bureaux in other departments as well as vertically with the Ministers and officials who carry responsibility for the overall functioning of the educational system.

The usual arguments about machinery of government make much less sense away from the Minister's office. In the extreme case, the scientist in his government laboratory may be very little concerned in the uses to which his work may eventually be put. For him, a change of responsible ministry may mean a good deal of irrelevant and meaningless disturbance. There will be trivial and possibly irritating changes in designations and filing systems. Professional contacts may be unable to find him in the *Civil Service Yearbook*. Moreover, he will have to learn how to win resources from a new establishment and organization division, who may play the game according to unfamiliar rules. The scientist may, in practice, be screened from much of this disturbance. But his administrative colleagues will not, and may well suffer the extra dislocation of a physical move to a new departmental building.

The fallacy is to assume that only one type of coordination is important. Any administrative task, such as the negotiation of teachers' superannuation or a cost-benefit study of road-pricing devices, can be viewed from at least three points of view: (a) its technical content, (b) its relationship with a major political purpose, and (c) the need for consistency with other major purposes. These are separate dimensions and it is unlikely that the same structural arrangements will serve all three. Technical expertise can best be secured by the selection and training of staff who pursue an integrated career in the field. Subordination to a major goal implies locating it in a department whose senior echelons are committed to the pursuit of that goal. Consistency with other goals implies interdepartmental coordination procedures and a supra-departmental authority to resolve disputes. According to the political and administrative needs of the time, any activity can be slotted into place along each of these three dimensions. The first is independent of the other two (although is has not been recognized as such in the past) and presents mainly career and training problems. The other two are much more closely interconnected, since it must be a matter of judgement whether any particular goal conflict is too important politically to be resolved by the internal processes of a large department at any particular time. In a very few cases, the relative advantages and disadvantages of different groupings could be compared systematically if research workers had access to the files of government departments in different parts of the United Kingdom. For example, in England, Wales and Northern Ireland social work services are closely associated with the National Health Service (and in Northern Ireland they are administered by the same field authorities). In Scotland, however, they embrace the probation service (a Home Office function in England) and are administered centrally not by the Scottish Home and Health Department but by the Scottish Education Department. There is room for an interesting study of the implications of these variations, both for policy integration and for the structure and cost of the relevant services.

Conclusions

We have looked at various aspects of the machinery of government problem – which is essentially about the way one set of tasks and functions is linked with others – from perspectives varying from overall policy coordination to the kind of expertise needed to carry out a specialized task. Both political and administrative considerations enter into the question of finding the best way of combining functions at a particular time.

The political aspects command most attention. The grouping of functions around key Ministers will reflect the primary concerns of the government of the day. The combination of several functions under a single Minister is a sound and elegant way of implementing political ideas about the primary context in which they should be regarded: by seeing and commenting on the sample of business that requires his attention, the Minister can, in Laski's phrase, 'inject a stream of tendency' into the department as a whole. This will not happen, of course, if the work of the department lacks underlying unity (which may be true of the DHSS); or if its functions have to be subdivided among Ministers of equal rank or opposing ambitions. Moreover, ideas about the most appropriate combination of functions will necessarily change from time to time, sometimes because of party ideology, sometimes because of changes in the context of government which demand political attention. The 1970 White Paper was intended to set the seal on the administrative experiments of the 1960s and to herald a period of administrative stability. Subsequent history confirms that departmental structures reflect the needs and political preferences of the time rather than abstract principles.

Senior administrators who underpin the Minister and work closely with him on policy need to share his frame of reference and to be exposed to the same range of material. Bridges begin to appear between areas of policy that are attended to by the same group of people. But there is no simple relationship between administrative functions and the focal points of ministerial responsibility. As one moves away from the political battlefield to day-to-day administration and executive management, the need for quite different patterns of specialization begins to appear. The administrator in charge of technical aspects of hospital building needs broad experience of clinical requirements and of project management, but it is relatively unimportant to him whether his Minister has other duties that incline him to regard a new hospital, say, as part of the economic infrastructure or as an instrument for achieving social equality. It does not usually make political sense to divide functions among Ministers according to the administrative techniques involved. But there may be advantages along that road in terms of efficiency and expertise. Just as in the case of planning, therefore, it may be necessary to find other ways of satisfying system requirements which are inconsistent with short-term political exigencies. Some of them will be explored in the next chapter.

Notes

1 There is a full account of detailed changes in each year since 1966 in B. C. Smith and J. Stanyer, 'Administrative Developments in 1967', *Public Administration* Vol. 46 (1968) pp. 239–79, and subsequent years (from 1972 by D. R. Steel and J. Stanyer; biennial after 1970).

2 *Report of the Machinery of Government Committee*, Cd. 9230 (1918). The Committee's terms of reference were 'to enquire into the responsibilities of the various Departments of the central executive Government, and to advise in what manner the exercise and distribution by the Government of its functions should be improved'.

3 J. M. Lee, *Reviewing the Machinery of Government, 1942–52: an essay on the Anderson Committee and its successors* (Birkbeck College, London, 1978).

4 For example, W. A. Robson, *Nationalized Industry and Public Ownership*, 2nd edn (London, 1962).

5 D. N. Chester and F. M. G. Willson, *The Organization of British Central Government 1914–64*, 2nd edn (London, 1968).

6 Sir David Milne, *The Scottish Office* (London, 1957).
7 *Royal Commission on the Constitution 1969–73*, Cmnd. 5460 (1973); *Democracy and Devolution: Proposals for Scotland and Wales*, Cmnd. 5732 (1974). Scotland and Wales Bills were introduced in the 1977–8 parliamentary session.
8 *H.C. Debs*, Vol. 763 (23 April 1968) cols 27–8.
9 *H.L. Debs*, Vol. 262 (4 February 1965) cols 1298–9 (Second Reading of Science and Technology Bill).
10 R. H. S. Crossman, *Diaries of a Cabinet Minister*, e.g. Vol. 3, 1968–70 (London, 1977), see index under 'Wilson, Harold – Cabinet' and '– Health and Social Services'.
11 *H.C. Debs*, Vol. 773 (21 November 1968) col. 1563.
12 D. Howell, *A New Style of Government* (Conservative Political Centre, London, 1970).
13 *The Reorganisation of Central Government*, Cmnd. 4506 (1970).
14 Sir Richard Clarke, *New Trends in Government* (London, 1971) pp. 1–6.
15 A. Clark, 'Ministerial Supervision and the Size of the Department of the Environment', *Public Administration* Vol. 55 (1977) pp. 197–204.
16 *The Reorganisation of Central Government*, op. cit., paras 8, 9.
17 H. Heclo and A. Wildavsky, *The Private Government of Public Money* (London, 1974) Chap. 3, 'Village Life in Civil Service Society'.
18 Cmnd. 4506, op. cit., para. 16.
19 *H.C. Debs*, Vol. 805 (3 November 1970) col. 890 (Mr A. Crosland).
20 Sir Richard Clarke, op. cit., pp. 40–2.
21 ibid., pp. 58–61, 65–8.
22 *Eleventh Report from the Expenditure Committee 1976–77*, H.C. 535. See also the Government's observations on the report, Cmnd. 7117 (1978).
23 *Social Insurance and Allied Services: report by Sir William Beveridge*, Cmd. 6404 (1942) pp. 145–8.
24 *Financial and other Circumstances of Retirement Pensioners*, Report on an Enquiry by the Ministry of Pensions and National Insurance with the cooperation of the National Assistance Board (London, 1966).
25 *H.C. Debs*, Vol. 725 (23 February 1966) col. 432.
26 *Fourth Report from the Estimates Committee 1964–65*, H.C. 274, Ministry of Pensions and National Insurance'; *Fourth Special Report 1965–66*, H.C. 32.
27 R. G. S. Brown, *The Management of Welfare* (London, 1975) Chap. 4, 'The Administration of Social Security Benefits'. See also 'O & M in Social Security', *O & M Bulletin* Vol. 23 (1968) p. 61.

28 Conservative Political Centre, *Putting Britain Right Ahead* (London, 1965).
29 R. G. S. Brown, op. cit., Chap. 3, 'The Department of Health and Social Security'.
30 R. H. S. Crossman, *Diaries of a Cabinet Minister*, Vol. 3, 1968–70 (London, 1977), see index under 'Home Office'.
31 *Report of the Machinery of Government Committee*, op. cit., p. 8.

XII
Management

The word 'management' has several meanings. The Fulton Committee's management consultancy group defined it as 'the formulation and operation of the policy of the enterprise' and distinguished 'four aspects which make up the total management task of the Civil Service: (a) formulation of policy under political direction; (b) creating the machinery for implementation of policy; (c) operation of the administrative machine; (d) accountability to Parliament and the Public'.[1]

This list seems to comprise all the work of government below political level. It closely resembles most definitions of senior administrators' tasks. In the Committee's report, however, 'management' has a more limited meaning: managers were said to be 'responsible for organization, directing staff, planning the progress of work, setting standards of attainment and measuring results, reviewing procedures and quantifying different courses of action' – duties which seem to cover only items (b) and (c) on the consultants' list.[2]

In this chapter we are concerned with management in this more limited sense. The Fulton Committee was very critical of the quality of this kind of management in the civil service. It believed that senior staff paid too little attention to this aspect of their work, preferring to regard themselves as 'advisers on policy to people above them, rather than as managers of the administrative machine below them',[3] and that various aspects of departmental organization hampered effective management of executive activities. In this chapter we will examine the effects of traditional civil service structures upon management and discuss some of the reforms that have been proposed to overcome them, notably the adoption of accountable management within departments and the transfer of executive activities from departments to semi-autonomous public bodies, a process generally known as 'hiving-off'.

Management in departments

Political factors have a major impact upon the nature of management in the civil service. The fact that ultimately the Minister is answerable to Parliament for everything that is done in his department makes it difficult to delegate responsibility to subordinates in the same way as happens in most other large organizations. This difficulty is reinforced by the importance attached to ensuring that all departmental spending is in accordance with parliamentary appropriation. This has led to the adoption of standardized financial procedures under the supervision of the Treasury and to the designation of the Permanent Secretary in each department as accounting officer. In this capacity he is liable to be called before the Public Accounts Committee to explain any irregularities, and this places limits on the extent to which financial responsibility can be devolved.

The political environment of the civil service has also contributed to the emergence of a distinctive style of staff management.[4] Traditionally this has always been closely linked to financial control. Thus establishments work – as personnel management in the civil service is generally known – was originally conceived as an instrument for limiting staff numbers, and this remains an important aspect, although it is now much wider in scope. One result of this tradition is that decisions on staffing also tend to be centralized. The Civil Service Department lays down recruitment policy and negotiates centrally on wages, conditions of service and promotion rules and procedures. Departments have some latitude in the implementation of these rules but this is closely circumscribed, not least because on most questions service-wide agreements have been negotiated with the staff associations. Within departments, too, staffing decisions tend to be taken centrally so that individual managers have little discretion in the deployment of staff.

As we saw in Part One, political factors also influence the career structure of the civil service. Given the need to maintain a career service, it is essential that staff have a sense of security and an expectation of fairness. At the top, where civil servants have the almost unbearable task of putting their knowledge and abilities at the disposal of Ministers with differing abilities and philosophies, they have enjoyed the protections of anonymity and virtual security against dismissal, thus encouraging them to give advice freely. Lower down the scale, regular movement between jobs and promotion rules based largely upon seniority reassure a civil servant doing a stint on a particularly trying or unrewarding block of work that the system will not allow him to be forgotten and that his career prospects will not be jeopardized. For all grades, centralized bargaining with the staff associations has resulted in procedures for discipline and promotion which offer considerable protection from arbitrariness and 'scapegoating'.

In this way a balance has been struck between the functional requirements of the civil service and the personal objectives of its staff. Much of the work of government calls for collaborative effort between staff of a kind which is facilitated by the non-competitive career system. This system also appears to suit the personal wishes of many officials. For instance, a survey of young administrators conducted by one of us in 1969–70 revealed that most of them did not seek a working environment that stressed economic rewards and keen competition but that they attached importance to social factors such as congenial colleagues and easy relationships with superiors and to psychological rewards such as the intrinsic interest of work and the scope given for initiative.[5]

In Part One, however, we discovered that the tasks of contemporary government are now extremely varied and that this variety is reflected in the staffing of the civil service and in the range of techniques employed. This has major implications for management. Organization theorists, such as Burns and Stalker, have demonstrated that the appropriateness of different types of internal management structure varies according to such factors as function and environment.[6] They found that a 'mechanistic' structure was well suited to work that was of a repetitive, routine nature but that it was less appropriate for work that was innovative and creative, where the environment was frequently unstable and where political viability could depend upon being able to cope with the latest challenge. In such circumstances they argued that a more flexible or 'organic' structure was needed. Their analysis points in the direction not of a uniform system throughout government but to a variety of systems related to differences in task and environment. Thus a mechanistic system may be needed in departments whose work consists of the application of rules and regulations on a standardardized, equitable basis and which is generally removed from politics. In other departments, where work is innovative and political involvement is frequent and unpredictable, an organic type of structure may be more suitable. For instance, instead of a new problem having to be referred to the top for a decision as to how it should be solved, everyone becomes involved and gaps are automatically filled as individual managers try to clarify the implications for their own ill-defined areas of discretion. Taken a stage further, it is likely that different systems will be needed at different levels in any one department. At policy-making levels, or in divisions dealing with planning, flexibility and informality may be desirable; at lower levels a clear and fairly formal structure of authority is more important.

Again, the fact that the system of staff management meets the aspirations of officials at administrative levels does not mean that it is appropriate throughout the service. Many junior civil servants work in areas that have little intrinsic reward and where, to promote efficiency, it may be necessary to allow individuals to identify themselves more closely with success and to enjoy specific rewards for specific performance. But any improvements in performance and morale obtained in this way need to be set against the lower satisfaction, and possibly lower performance, of the less successful. Moreover, the mechanics by which merit would be assessed could have all kinds of undesirable side-effects. For instance, they might lead to excessive importance being attached to those aspects of a job that could be measured (typically quantity rather than quality and speed rather than effectiveness). Problems might also arise in finding staff to work in those areas where such rewards were difficult to obtain. And the introduction of competition might affect the *esprit de corps* of the service as a whole, thus harming those areas of work where collaborative effort was still needed. In other words, the system requirements of individual parts of the civil service need to be weighed carefully against those of the service as a whole.

Particular attention has been paid by advocates of managerial reform to those parts of government where work is primarily executive in character. In these areas political factors are generally muted and the pursuit of efficiency in the use of resources is a major aim of management. Their effectiveness in achieving this aim can in theory be gauged relatively easily by relating the level and quality of the output of goods or services produced under their direction to the level and quality of the input of resources they receive. However, the conventional system of management in departments hampers the achievement of this kind of efficiency. The blurring of responsibility for decision-making makes it difficult to hold a manager accountable for performance if he has little or no freedom to vary centralized rules about either money or manpower. Nor can he be rewarded or punished for succeeding or failing to meet his targets as long as he is secure in his job and subject to promotion rules that are based primarily upon seniority. For these reasons, the Fulton Committee and others have proposed that departments should be reorganized so as to permit the application of the principles of accountable management to executive work. In the next section the steps that have been taken to implement this proposal will be examined in order to see how far this style of management can be adopted within the departmental framework.

Accountable management

The Fulton Committee defined 'accountable management' as 'identifying or establishing accountable units within government departments – units where output can be measured against costs or other criteria, and where individuals can be held personally responsible for their performance'.[7] It thought that output could be measured against cost in any case where large numbers of similar operations were performed, such as dealing with applications, handling individual employment problems at local offices or handling stores or supplies. Those in charge of such units 'should be given clear-cut responsibilities and commensurate authority and should be held accountable for performance against budgets, standards of achievement and other tests'.[8]

Accountability in this sense demands that the costs of particular activities are identified so that performance can be assessed by comparing actual with planned expenditure. The traditional system of budgeting in Britain is not very helpful in this respect. Its main features were laid down in the nineteenth century and were designed to ensure regularity in the expenditure of public funds. Departments therefore prepare estimates and statements of expenditure in input terms (staff, equipment, supplies, etc.). This information is now related to the broad functional categories of PESC, so that it is possible to discover how much is spent on particular activities such as social security or the health service, but it is of little use for management accounting. For this purpose, it is essential that expenditure is subdivided in a way which corresponds with managerial authority, thus making it possible for the output of individual divisions to be related to the input of resources they receive.

More sophisticated tests of performance require expenditure to be related to particular objectives, the achievement of which can be measured in quantitative terms. Budgeting techniques of this kind, known as Planning-Programming-Budgeting, were pioneered in the United States in the Department of Defense, and in 1965 were applied throughout the Executive Branch. Their main function, however, was to improve the planning of public expenditure by increasing the amount of information available to decision-makers, rather than to serve as an instrument of management. In Britain the approach to PPB, generally known here as 'output budgeting', has been more cautious and even less related to management.[9] In central government various experiments – for instance in the Ministry of Defence – have succeeded in clarifying the costs of various policy options, but they have not yielded information that is useful for management purposes. Output budgeting has been more extensively applied in local government but again it has been used mainly to assist in decision-making.

In any case, it is clear that large areas of government are not appropriate for the introduction of quantitative means of assessing performance. In this kind of field, however, another technique known as 'management by objectives' has been advocated as a means of improving managerial efficiency. Under this system the head of a branch agrees with his superiors and subordinates a programme of objectives, with priorities and deadlines. Each individual thus knows the extent of his responsibilities and the limits of his authority. By regularly monitoring progress, the effectiveness of the branch and the contribution of its individual members can be more objectively assessed.[10]

Since Fulton, some progress has been made towards introducing the principles of accountable management.[11] A major step forward has been the development of the concept of the departmental agency, the first two of which were the Procurement Executive in the Ministry of Defence and the Property Services Agency in the Department of the Environment. A departmental agency is an identifiable unit within a department, still under the direction of a Minister who is answerable for its activities to Parliament and still staffed by civil servants, but distinguished from the conventional pattern of departmental organization by having its own executive head and accounting officer, and by a large degree of freedom in staff management.

Within a departmental agency it is thus easier to get away from traditional accounting methods and staffing patterns, both of which stand in the way of the effective allocation of responsibility. The Property Services Agency provides a good example.[12] As we saw in Chapter IV, it has a structure of command in which responsibilities are clearly defined at each level. Against this background, accountable management has been taken furthest in the Supplies Division. It was established in 1976 as a separately accountable unit with its own trading fund. It is therefore freed from the procedures associated with the control of normal vote expenditure. It is charged with the full cost of services provided to it by other parts of the PSA and other departments and it supplies its goods and services to its clients for repayment. It has been set a financial objective and will produce trading accounts at regular intervals. Its performance will also be monitored by means of various quantitative indicators. This system has not only been applied to the Division as a whole; it has also been introduced in a more limited form for the individual units within it.

In other parts of the PSA this sort of system has not been found practicable. However, much work has been done to define aims and objectives for key levels of command, to devise performance indicators and to generate financial information of a kind which can be used for control purposes.

Equivalent developments have occurred in other departments. Trading funds have been established for most of the quasi-commercial activities that have not been hived-off, such as the ordnance factories, the Royal Mint and the Stationery Office. Where achievement can be measured in quantitative or financial terms, management accounting is being used increasingly to supplement traditional vote accounting, for instance in the job-finding and training agencies which are under the aegis of the Manpower Services Commission. Elsewhere, there has been a programme of experiments with 'management by objectives' covering many different types of work, the largest of which has been in the regional and local office organization of the DHSS.

Political and administrative limits

Most of the techniques associated with accountable management were pioneered in the private sector, and the question arises as to how far they can be applied successfully in public organizations. In industry it is often possible to define constraints fairly clearly in financial terms and to measure results unambiguously in terms of profitability and growth. This is much more difficult in the public sector, as many of the experiments with output budgeting have indicated. What, for instance, are the objectives of an educational institution? If the answer to this question is not to be so vague as to be useless for management purposes, it raises social and political issues which cannot be reduced to a simple statement of objectives. Even if this could be done, it is far from easy to monitor progress towards achieving objectives. There is no simple equivalent of profitability in the public sector. It may be possible to devise proxy indicators of success – in the field of secondary education, for instance, the pupil/teacher ratio might be used – but these can at best only be rough guides to achievement and they may be positively misleading.[13] In any case it is very difficult to isolate the work of particular units from their wider environment. Since political currents are unpredictable – and the effects of a change of government are particularly so – it is almost impossible in practice to formalize the 'external factors' to which civil service managers should pay attention. It is not surprising, therefore, that accountable management has been introduced in areas which are fairly remote from politics. Moreover, there are few areas which can be entirely insulated. For instance, the experience of the PSA has been that all its activities have been the subject of continuing political interest, not only because they involve the spending of public money but also because of public interest in such matters as standards of design.[14]

Even if the technical problems could be overcome, it is doubtful whether any of those directly involved in public administration would allow these procedures to be implemented fully. In industry it is often possible to delegate wide powers over staff and money, subject to overall budgetary control and to assessment of performance after the event. The accounting officer of a department, however, is likely to have to satisfy the Comptroller and Auditor General that money has actually been spent as Parliament authorized. Although the Public Accounts Committee is increasingly concerned with the general efficiency of departmental spending it still frequently focuses its attention upon fairly small examples of error and inefficiency.[15] This explains why the establishment of a trading fund is such an important step towards the introduction of effective delegation of responsibility. But this can only really be done in quasi-commercial fields, of which there are now very few that are the responsibility of central departments. For vote expenditure, the system of parliamentary control could certainly be improved but it is unlikely that MPs would agree to any reforms that significantly weakened their ability to question minor items of expenditure if they had political implications.

Nor is it just for financial reasons that effective delegation would be difficult to achieve. To be implemented fully, accountable management necessitates the use of financial rewards to encourage efficiency and the delegation to managers of power to deploy their staff. It is most unlikely that the staff associations would agree to abandon the present system of centralized negotiations on such matters as pay and promotion. Some idea of the importance attached by staff to these procedures, and of course to the benefits they produce, can be gauged from the battle waged and won by officials working in the employment services to retain civil service status when their work was transferred from the Department of Employment (DE) to a semi-autonomous agency.

Nor is it clear that such a change would benefit the civil service as a whole. Extensive introduction of accountable management would adversely affect the system of staff management which, as we have seen, is closely linked to the political environment of the service. For instance, the development of strong line management would weaken the much-admired system of centralized staff relations. Similarly, a more competitive career structure could not be achieved without affecting the solidarity of the service and the sense of commitment shown by most civil servants. This was a fear expressed by the first Chief Executive of the PSA, who in other respects favoured the adoption of a commercial approach to government operations. He believed that the unity and *esprit de corps* of the civil service, both of which are important for a large part of its work, would be eroded by placing too much emphasis on performance indicators and precise tests of individual merit.[16]

It is not that the civil service has failed to make easy and obvious arrangements like those sometimes found in industry, but that it has found a different type of solution (and perhaps in some ways a better one) to a common problem. There are also two different approaches to managerial responsibility. One approach is to find a man able to do a job, give him the resources he asks for and leave him to get on with it. The other is more subtle; it involves appointing a man to fill a niche in an organization, to inherit a set of practices and a group of staff who will go on doing what they did under his predecessor until stopped. It may take the second man longer to make his mark, but work flows on in the meantime and there is likely to be less disruption if he turns out to be a misfit or has a breakdown.

Finally, it is far from certain that Ministers are willing to accept the limitations imposed by the delegation of responsibility to officials. The principle of accountable management implies that a Minister would normally decline to intervene in a matter where a civil servant was acting within his delegated authority. It is almost impossible to imagine Ministers accepting this degree of self-restraint; it is even less likely that MPs would allow them to get away with it, particularly when things went wrong. And once the political head of a department had intervened, it would be extraordinary if his civil servants did not give priority to meeting his wishes. In which case they could not be penalized for failing to meet strictly managerial objectives because they had spent their energies dealing with political inquests or because they had been compelled to implement ministerial instructions.

Hiving-off

The political and administrative problems associated with delegating authority within departments have led many observers to the conclusion that executive activities cannot be run efficiently by departments and that they should be hived-off to semi-autonomous bodies. The term 'hiving-off' is of recent origin, but the idea has a longer history. Semi-autonomous bodies existed in the nineteenth century, but their importance grew rapidly in the years after the First World War. Organizations such as the BBC and the London Passenger Transport Board, where it was felt vital that political neutrality should be maintained, were early examples of such bodies. Recognition of the importance of managerial autonomy led the Labour Party in the 1930s, under the influence of Herbert Morrison and others, to decide that the management of any industries taken into public ownership should be entrusted not to ministerial departments but to *ad hoc* bodies, so as to free them from 'those undesirable pressures associated with both public and private Parliamentary strategy, political lobbying and electoral "blackmail".[17] This decision was implemented between 1945 and 1950 when a number of key industries were nationalized; they were, however, subject to more public control than Morrison had originally envisaged. Similar bodies, varying widely in the degree of their autonomy, have been created in many other new areas of state social and economic intervention.

During the 1960s an increasing amount of attention began to be paid to the possibilities of transferring activities from departments to *ad hoc* agencies. This had been discussed intermittently in relation to the Post Office since the 1930s and was eventually implemented in 1969. It was also recommended by a committee of enquiry into the air transport industry, and in 1971 a Civil Aviation Authority was established, one of whose purposes was to assume most of the responsibilities of Ministers in connection with the regulation of civil aviation. More generally, the idea was taken up, as we have seen, by the Fulton Committee, and it was also one aspect of the review of government activities undertaken by the team of businessmen brought into the civil service in 1970. To date, the only major change in this field resulting from their work has been the transformation in the size and character of the DE which occurred in 1973 and 1974, through the transfer of its job-finding, training, health and safety, and conciliation and arbitration services to three independent agencies: the Manpower Services Commission, the Health and Safety Commission and the Advisory, Conciliation and Arbitration Service (ACAS).

There are thus a considerable number of semi-autonomous bodies in existence, many of them performing important governmental functions. The task of classification is very difficult as their constitutions vary widely. The following list attempts very roughly to group government organizations according to their proximity to ministerial and parliamentary control.

1 Closest to the parliamentary system are the conventional Whitehall departments, headed by a Minister and under the immediate policy direction of the Cabinet.
2 Still formally within the departmental framework but enjoying some autonomy are various departments and agencies headed either by boards or by individual officials. Some of these are

long-established, for instance the Boards of Inland Revenue and of Customs and Excise; others such as the Property Services Agency and the Procurement Executive are of recent origin. They are subject to policy direction from Ministers but enjoy some financial autonomy and are independent in day-to-day matters unless they have major political implications. In the same category, although different in many other respects, are the regional and area health authorities which manage the NHS under the overall supervision of the Secretary of State for Social Services.

3 A third group of bodies, such as the Civil Aviation Authority, the Monopolies and Mergers Commission and the Price Commission, relieve Ministers of responsibility for investigations and policy recommendations of a quasi-judicial nature.

4 Next are a number of agencies through which the spending of public money and the regulation of private activities is entrusted either to experts in the relevant field or to the representatives of affected interests. In the first category are the Research Councils, the University Grants Committee and the Arts Council which enable the distribution of funds in particular areas to be removed from the political arena; in the second are bodies such as the Manpower Services Commission and ACAS. In both cases semi-autonomous status not only frees these activities from direct parliamentary intervention but may also increase the likelihood of decisions being accepted, by bringing those who are affected formally into the decision-making process.[18]

5 Fifthly, there are the many *ad hoc* bodies engaged in commercial or quasi-commercial activities. These include the nationalized industries proper (British Rail, British Steel, etc.), companies such as Rolls-Royce and British Leyland that are publicly owned, and other bodies such as the UK Atomic Energy Authority, the BBC and the Bank of England.

6 Finally, there is a category of bodies lying in the 'no-man's-land' between the public and private sectors. Some are partly publicly owned, for instance companies such as British Petroleum, Ferranti and International Computers. Others are private bodies

that are used by the government to perform public functions. These may have been created specially for this purpose in circumstances in which the government did not want to be openly involved, for instance the British Board of Film Censors. Alternatively they may be private organizations which, either because they depend upon government patronage, or voluntarily, agree to act as a 'chosen instrument' or agent for the government. In this category are firms which are dependent upon the government for orders.

This kind of classification can only be very tentative, largely because little is known about the precise effects of hiving-off or about the consequences of different features of their organization. The legal status of a body is by no means an infallible guide to the extent of its autonomy. There are parts of government departments which in practice are further from ministerial and parliamentary supervision than many ostensibly autonomous bodies; equally, bodies which have similar legal status, indeed in some cases with almost identical constitutions, may vary widely in the degree of their independence.

Unfortunately this is a field of study which has only recently attracted much attention. As long ago as 1953, D. N. Chester suggested a number of key points which he considered were important in determining a body's independence: (1) the extent to which it had its own independent source of annual income and could finance its borrowing in the market on its own credit; (2) the method of appointment and security of tenure of the members of its controlling board; (3) the powers of control given to Ministers; and (4) the extent to which its staff was subject to civil service rules.[19]

However, it was only in the 1970s that serious attempts were made to apply this kind of analysis to the experience of existing semi-autonomous bodies, notably by a team working under the aegis of the Carnegie Corporation of New York.[20] Their studies have suggested that most classifications, including our own, oversimplify the position, and have revealed a need for further investigation on a wide scale. Nevertheless, Chester's analysis does provide a framework for general discussion, making use of the evidence that is available, of the benefits and problems involved in hiving-off.

The establishment of a semi-autonomous body insulates a particular activity from the full force of ministerial and parliamentary control. The instrument establishing the body, usually a statute, specifies the powers of Ministers to intervene in its affairs; in other respects the board which is entrusted with its management is free to act independently within broad terms of reference laid down by the government. In Parliament, MPs can only question the Minister about the exercise or non-exercise of his powers; they cannot ask about matters which are the responsibility of the board. Select committees are able to investigate the activities of *ad hoc* bodies but their enquiries can only affect any particular body occasionally and their impact is therefore less direct than it is in most government departments (see Chapter v).

Hiving-off is not only advocated in order to avoid the direct effects of political interference; it is also seen as a means of escaping from many of the features of departmental organization which, as we saw earlier, are closely related to the system of political accountability. First, a semi-autonomous body which owns revenue-bearing assets and is financially self-supporting is freed from the close control which is exercised over expenditure that is financed out of annual parliamentary appropriations. This freedom also has a general effect upon an organization's approach to its duties. For instance, it is likely to be more prepared to take risks and to concentrate upon the development of services rather than upon budget balancing and the maintenance of 'public authority' standards of equity.[21]

Secondly, semi-autonomous bodies have greater flexibility in staffing. Their limited terms of reference and freedom from direct political accountability make it possible to give specialist staff a greater role in decision-making. In the past they were also able to pay more than normal civil service rates and to vary conditions of service in order to recruit the staff they needed. At present, however, this freedom is limited by government pay policy which applies throughout the public sector. Generally, decisions are affected by the previous experience – and to some extent by the career outlook – of an organization's staff and by the frequency with which different factors are brought to their notice. Even within government departments, there are areas where political factors intrude so seldom that staff specializing in, say, management services get into the habit of working from purely technical premises. This would apply even more if their careers were limited entirely to the application of a particular technique to a particular objective and if their frame of reference was directed exclusively to the organization in which they were working rather than to a wider service. On the other hand, the effects of organizational change can be exaggerated. For instance, a recent study has shown that the transfer of the Post Office from a government department to a public corporation had little effect upon the way in which the staff approached their work.[22]

(3)   Thirdly, semi-autonomous bodies have more flexibility in experimenting with new administrative methods and with different organizational patterns. There are, for example, various techniques for decentralizing authority and responsibility to unit managers, giving them discretion to find the best way of achieving an agreed objective within a given budget. (This provides them with an incentive to concentrate on efficiency and to have less regard for incidental repercussions: thus a site manager who is trying to build a new factory in a development area is not concerned about the long-term effects on the local economy of paying high wages to labourers during the operation.) They are more easily applied within an organization which is devoted to a single measurable goal and whose detailed operations are not likely to be challenged by higher authority because of their incompatability with other goals. Similarly, it is simpler for a semi-autonomous agency to adopt an internal management structure that is suited to its tasks and its environment.

Constraints

In practice, however, it is not easy to obtain many of these benefits while at the same time retaining some control over activities that of course remain in the public sector. In particular it has proved very difficult to find a satisfactory means of relating the work of semi-autonomous bodies to other national objectives, without jeopardizing the autonomy which hiving-off was intended to secure. In conventional departments the ultimate sanction for consistency and attention to general values not related to the task in hand is the constant threat that any action will be exposed to parliamentary criticism. Hiving-off deliberately excludes this sort of political audit. It also makes integration more difficult by institutionalizing goal achievement. Price has shown how, in the United States, the existence of the Atomic Energy Commission made it difficult to ask proper questions about the cheapest way of meeting certain objectives, since officials of the Commission saw it as their duty to promote the use of nuclear fuel and used sympathetic Congressmen to advance their claims; a development like the nuclear submarine was taken beyond the point that the Department of Defense would have chosen or the President's Science Advisory Committee recommended.[23] The UK Atomic Energy Authority may similarly have 'over-egged the atomic pudding' in discussion of the future energy requirements of this country, although its influence has been moderated by the existence of equivalent agencies promoting other sources of energy.

The more subject-centred an agency is, therefore, the more difficult it will be to coordinate its activities with other national aims. Once a chain of such bodies has been set up, each with a body of staff committed to a particular goal, it is very hard for Ministers to ensure that their priorities are observed. Nor is it easy for them to alter the pattern of agencies as their political needs change. With conventional government departments, and a staff of reasonably interchangeable generalists, it is not difficult to set up a new department very quickly or for a new government with different ideas to wind it up. It is much more difficult to do this with semi-autonomous agencies each of which has its own corporate set of values and its own pride in its place in the governmental system. The creation of separate agencies thus affects adversely one of the features of British government that has attracted widespread admiration: the flexibility of Ministers in taking prompt action and in altering the machinery of government.

In theory the activities of semi-autonomous agencies are integrated with national objectives by means of certain ministerial powers of direction and by the retention of limited parliamentary oversight. Some idea of the practical problems involved in devising a framework which reconciles the needs of public accountability and those of managerial autonomy can however be gained from the experience of the nationalized industries during the last thirty years. As far as Parliament is concerned the problems have not been too serious. In 1956 a Select Committee on Nationalised Industries was established to provide a direct link between MPs and the industries. It conducts regular enquiries into individual industries and occasionally examines general problems. In general it seems to have worked to the satisfaction of both sides. The industries acknowledge that on the whole the Committee has succeeded in striking a balance between asking questions and expressing opinions on the one hand and interfering in managerial decisions on the other, and they believe that it has usually taken a sympathetic view of their problems. However, relations have not always been easy, as was clear from the bitter row between the Committee and the British Steel Corporation in 1978 over the Corporation's handling of its financial problems.[24]

The Select Committee's work has also generally been regarded by MPs as useful. Nevertheless, there are many MPs who feel that Parliament does not have the influence over management that it ought to have. These problems would almost certainly be exacerbated if a large number of activities which are at present the responsibility of Ministers were to be hived-off. In the case of the nationalized industries, market and consumer tests of performance compensate in part for the weakening of traditional forms of accountability. Such tests cannot be applied to activities such as the running of employment exchanges – which has been hived-off – or the handling of tax cases, which is a candidate for transfer. Nor is the need for these activities to be insulated from politics so obvious. Moreover, the success of the Select Committee may partly be due to the fact that all its dealings are with semi-autonomous bodies. Already there is some evidence to suggest that other select committees are less aware of the special position of those who manage bodies such as the Manpower Services Commission, and have tended to treat them in the same way as they treat government departments.

Much more troublesome has been the relationship between

Ministers and the industries. In principle it ought to be relatively
straightforward for Ministers to set objectives for each industry
which take account of the public interest, and then to use these
targets as a means of monitoring their progress. This has indeed
been tried on a number of occasions. For instance, in 1961 the
Government laid down financial objectives for each industry and
later these were supplemented by guidance on the criteria to be
used in investment appraisal and pricing policy.[25] In addition,
certain major decisions, such as closing a railway line or embarking
upon a major new project, have remained subject to procedures
that allow public debate and ultimately provide for ministerial
sanction.

This kind of framework, however, has not worked in practice.
Politicians have found it hard to settle upon the aims of the
nationalized industries and economists have disagreed on the
manner in which these aims should be specified in measurable
form.[26] Nor has it been easy to sustain such a framework under
the pressure of events. Thus in 1973, at the end of an enquiry
into the control of capital investment, the Select Committee concluded that the Government had failed to meet its objective 'of
exercising its control publicly and according to well-defined
ground rules, without interfering with the management functions
of the industries themselves'.[27] In large part this has happened
because of the importance of the industries as employers, suppliers
and customers and because of the economic and social implications
of almost all of their decisions. This has been highlighted in the
1960s and 1970s by intense political interest in their pricing
decisions and wage settlements. But Ministers have also been
reluctant to confine themselves to strategic questions because it
is very often minor decisions that have political repercussions both
nationally and in particular constituencies.

These problems led the Government in 1975 to institute a
general enquiry by the National Economic Development Office
into the control of the nationalized industries. Its report, published
in 1976, confirmed the unsatisfactory nature of the relationship
between Ministers and most of the industries.[28] It therefore
recommended a radical change in the institutional framework with
the establishment of a policy council for each industry. This would

be composed of representatives of the main groups concerned with the industry – government, trade unions and customers – and some independent members, and its purpose would be to set objectives, to monitor progress and generally to act as a buffer between the government and the management board of the industry. Thus proposal has been rejected by the Government, which has chosen instead only to make modifications in the existing framework.[29]

It is unlikely, however, that organizational tinkering, even of the fairly radical kind proposed by NEDO, can solve the fundamental problem. Those in charge of the industries have little alternative other than to implement ministerial wishes, almost regardless of the formal division of responsibility, as they know that Ministers hold most of the cards and that ultimately they can remove them from office. This would change only if there was radical constitutional change in which the boundaries of different public organizations were defined more clearly and some form of independent arbitration was provided. Failing this, the full benefits of semi-autonomous status can be gained only through self-denial on the part of politicians.

In social services there is a more fundamental problem of defining basic objectives. What is the equivalent of profitable return on investment for an area health authority? What terms of reference should be given to an autonomous social security organization: should it be compelled to structure its schemes so as to encourage redeployment or to discourage voluntary cessations, to favour the needy or to reward the thrifty, to cut down on overheads or to provide advisory and 'convenience' services for the public? These are primarily political questions to which there is no unequivocal answer. They can be resolved only through changing political judgements about the correct balance of priorities in the circumstances of the moment.

It is easier to ensure the consideration of 'external benefits' within a government department. Political direction by a Minister, overall accountability to Parliament, the unwritten assumptions that underlie bargaining with the Treasury and (above all) the ethos of senior administrators all tend to set ill-defined but well-understood limits on the extent to which a particular goal will be pursued without regard to its repercussions elsewhere. Formal procedures, particularly those concerned with financial control and parliamentary scrutiny, play a part in this, but it is a relatively small one.

It would be useful to test the effect of locating a function in a government department rather than elsewhere if a suitably controlled situation could be found. For example, government departments, local authorities, health authorities and nationalized industries all purchase large quantities of equipment and place large-scale contracts for goods and services. A comparative study of something as simple as tendering procedures might indicate how far purely managerial considerations were affected by wider considerations (employment given to disabled persons, the technological development of the industry, local employment situation in the supplier's area, etc.) in the different types of organization and through what machinery.

Conclusion

The prospects for extensive delegation of responsibility within departments appear, therefore, to be fairly limited. Political needs rule out fundamental changes in the structure and staffing of departments, except in a few special fields which for various reasons are largely immune from ministerial intervention and detailed parliamentary review. This is not, however, to deny the importance of promoting managerial efficiency in government. A high proportion of civil servants are doing fairly routine work to which general efficiency techniques can be applied. Indeed, the civil service has an impressive record in pioneering techniques such as organization and methods and work study. Initially these were applied mainly to low-level, clerical work. But since Fulton their application has been widened. Most departments now have high-level management services units responsible for reviewing organization and promoting efficiency, and management is a major element in the training of senior staff. More resources have been devoted to personnel management and greater emphasis is now laid upon the planning of individual careers and the wider aspects of this work.[30] Tremendous strides have also been made with the application of quantitative techniques of control in fields ranging from the day-to-day operations of schools and hospitals to more complex problems in transport and defence.

However, there are limits to the extent to which managerial efficiency can be taken within the departmental framework. They are too exposed to political turbulence, and the political requirements of Ministers are bound to take precedence over routine executive work. Their pattern of staffing is also inevitably determined primarily by policy and political needs. Moreover, as the scope and complexity of government has grown, it has become all the more important that Ministers and their advisers should be relieved of routine work so that they can concentrate their energies upon the work of making and reviewing policy, which they alone can undertake.

Such relief can be achieved only through hiving-off. In many departments the execution of policies has for some time been delegated to outside agencies (health authorities, local authorities, public industrial corporations), and any opportunities for extending this process need to be explored. Semi-autonomous status has particular advantages for the management of executive activities in that it gives managers flexibility in staffing and financial matters. However, it carries the disadvantages that have been outlined in this chapter. Functional agencies have to be linked to the rest of the system by formal constraints. It is more difficult to reshuffle established agencies when needs change than it is to reallocate functions among departments of a unified civil service. The tendency of staff to identify with their organization, especially if they have no other career outlet, may be a prescription for dynamic administration or a form of organizational disease, according to the circumstances and your point of view. These sorts of disadvantages can be tolerated only if they are outweighed by the gains: more research is needed into the balance of advantage.

Nor is it easy to devise a framework which provides opportunities for Ministers to exercise control on key issues and for Parliament to ask questions and exert some influence, without jeopardizing the independence which was the purpose of hiving-off in the first place. New techniques are certainly available which may assist in overcoming some of the problems that have been associated with hiving-off in the past. But ultimately the pursuit of delegation, whether hiving-off or accountable management, comes into conflict with the traditional demand for unlimited political accountability. This fact of life can be altered only by a change of attitude on the part of politicians or by constitutional reforms which impose strict limits upon their ability to interfere.

Notes

1 Fulton Report, Vol. 2, para. 303.
2 Fulton Report, Vol. 1, para. 18.
3 ibid.
4 The system of staff management is outlined in J. Garrett, *The Management of Government* (London, 1972) Chaps 1 and 8. See also Sir William Armstrong, *Personnel Management in the Civil Service* (London, 1971).
5 R. G. S. Brown, 'Fulton and Morale', *Public Administration* Vol. 49 (1971) pp. 185–95.
6 T. Burns and G. M. Stalker, The Management of Innovation (London, 1966). Burns and Stalker identified the polar types of 'mechanistic' and 'organic' forms of organization after a study of firms adapting to changing market and technological conditions, mainly in the electronics industry.
7 Fulton Report, Vol. 1, para. 150.
8 Fulton Report, Vol. 1, para. 154.
9 These experiments are discussed in Garrett, op. cit., Chap. 4.
10 Fulton Report, Vol 1, paras 155–6.
11 *Eleventh Report from the Expenditure Committee 1976–77*, H.C. 535, Vol. II (I), pp. 21–4.
12 *Expenditure Committee*, op. cit., Vol. II (I), pp. 285–7. See also J. G. Cuckney, 'The Commercial Approach to Government Operations', *Management Services in Government* Vol. 29 (1974) pp. 121–9.
13 These problems are discussed by Rudolf Klein in 'The Politics of PPB', *Political Quarterly* Vol. 43 (1972) pp. 270–81.
14 Cuckney, op. cit., p. 127.
15 See Ann Robinson in S. A. Walkland and M. Ryle (eds), *The Commons in the Seventies* (London, 1977) Chap. 7.
16 Cuckney, op. cit., pp. 128–9.
17 H. Morrison, *Socialisation and Transport* (London, 1933) p. 137.
18 Sir James Dunnett, 'The Civil Service: Seven Years after Fulton', *Public Administration* Vol. 54 (1976) p. 376.
19 D. N. Chester, 'Public Corporations and the Classification of Administrative Bodies', *Political Studies* Vol. 1 (1953) pp. 34–52.

20 D. C. Hague, W. J. M. Mackenzie and A. Barker, *Public Policy and Private Interests* (London, 1975).
21 Sir Geoffrey Vickers, *The Art of Judgment* (London, 1965) Chap. 13.
22 D. C. Pitt, 'Bureaucratic Adaptation: The British Post Office. A case study of the telecommunications function' (Manchester University Ph.D. thesis, 1977).
23 D. K. Price, *The Scientific Estate* (Cambridge, Mass., 1965) p. 224.
24 *Fifth Report from the Select Committee on Nationalised Industries 1977–78*, H.C. 238.
25 *The Financial and Economic Obligations of the Nationalised Industries*, Cmnd. 1337 (1961); *Nationalised Industries. A Review of Economic and Financial Objectives*, Cmnd. 3437 (1967).
26 See, for example, the views of Christopher Foster in J. A. G. Griffith (ed.), *From Policy to Administration* (London, 1976) Chap. 7.
27. *First Report from the Select Committee on Nationalised Industries 1973–74*, H.C. 65, para. 108.
28 National Economic Development Office, *A Study of UK Nationalised Industries* (London, 1976).
29 *The Nationalised Industries*, Cmnd. 7131 (1978).
30 See, for example, the report of the Wider Issues Review Team, *Civil Servants and Change* (London, 1975).

XIII
Ministers
and their staff

Review of argument

In earlier chapters, the present structure of the British civil service and its relationship to the political system have been described. We started by looking at the changing task of public administration, and saw that the essential problem was one of meeting incompatible demands. The administrative structure and individual public servants have to serve different purposes at the same time. It is partly a clash of goals – the expansion of health services and of road building programmes somehow have to be reconciled with one another and with the overall economy goal. But it is also a clash of operating modes – different parts of the total job demand different standards of relevance and a different administrative approach. The qualities needed to streamline a school building programme are not those needed to negotiate an incomes policy nor to help a Minister deal with criticism in Parliament. There is a tension between a Minister's need for loyal servants and the need for those concerned with a developing service to take forceful initiatives; between meticulous attention to detail and the courage to take entrepreneurial risks; between central coordination and flexible, speedy decision-making.

The brief survey of administrative theory in Part Two helped to clarify the problem by demonstrating the need for organizational choice and compromise. Within an organization, individual decisions can be slanted by controlling staff selection, training and career development and also by modifying the administrative structure so that appropriate factors are given prior attention. Human limitations make it impossible to achieve more than a limited amount of sensitivity in any one group of people. When too much is expected of a single piece of administrative machinery, there must be compromise. If a compromise is not reached deliberately, a point of equilibrium will be determined by the strength of competing pressures. (For example long-term planning will inevitably take second place to parliamentary business if the same people are responsible for both.) Alternatively, tasks can be divided and different aspects allocated to different parts of the machine, but in that case some coordinating mechanism is required. We saw that political accountability is an important coordinating device in the public sector – to the extent that less accountability means less integration – but that lay control has certain characteristics, both useful and potentially harmful, which compel attention to the exact part played by a lay assembly in the policy-determining system and to the stage in policy-formulation at which it is exercised.

Using this framework we have examined some particular problems in British public administration. The scope of government activity and the complexity of many of its tasks have increased so much that an administrative system fashioned in an earlier age has been placed under very great strain. A good deal of adaptation has taken place within the system as a more or less spontaneous reaction to changing circumstances. Ministers have had to delegate more to their officials, new departments have been created, and the civil service has grown both in size and diversity. But there have also been more deliberate attempts to reform administrative structures and processes to cope with new demands. New planning techniques have been introduced both to increase the amount of information available to decision-makers and to strengthen the influence of longer-term considerations in policy-making. There have been experiments in the grouping of functions between departmental Ministers, designed to integrate decision-making on related issues. Changes have been made in the administrative structure in order to provide greater freedom in the management of executive activities. We have found that for a number of reasons the effectiveness of these reforms has varied. But our analysis of them has constantly returned to the necessity of organizational choice in order to balance the conflicting functions of the administrative system.

So far in Part Three we have concentrated mainly upon structural problems. But each of the issues we have discussed has major implications for the staffing of the civil service. The development of planning calls for new skills and for changes in the deployment of staff so as to ensure that long-term considerations are not always subordinated to short-term demands. Changes in the distribution of functions between departments affect the way in which officials approach their work, and developments such as the creation of 'giant' departments alter the balance between different aspects of the workload of particular officials and affect their career opportunities. Hiving-off and accountable management have been advocated as a means of modifying the environment in which officials work and of giving specialist staff a greater role in management.

In this final chapter we will concentrate upon the question of staffing by considering the sort of staff assistance that Ministers need, as part of a final general discussion of the administrative process. Traditionally, a Minister's closest advisers and assistants have been generalist administrators. Their role has, however, been under strong attack for some time. As we saw in Part One, one of the Fulton Committee's principal objectives was the abolition of the generalist, and although none of the reforms of the 1970s has fundamentally altered the kind of staff support given to Ministers it has remained a very controversial topic. In 1977 the Expenditure Committee received much the same evidence on this question as its predecessor had ten years' earlier, for instance from the Institute of Professional Civil Servants attacking the subordinate position of specialists, and from the Society of Civil and Public Servants criticizing the Administration Trainee scheme on the grounds that it placed too much emphasis on academic qualifications in preference to practical experience of government work.

The traditional pattern

In the traditional administrative system, the generalist performed a key role. Within his department his expert knowledge of administrative structure and process facilitated the translation of the Minister's political ideas into workable schemes, and his detached judgement provided a link between the broad objectives of the politician and the more specific orientation of the sectional and specialist interests of professional colleagues and outside groups. In Whitehall generally his breadth of experience facilitated inter-departmental coordination. Many of his functions have been mentioned in earlier chapters but it is worth recapitulating and reformulating them here.

1 The general administrator is in the first instance a *facilitator*. If the politician (or the expert) provides ideas and motive force someone has to ensure that decisions are properly recorded, processed and implemented. This is partly a secretarial function. It becomes more complex when implementation involves securing financial allocations, obtaining formal authority from Cabinet committees, preparing amending regulations for approval by Parliament and perhaps referring proposals to interested parties. Such a role calls for knowledge of the system and some sense of what is possible. It does not demand sympathy with political objectives, nor does it call for a great deal of technical knowledge of the field.

2 A more demanding role for the general administrator is that of *mediator*. It becomes especially important when political or financial constraints have to be placed on technical initiative. The task of the mediator is to discover what is politically and financially possible and then to persuade specialist colleagues and outside groups to work within these constraints. However, if it is made clear that these limits are intolerable, the mediator will try to have them eased. This mediating role is frequently performed by Ministers, but they need advice and assistance. To do this successfully, a knowledge of the machine and a fairly sophisticated understanding of different value systems are necessary. The mediator needs not only to be attuned to his

Minister's wishes and to be familiar with the relevant professional or sectional interests but at the same time to be aware
of the conventions of a collegiate system of decision-making and
of the requirements of the system of financial control.

3 Somebody, however, has to take decisions. There is a need for
arbiters. Again, this is ultimately a political function. But the
time of Ministers is limited and they need assistants both to
take decisions on their behalf and to narrow the field and
sharpen the issues involved in questions coming to them for
decision. This role demands the ability to compare and reconcile
conflicting priorities. In short, the successful arbiter must
possess the power of judgement. However this is a quality which
is difficult to define, and there is little agreement as to how
it can be attained. At one extreme are those who believe that
it is an innate quality and that all that needs to be done is to
devise selection procedures which identify those who possess
it. At the other are those who deny its existence and believe
that decision-making can be reduced to terms in which problems can be solved by the application of objective techniques.
Generally, however, it is argued that the politician, or his
adviser, needs to be able to use whatever techniques are available but that he needs to remain sceptical of 'formulae' and
to have the flair to choose between objectives which often
cannot be reduced to simple terms.

The selection, training and career management of administrators
in the civil service have traditionally been geared to the performance of these functions and, as we have seen, they have not been
changed fundamentally, despite the criticisms of the Fulton
Committee. The Civil Service Selection Board tests are based upon
a job analysis of the post of Assistant Secretary, originally conducted soon after the war but modified to take account of changing
requirements, which indicated that administrators needed a mixture of academic and practical ability: they had to be able to sense,
isolate and define problems; to formulate solutions to them; to
accomplish these solutions through people and through paper; and
'to persist in so doing'.[1] General knowledge of the machine and
the acquisition of administrative wisdom is developed through a

fairly mobile career, in which administrators pick up bits of experience from one branch and apply it in another. Communication between departments is facilitated by inculcating, through common training and cross-postings, a shared set of values against which administrators can interpret the changing requirements of a complicated coordinating machine, part legal, part administrative and part political, whose convictions are nowhere codified and are constantly being modified, without serious breakdown in communication. This sort of mixed experience has in the past helped administrators to develop a political sense and an awareness of the possible. They have become quasi-politicians, dealing with Ministers as informed laymen communicating with the slightly less informed.

The future of the generalist administrator

It is generally accepted that administrators selected and trained in this way are highly proficient at operating the government machine and in serving Ministers – that they perform the functions of *facilitator* and *mediator* effectively. These roles, however, are not sufficient to account for their pre-eminence in the service. In many professional organizations, including some scientific establishments staffed by civil servants, generalists performing these tasks are responsible to scientifically qualified superiors.[2] Rather, it is the function of arbitration which lies behind the dominant position of generalists in most departments. It is here that their intellect, political flair and detached judgement – qualities which other staff may possess in less measure because they have been selected and trained on different criteria – have been regarded as essential.

Since about 1960, however, it has frequently been alleged that generalists are no longer capable of performing this role adequately.[3] It is argued that the business of government is now so complex that they are unable to understand much of the material that is presented to them for approval and that decision-making frequently involves the use of techniques which require extensive training and practice to master. There is a danger, therefore, that decisions will be taken without a proper understanding of their

implications and that techniques will be applied without an awareness of their limitations. Alternatively, an administrator who is
out of his depth may be reluctant to reach a decision at all. This
adds to the frustration of the experts, who in any case have to
spend much of their time attempting to explain what they are doing
to such laymen, thus being distracted from more important work
for which they have primarily been employed. Nor is the
generalist merely out of his depth within his department. Many
areas of administration are now highly specialized, and the successful administrator needs to be able to speak the language of those
with whom he is dealing and to be aware of current developments in the field.

On these grounds the philosophy of the generalist and the part
that such officials play in the civil service has come under attack
from many quarters. On the one hand, a larger role has been
advocated for specialist civil servants in policy-making and
management. However, it is evident that most specialists would
not want to take over entirely from their administrative colleagues
and that they could do so only to the detriment of their specialist
expertise. It is therefore accepted that some officials should concentrate upon administrative work but it is argued that if they
are to do this effectively they need to specialize themselves in order
to develop 'a real understanding of, and familiarity with, the
principles, techniques and trends of development in the subject-
matter of the field in which (they are) operating'.[4]

The arguments for such administrative specialization are very
plausible. Although little systematic research has been done in
the civil service on the work that administrators actually do,
comparable with the studies conducted in industry by Rosemary
Stewart and others, no one would dispute that the skills needed
in different posts vary very widely.[5] However, any change in the
recruitment and training of administrators which was designed to
take account of this variety might well make them less able to
perform other parts of their work. It is not realistic to expect all
civil servants individually to become equipped as specialists (a)
in the problems of a specific service, (b) in management techniques
and (c) in operating a highly complex piece of machinery for taking,
justifying and coordinating political decisions. Greater emphasis

on (a) and (b), as was advocated by Fulton, would be likely to lead to weakness in (c). This can be seen by returning to our classification of administrative functions.

As a *facilitator*, the administrator who specialized would be in a better position to grasp the essentials of particular problems in his field. He would be able to acquire an expert knowledge of the relevant parts of the legislative machine and would still presumably have been selected partly for his fluency on paper. He might, however, be less able, because of his narrower career, to see the value of an administrative procedure that had worked well in a different field, and his more limited experience might make him less useful in assisting his Minister to perform the full range of his duties as a member of the government.

As a· *mediator* he would still know the rules governing the extraction of money from the Treasury and the grant of powers from the legislature. In bargaining over these things he would be likely to argue strongly on behalf of a service to which he was committed and be reluctant to accept external disadvantages to what he was advocating. He would thus be a difficult adversary for those responsible for coordinating the work of departments in the Treasury and elsewhere. As a result, the work of government would probably be less well integrated. An administrator brought up exclusively in a specialist field would be bound to identify with it. Already there is a risk that a civil servant in, say, the Ministry of Agriculture, his shoulders bowed with years of patient negotiation with the National Farmers' Union, is so acutely aware of their interests that he becomes incapable of looking at agricultural problems in the light of wider issues.

It is as an *arbiter* that the specialist administrator would probably be least effective, because all his training and experience would have been geared towards a special group of interests. Specialization would thus have the effect of limiting the ability of administrators to apply the elusive quality of judgement to the proposals of their specialist colleagues and the views of affected groups. It would leave politicians very much on their own in taking an overall view of questions which have wider implications. The effect of undermining the generalist nature of administration might well be to place a greater load on Ministers for overall appraisal.

Some would see it as an advantage that the system should compel Ministers to play a positive role in evaluating expert advice, in dealing with outside groups and in resolving interdepartmental disputes. Indeed, the quasi-political role of senior civil servants has frequently been criticized.[6] However, the problem is that ability to perform these tasks is only one of the criteria for appointment to ministerial office. Moreover, as we saw in Part One, the pressure on Ministers is already so great that it would seem unwise to reduce the quality of their support unless the demands made on them could also be limited. With a weak Minister, there could be an unpleasant vacuum between the political and executive systems which is at present filled by senior administrators.

This sort of analysis can also be applied to the more radical proposal that specialists should supplant generalists. Again it is the task of arbitration which is crucial. There is no reason why specialists should not undertake the functions of *facilitator* and *mediator* should they wish to do so and were they prepared to work within the system of political and financial control. It is doubtful, however, that, given these conventions, they would be able to assist in choosing between alternative proposals by relating them to the Minister's own priorities and to the needs of the government as a whole.

In short, therefore, those who have advocated the erosion of the generalist character of administration in the civil service have failed to recognize the problem of organizational choice that has been outlined in this book. The Fulton Committee proposed strengthening the managerial efficiency of government departments through changes in their structure and staffing, but it failed to clarify the cost that would be incurred in terms of other aspects of departmental performance. In this instance, the Committee paid insufficient attention to certain aspects of the administrator's function which would inevitably be affected adversely by its proposal for greater specialization.

This is not to argue that the Fulton proposals were without any merit or that the traditional pattern of administration in the civil service cannot be improved. The point is only that it is essential to take account of all the tasks that any group of staff undertake before deciding what skills are needed and how they can best be obtained. In the case of administration in the civil service, it seems likely that there is such variety of work that different departments will need distinctive patterns of staffing, and that within any particular department there will be a need for different types of administrator. For instance, in most conventional 'purpose' departments a need might be identified for three types: (a) managerial specialists to work in executive divisions, including personnel and organization; (b) specialized administrators, perhaps younger, and with training and ability to enable them to contribute to long-term planning; and (c) administrators recruited and trained in the traditional manner, to provide secretarial support for Ministers. But this is only speculation. The actual needs of departments can be identified only through detailed analysis of their work. A limited enquiry of this kind was undertaken by the Civil Service Department in 1969.[7] It revealed that their requirements varied so much that a twofold division of administrative work, along the lines proposed by Fulton, was not practicable. The case for further specialization by administrators was accepted but little progress has been made in following this up. Moreover, even when departmental needs have been identified, difficult questions remain as to how the necessary skills are best obtained.

So far this discussion has been conducted in very general terms. However, in recent years various developments have occurred which have underlined the limited nature of the Fulton Committee's picture of administration in the civil service and which have spotlighted the contribution that the generalist is still able to make. First, more explicit attention has been paid to the nature of the political support that Ministers need. Secondly, attempts have been made to strengthen the centre of government which have focused additional attention upon the sort of staff needed to undertake the politically sensitive work of policy coordination.

A political secretariat

Traditionally in Britain Ministers have looked exclusively to career officials for staff support. Senior civil servants, ultimately the Permanent Secretary, have given a Minister advice on the decisions he has to take, and a small private office, composed entirely of officials, has provided him with general assistance on such matters as arranging meetings, handling correspondence and drafting speeches. The only 'political' support has come from junior Ministers and Parliamentary Private Secretaries who are themselves members of Parliament.

This system has come in for extensive criticism in recent years from those who believe that in such a system a Minister is heavily outbalanced by the civil service and needs the assistance of those who are committed to him personally and politically. This argument has taken two forms. One is that anonymous and faceless secretaries, with no political commitment, are incapable of taking initiatives and leading a Minister towards dynamic new policies.[8] The other version is that senior members of the civil service élite have strong political views of their own, which condition the advice they choose to give to Ministers.[9] But the implications are the same: that Ministers should be free to bring in temporary staff both to advise them on policy and to assist them generally in the performance of their departmental and other duties. Nor is it felt that junior Ministers and Parliamentary Private Secretaries can provide this kind of support as they have other loyalties and commitments. Moreover, increasingly the former have clear responsibilities of their own within the department.

Many of those who have argued in this way have looked favourably upon the 'ministerial cabinet' in France.[10] This is a small group of personal staff appointed by each Minister to act as a bridge between the political world and the administration. Most *cabinets* have between ten and twelve members, the only major exception being that of the Prime Minister which is almost three times as large. Members of the *cabinet* help the Minister with his political relationships (dealing, for instance, with members of the National Assembly), with his constituency affairs and with his political party. They provide a link between the Minister and the quasi-independent 'directorates' that make up a French department. In this respect they combine some of the non-managerial functions of the British Permanent Secretary (who generally does not exist in France) with those of the private office. They also serve as a permanent brains trust at the immediate disposal of the Minister. Although 80 per cent of the members of *cabinets* are career civil servants, they are committed to their master and relationships are generally very close.

In fact, as frequently happens, change in Britain has occurred in a piecemeal manner. Since 1964 the practice of Ministers bringing in personal aides has grown steadily. By 1977 there were 26 special advisers, as they are now generally known, working in most but not all major departments. Generally one, or occasionally two, advisers were working for any particular Minister but there were five in the DHSS and the Prime Minister had a team of six advisers.

The sort of people recruited in this way can be divided into two categories, although it is not always easy in practice to distinguish clearly between them. First, there have been experts, most of whom have been involved in the preparation of party policy and who have been appointed to assist in its implementation. Thus, at the highest level, A. H. Halsey, a distinguished left-wing sociologist, was appointed by Anthony Crosland as research adviser in the DES in 1965; similarly Brian Abel-Smith, Professor of Social Administration at the London School of Economics, has twice been brought in by Labour Ministers as an adviser in the DHSS. Many of the economists appointed in 1964 were quasi-political, as were a number of the appointments made by the Conservative Government in 1970. The principal tasks of advisers of this type are to examine papers as they go to Ministers in order to advise them of problems, especially those having party political or electoral implications, and to contribute to the planning of policy.[11]

Secondly, Ministers have appointed younger and less experienced personal assistants to help them generally in coping with the burdens of office by supplementing the work of the private office and undertaking tasks, such as political liaison, which career civil servants cannot easily perform.

Despite a number of problems, on matters such as the access of special advisers to confidential papers and their freedom to participate openly in party and constituency affairs both for their political masters and on their own behalf, this system has gained widespread acceptance. It is favoured by politicians of all political parties, whether of ministerial rank or on the backbenches. Most of the initial qualms of senior civil servants have also been allayed. In part this may be because the number of advisers has not been sufficient to constitute a serious threat to the relationship which civil servants have traditionally enjoyed with Ministers. But it is also a reflection of the fact that in general special advisers complement rather than supplant civil servants by providing advice and support of a kind which career officials cannot offer.

The introduction of outside advisers who enjoy very close relationships with Ministers does of course introduce an element of competition. As one civil servant in the DHSS put it: 'Nothing of major importance is decided without a political adviser being present at the meeting that decides it.'[12] Nor can a permanent civil servant give a Minister the same sort of commitment that he expects from an adviser whose position is entirely dependent upon his patronage. But the career official does have a number of considerable assets which the temporary adviser cannot match. Special advisers cannot provide the continuity and experience which is available to a Minister in his private office and from his senior officials. Too much dependence upon such advisers could result in decisions being taken without full regard to their consequences, many of which can only be known to those who have long experience of working in government and in particular areas of activity. Decisions also need to be taken not only in the light of their effects within the Minister's own area of responsibility but of their consequences for other departments and the standing of the government as a whole. It is important therefore that Ministers should be advised of the wider implications of possible courses of action, a task which members of a service-wide cadre of officials are well placed to undertake.

Some doubts have been expressed as to the calibre of many special advisers.[13] Their position is inevitably a rather vulnerable one, dependent upon ministerial patronage and the survival in office of both Minister and Government. Their relationship with Ministers is largely a confidential one, and it is hard to see what attractions such a post, lacking both public recognition and a career outlet, could offer to candidates of experience and ability unless (like Brian Abel-Smith) they had strong commitments in a particular policy area. Such a system seems to work well in Washington; but Britain has no 'in-and-outer' tradition and a much less flexible career structure, both in government and in the universities. As a result it is likely that most recruits to these posts will be young and inexperienced – many of them seeing the position as a stepping-stone to their own political careers – who could well prove to be more of a handicap than an asset to Ministers by providing a source of friction in his relationship both with his political colleagues and the administrative machine. This points to another danger: that of abuse. Staff brought in on an *ad hoc* basis, enjoying very close relationships with Ministers and with access to confidential papers, but without being subject to the 'rules and understandings' that are inculcated by membership of a career service, could easily abuse their position.

Thus, although it is likely that the installation of special advisers will become an accepted feature of administration, the need for career officials as close advisers is not going to disappear. Given the constitutional framework in which they operate, Ministers need advisers who are familiar with the implications for their work of individual and collective ministerial responsibility. In other respects too it may well be that the qualities of loyalty, self-effacement and administrative and political wisdom will come more easily from career administrators. A clear lesson is to be learned from the fact that such a high proportion of members of French 'ministerial cabinets' are career civil servants and that even in Washington many posts which are theoretically political are filled by career officials.[14]

Central coordination of policy

Apart from quasi-political secretarial duties, three fundamental requirements have to be met by the administrative machine as a whole: (a) effectiveness and economy in pursuit of particular goals (without prejudice to the pursuit of other goals); (b) some means of injecting political values, and a respect for other goals, into (a); (c) an apparatus which allows major political decisions to be taken by bringing disparate goals together, evaluating them and where necessary suggesting changes of direction.

The first two requirements have been discussed at length. The first calls for the institutionalization of goals in agencies and departments with specialized staff, some of whom work on long-term questions in planning units. The second is provided through the mechanisms of political accountability. The third requirement presents the greatest challenge to organization – it raises questions about the machinery of government, the distribution of functions between departments, the role of the central coordinating machine, and the staff who work in it.

Since 1960, as we have seen in earlier chapters, a considerable amount of attention has been paid in Britain to improving the central coordination of government. First, planning and control of public expenditure have been extended through the introduction and refinement of the Public Expenditure Survey System. Secondly, central control of manpower and of organization has been strengthened by the creation of a new department, the Civil Service Department, charged exclusively with this responsibility. And thirdly, the position of the Cabinet, traditionally the apex of the policy-making system and the final arbiter in cases of disagreement between Ministers, has been bolstered by developments in the Cabinet Office and by the creation of the CPRS.

Before considering the implications of these changes for staffing, it is necessary to elaborate upon the developments in the Cabinet Office. Traditionally it has been concerned more with the smooth movement of paper than with the evaluation of policy, its main function being to service the Cabinet and its committees, taking minutes and recording decisions which are transmitted throughout Whitehall. During the 1960s, however, the Cabinet Office began to emerge as a more positive instrument of coordination. It provided the base for two of the Labour Government's senior advisers, and the Central Statistical Office, which since its inception during the Second World War has been part of the Cabinet Office, was strengthened. This trend continued after 1970 with the establishment of a European Unit, first to oversee the negotiations with the EEC and then to coordinate the work of other departments in dealing with the institutions of the EEC. For a short time there was also a unit on devolution. Most important, however, was the creation of the CPRS in 1971, which 'physically and constitutionally' is part of the Cabinet Office.[15]

Most of these developments may be said to have bolstered the central position of the general administrator. In Chapter III we noted that the most able administrators were generally posted to one of the three central departments – Treasury, Civil Service Department and Cabinet Office – during their journey to the top. Thus, if the role of these departments has been strengthened, so has the influence of those who are the most 'generalist' in the civil service. Nor have the changes in the role of the central departments been accompanied by alterations in their staffing. For example, in 1977 the official in charge of the divisions of the Treasury which are responsible for the control of public expenditure was a classics graduate from Oxford whose working life had been spent almost exclusively in the Treasury.

In many ways the CPRS is a symbol of the importance which is still attached to generalist virtues. It has about sixteen to nineteen members, half of whom are career civil servants on secondment from their departments and the rest recruited from outside – from universities, industry, financial institutions and international organizations. Among its staff there are a number of specialists, for instance economists and scientists, but others are high-flying members of the Administration Group and bright outsiders, few of whom have obviously relevant qualifications and experience. But the CPRS is in the generalist tradition in a more fundamental way.[16] Its whole *raison d'être* is the belief that a group of highly intelligent people who have little or no previous knowledge or experience of an issue have a contribution to make to its resolution. In some cases those who are chosen to conduct particular enquiries have appropriate qualifications; but this is not invariably so and, in any case, the important point is that they are outsiders who bring a fresh outlook to bear on a problem. Nor does the CPRS have extensive research and information-gathering services of its own. In the generalist manner it depends upon others for information, relying upon the intellect of its members and their power of judgement to assess the arguments of experts.

The other striking feature of the CPRS is the fact that all its work is intensely political in the sense that it advises Ministers on priorities and relates particular decisions to the overall strategy of the government. This very sensitive task is not performed by advisers who are openly committed to a particular political party, but by a group composed partly of career officials and the rest (with only one obvious exception) of members selected on the basis of their ability rather than political affiliation. Since 1974 some of the more overtly political work has been transferred to the Prime Minister's Policy Unit, whose members are all committed supporters of the Government, but the role of the CPRS has not radically changed. It remains a symbol of the willingness of Ministers in Britain to depend upon impartial staff for advice on matters which are very close to their political choices.

Developments in the field of central coordination during the last twenty years thus point to a continuing recognition of the usefulness of advisers in the traditional mould, able to communicate easily with non-expert politicians, politically sensitive and strong in what one observer called 'more general qualities of judgement and decisiveness, and the ability to understand how the reshaping of values may be embodied in and implemented by public policy'.[17] For such people the main requirement apart from basic ability is probably wide experience of quasi-political work in different contexts – in other words, a career pattern similar to that of a high-flier in the Administration Group.

This kind of work is only one of the administrator's tasks. Others require different skills which point to other patterns of recruitment and career management. It may well be that many administrators need to specialize either in particular areas of activity or in particular forms of administration. But in so doing they will become less proficient in other parts of their work.

Some of the attempts to substitute for, or complement, the generalist administrator, like the predominance given to economists in 1964–70 and to business experts in 1970–4, have had fairly limited success. But the increasing politicization of what were once thought of as administrative issues, as well as the growing burden on Ministers, suggest that the role of the political adviser, both in policy and in private office functions, will become increasingly important.

Conclusion

In this chapter a single aspect of the staffing of the civil service has been examined in order to illustrate the nature of the administrative process and to reinforce some of the central arguments of this book. In the first case, we have seen that the political needs of Ministers both individually in their departments and collectively in the Cabinet account to a large extent for the continuing importance of generalist administrators among their staff. Here, as in all the other areas discussed in Part Three, political relationships limit the options for administrative reform. Secondly, the need for organizational choice has again been apparent, and we have attempted to clarify the issues involved and to suggest how the consequences of change can be assessed. Argument and experiment on all the issues discussed in this book are certain to continue in the future. It is our belief that systematic research, undertaken in the light of theoretical writing on organizations both public and private, has much to contribute to this debate and hopefully to the solution of many of the problems in public administration.

Notes

1 Civil Service Commission, *Memorandum on the Use of the Civil Service Selection Board in the Reconstruction Examinations* (London, 1950).
2 For instance, in the Royal Aircraft Establishment at Farnborough a central administrative unit, headed by an Assistant Secretary, is responsible to the scientific director.
3 See Chapter IV.
4 Fulton Report, Vol. 1, para. 41.
5 This point is discussed by Lewis Gunn in his 'Six Questions about Management Training' in R. A. W. Rhodes (ed.), *Training in the Civil Service*, Joint University Council for Social and Public Administration (London, 1977).
6 For instance by Labour MPs on the Expenditure Committee, *Eleventh Report from the Expenditure Committee 1976–77*, H.C. 535, Vol. I, p. lxxix.
7 The findings of the survey are outlined in the Civil Service National Whitley Council's report, *Fulton: A Framework for the Future* (London, 1970) pp. 15–17.
8 See, for example, *Expenditure Committee*, op. cit., pp. lxxx–lxxxi.

9 See, for example, J. Haines, *The Politics of Power* (London, 1977).

10 The system of 'ministerial cabinets' is outlined in E. N. Suleiman, *Politics, Power and Bureaucracy in France* (Princeton, N.J., 1974).

11 The role of special advisers was set out in a statement by the then Prime Minister in 1975 which is included in H. Wilson, *The Governance of Britain* (London, 1976) pp. 202–5. See also J. E. Mitchell, 'Special Advisers: A Personal View', *Public Administration* Vol. 56 (1978) pp. 87–98.

12 Quoted in *Health and Social Service Journal* (16 September 1977) p. 1320.

13 These problems are discussed by R. Klein and J. Lewis in 'Advice and Dissent in British Government: The Case of the Special Advisers', *Policy and Politics* Vol. 6 (1977) pp. 1–25.

14 Suleiman, op. cit., p. 203; D. Mann, *The Assistant Secretaries: Problems and Processes of Appointment* (Washington D.C., 1965) Chap. 2.

15 See Chapter x, pp. 245–7.

16 The distinctive contribution of the Central Policy Review Staff is discussed in H. Heclo and A. Wildavsky, *The Private Government of Public Money* (London, 1975) Chap. 7.

17 Fulton Report, Vol. 1, p. 102 (reservation by Lord Simey).

Guide to
further reading

A complete bibliography for the ground covered in this book would be too long to be helpful. The reader who wishes to pursue a topic in more detail, or to check our interpretation, has at least a starting point in the endnotes to each chapter. Author references can be traced through the name index. The following suggestions for further reading are limited to selected books which are important in themselves or are fairly readable (and sometimes both).

Everyone should read the two civil service classics: the Northcote–Trevelyan *Report on the Organisation of the Permanent Civil Service*, C. 1713 (1854), reprinted in 1968 as Appendix B to the Fulton Report; and the Haldane *Report of the Machinery of Government Committee*, Cd. 9230 (1918). Their modern successors have a shorter life-expectancy. But no permanent harm will result from reading the Fulton Committee's *Report on the Civil Service 1966–68*, Cmnd. 3638 (1968) or the White Paper on *The Reorganisation of Central Government*, Cmnd. 4506 (1970), provided that they are interpreted in the light of our comments.

On the historical development of the civil service in the nineteenth century, H. Parris's *Constitutional Bureaucracy* (London, 1969) and M. W. Wright's *Treasury Control of the Civil Service 1854–1874* (London, 1969) are probably the best sources. Good first-hand accounts of the civil service in the twentieth century are provided by H. E. Dale in *The Higher Civil Service of Great Britain* (London, 1941), which deals with the years just before the Second World War, and by C. H. Sisson in *The Spirit of British Administration*, 2nd edn (London, 1966), which covers the decade after the war.

There are now a large number of good general surveys of the British system of government. Particularly useful for the reader whose primary interest is in public administration is A. H. Hanson and M. Walles, *Governing Britain*, 2nd edn (London, 1975). The institutional reforms of the 1960s and 1970s are surveyed by Frank Stacey in his *British Government 1966 to 1975: Years of Reform* (London, 1975). A rather different introduction to British politics and government, which concentrates upon the policy-making process, is provided by Brian Smith in *Policy-Making in British Government* (London, 1976).

Specifically on the contemporary system of public administration in the United Kingdom, Brian Smith and Jeffrey Stanyer's *Administering Britain* (London, 1976) is a first-rate general text, which discusses decentralized as well as central administration. Otherwise there are few general surveys. R. A. Chapman and A. Dunsire's *Style in British Administration* (London, 1971) is a useful collection of readings, some of which are difficult to obtain in their original form.

To keep track of current developments in British administration it is necessary to consult official publications. Particularly important for the topics covered in Part One are the annual reports of the Civil Service College and the Civil Service Commission, and the annual publication *Civil Service Statistics*. These and other official papers are available from HM Stationery Office, which publishes daily, monthly and annual lists of its publications. The more important publications dealing with public administration are noted in the quarterly issues of *Public Administration*, the journal of the Royal Institute of Public Administration. Since 1968 this journal has also included a survey of administrative developments, initially annually and, since 1973, biennially. Useful information on developments in the civil service since 1968 is contained in the evidence to the House of Commons Expenditure Committee enquiry, H.C. 535 (1976–77).

Sadly, informed discussion and analysis of current issues in British central administration is all too rare. Our endnotes refer to a number of useful articles but problems of access have generally hindered academic research. Special mention can be made of the work of two American academics, H. Heclo and A. Wildavsky. The focus of their book, *The Private Government of Public Money* (London, 1974) is on the system of public expenditure control, but they have also succeeded in providing a lucid account of many wider aspects of the administrative system. Nor have the large gaps in our knowledge been filled by civil servants, most of whom are reluctant to reflect upon administrative issues in public. One exception was Sir Richard Clarke, whose *New Trends in Government* (London, 1971) is a useful commentary by an insider on a number of recent developments. Officials also contribute occasional articles to journals such as *Public Administration* and *Management Services in Government*. Hardly surprisingly, politicians are more forthcoming, but their memoirs generally pay scant attention to administrative questions. There are exceptions, however. Particularly noteworthy is Richard Crossman, whose academic interest in the working of the system of government was maintained when he became a Cabinet Minister in the 1960s. This interest is reflected in his series of Godkin lectures, published under the title, *Inside View* (London, 1972) and in his diaries, *The Diaries of a Cabinet Minister* (3 vols, London, 1975, 1976, 1977). The latter provide a unique record of the life of a Minister and of his relationships with his colleagues and his advisers; but they need to be treated with some caution as Crossman's recollection and interpretation of events have not gone unchallenged.

On organization theory it is difficult to pick out a few books from the large number that are now available. Good general introductions by British authors are Tom Lupton's *Management and the Social Sciences*, 2nd edn (London, 1971), Rosemary Stewart's *The Reality of Management*, 2nd edn (London, 1967) and John Child's *Organization: A Guide to Problems and Practice* (London, 1977). More comprehensive surveys, largely American and most of which contain full bibliographies, include: J. G. March and H. A. Simon, *Organizations* (New York, 1958); A. Etzioni, *A Comparative Analysis of Complex Organizations*, 2nd edn (Glencoe, Ill., 1975); P. B. Applewhite, *Organizational Behavior* (Englewood Cliffs, N.J., 1965); P. M. Blau and W. R. Scott, *Formal Organizations*, 2nd edn (London, 1966); B. M. Gross, *The Managing of Organizations* (London, 1968); N. P. Mouzelis, *Organization and Bureaucracy*, 2nd edn (London, 1975). All these authors present their own distinctive points of view, as well as reviewing the field. Any one survey may therefore give an unbalanced picture. The most comprehensive work on policy-making is Yehezkel Dror's *Public Policymaking Re-examined* (San Francisco, 1968), which includes a massive bibliography.

A number of books are now available that attempt, as we have done, to apply theories of management and organization to the problems of public administration. A path-breaking study is Sir Geoffrey Vickers's *The Art of Judgment* (London, 1965) which seeks to understand the processes of judgement and decision in policy-making. Closer to our own approach is that of Michael Hill in his *The Sociology of Public Administration* (London, 1972) in which developments in organizational sociology are applied to issues such as administrative discretion, authority, bureaucracy and professionalism. Andrew Dunsire's *Administration:The Word and The Science* (London, 1973) contains an examination of the various bodies of theory and research that constitute administrative science and of the contribution they can make to our understanding of public administration. In his *Administrative Theories and Politics*, 2nd edn (London, 1977), Peter Self relates certain theories of the administrative process to various issues of administrative organization and behaviour with an emphasis on the politics of administration. Finally, Desmond Keeling's *Management in Government* (London, 1972) which is much wider in scope than its title suggests, contains a very thorough analysis of the nature of decision-making in government, drawing particularly upon the work of economists.

Name Index

Abel-Smith, B., 330, 331
Abramovitz, M., 44, 45
Adamson, Sir C., 111, 124
Albrow, M., 172
Allen, Sir D., 95
Anderson, Sir J., 45, 271
Applewhite, P. B., 172, 195, 340
Arbuthnot, G., 25
Argyris, C., 168, 172
Armstrong, Sir W., 64, 215, 317

Balogh, Lord, 110, 111, 124
Barker, A., 215, 318
Barker, Sir E., 106
Beer, S. H., 253
Bell, D., 13
Bellinger, Sir R., 111
Bentham, J., 24
Berkeley, H., 221
Berrill, Sir K., 109, 111
Blau, P. M., 197, 340
Booth, W., 24
Boyle, Sir E., 64
Bray, J., 227
Braybrooke, D., 196
Brech, E. F. L., 48, 171
Bridges, Sir E. (later Lord), 28, 41, 191,
    206, 271
Brittan, S., 42, 63, 124, 261
Brooke, H. (later Lord), 218, 219
Brown, G., 50, 147

Brown, R. G. S., 196, 234, 293, 294
Bruce-Gardyne, J., 124, 149, 274
Burke, E., 22
Burn, D., 263
Burns, T., 12, 166, 257, 297–8

Cairncross, Sir A., 109
Callaghan, J., 219
Campbell, G. A., 37
Catherwood, Sir F., 111
Chadwick, E., 26, 27
Chapman, B., 63, 123
Chapman, R. A., 65, 95, 339
Chapman, V., 206, 215
Chester, D. N., 292, 308
Child, J., 172, 340
Clark, Sir A., 39
Clark, A., 94, 150, 293
Clarke, Sir R., 264, 277, 281, 339
Cockfield, Sir A., 111
Cohen, E. W., 44
Compton, Sir E., 135
Coombes, D., 150
Crick, B., 151
Cripps, Sir S., 35, 48
Critchley, T. A., 37, 43
Crosland, A., 64, 281, 330
Crossman, R. H. S., 64, 124, 131, 149, 285,
    293, 294, 340
Crozier, M., 172
Cuckney, J. G., 124, 317

Cyert, R. M., 172, 195
Dale, H. E., 30–1, 37, 43–4, 338
Dearborn, D. C., 195
Devons, E., 37
Dickson, W. J., 172
Donnison, D. V., 204, 206
Downs, A., 185
Dror, Y., 176, 192, 340
Dubin, R., 257
Dugdale, Sir T., 39
Dunnett, Sir J., 317
Dunnill, F., 37
Dunsire, A., 199, 339, 340

Eliasberg, V. F., 44, 45
Etzioni, A., 195, 340

Fayol, H., 158–9, 166
Fisher, Sir W., 23, 30
Foster, C. D., 111, 318
Fox, C., 22
Franks, Lord, 37
Friend, J., 193
Fry, G. K., 242
Fulton, Lord, 50

Garrett, J., 172, 317
Gawthrop, L. C., 185
Godber, Sir G., 112
Greaves, H. R. G., 26, 33, 42
Grebenik, E., 82
Greenwood, R., 196
Gregory, R., 152
Griffith, J. A. G., 234, 318
Gross, B. M., 340
Grove, J. W., 187
Gunn, L. A., 336

Hague, D. C., 215, 318
Haines, J., 149, 337
Haire, M., 195
Halsey, A. H., 330
Hanson, A. H., 151, 339
Headey, B., 215
Heaton, R. N., 95
Heclo, H., 293, 337, 339
Hickson, D. J., 172
Hill, M. J., 172, 340
Hinings, C. R., 172, 196
Hood, C. C., 171
Houghton, Lord, 283
Howell, D., 293
Hussey, D., 196
Hutchesson, P., 152

Johnson, N., 64, 94, 151, 152
Jones, K., 264

Kaldor, Lord, 110, 111, 124
Kavanagh, D., 150
Keeling, D., 341
Kingdom, T. D., 64, 132, 147
Klein, R., 149, 317, 337
Kogan, M., 64, 215

Laski, H. J., 31, 291
Lee, J. M., 226, 292
Leemans, A. F., 94
Lever, H., 151
Levin, P. H., 186
Lewis, J., 149, 337
Lindblom, C. E., 191–2
Lupton, T., 12, 173, 340

Macaulay, Lord, 22
Mackenzie, W. J. M., 158, 187, 215, 318
Mackintosh, J. P., 142
Mair, R., 95
Mann, D., 337
Mansergh, N., 264
March, J. G., 172, 185, 195, 196, 340
Marre, Sir A., 136, 137
Marshak, J., 179, 195
Marshall, G., 150
Maxwell-Fyfe, Sir D., 39
Mayo, E., 172
Mellish, R., 219
Meyjes, Sir R., 111
Milne, Sir D., 293
Mitchell, J. E., 149, 337
Morrison, H. (later Lord), 35, 40, 48, 64, 305–6
Morton, W. W., 64
Mouzelis, N. P., 170, 340
Munro, C. K., 42

Neild, R., 63, 111
Newman, Sir G., 27
Nicholson, M., 63
Northcote, Sir S., 22

Parker, R. S., 199, 201
Parris, H., 44, 338
Pile, Sir W., 264
Pitt, D. C., 318
Playfair, Sir E., 55, 64, 231
Plowden, Lord, 35, 48
Plowden, W. J. L., 264
Pollitt, C., 263, 264
Posner, M., 111

Powell, J. E., 64, 215
Price, D. K., 123, 224, 229, 311
Pugh, D. S., 166

Ranson, S., 196
Ratcliff, A. R. N., 263
Razzell, E. J., 95
Redcliffe-Maud, Lord, 124
Regan, D. E., 116
Rhodes, G., 264
Rhodes, R. A. W., 95, 196, 336
Richards, P. G., 234
Ridley, F. F., 120, 123
Robinson, A., 151, 317
Robson, W. A., 173, 292
Roche, J. P., 234
Roethlisberger, F. J., 172
Roll, Sir E., 124
Roosevelt, President F., 157
Rose, R., 150, 234
Rothschild, Lord, 251
Rowntree, S., 24
Ryle, M., 150, 151, 152, 317

Sachs, S., 234
Sayre, W., 173
Schon, D. A., 167, 222
Scott, W. R., 197, 340
Seale, J. R., 263
Self, P. J. O., 185, 196, 198, 341
Sharpe, L. J., 234
Sheriff, P., 95
Simey, Lord, 337
Simon, H. A., 12, 172, 173, 184, 185, 195, 211, 213, 340
Sisson, C. H., 37, 54, 119, 338
Sleigh, J., 95
Sloman, M. B., 82
Smith, B. C., 93, 95, 292, 339
Snow, Lord, 275
Soskice, Sir F., 113
Spiers, M., 172

Stacey, F. A., 150, 151, 339
Stalker, G. M., 166, 257, 297–8
Stanyer, J., 93, 292, 339
Steel, D. R., 292
Stevens, A., 95
Stewart, R., 325, 340
Subramaniam, V., 94, 107, 199, 201, 213
Suleiman, E. N., 337
Summers, Sir S., 219

Taylor, B., 196
Taylor, F. W., 158, 159, 163
Thatcher, M., 127, 243
Thomas, H., 63
Thompson, J. D., 167
Thompson, V. A., 265
Thorpe, J., 274
Train, C. J., 264
Trevelyan, Sir C., 22, 26
Tuden, A., 167

Urwick, L., 171

Vernon, R. V., 264
Vickers, Sir G., 173, 250, 318, 340

Walker, N., 37
Walkland, S. A., 150, 151, 152, 317
Walles, M., 339
Weber, M., 159–60, 163, 166, 179, 210
Wheare, K. C., 22, 45, 264
Wildavsky, A., 293, 337, 339
Wilding, R. W. L., 65
Wilkins, L. T., 183
Williams, Sir L., 95
Willson, F. M. G., 292
Wilson, H., 64, 151, 274, 276, 293, 337
Wood, B., 124
Woodward, J., 12, 166
Wright, M. W., 152, 263, 338

Young, H., 150

Zuckerman, Lord, 112

Subject Index

administration, the general interest in, 201–3; public and private, 197–201
Administration Group, 67–91, 97, 104, 207, 334, 335; career structure, 86–91; recruitment, 73–80; size 67–8; structure, 68–72; training, 80–6
Administration Trainees, 69, 70, 72, 74, 75–80, 82–6, 88–9, 321
Administrative Class, 26, 29–30, 37–8, 61, 99
Advisory, Conciliation and Arbitration Service, 306, 307
advisory committees, 207–8, 249
Agriculture and Fisheries, Ministry of, 39, 139, 142, 268, 326
American Civil Service, 79, 106, 107, 108, 131, 332; see also USA
anonymity, 126, 127, 131–4
Arts Council, 307
Assheton Report (1944), 52
Assistant Principals, 61, 75, 77, 81, 90
Assistant Secretaries, 26, 31, 38, 41, 43–4, 55, 69, 70, 74, 85, 90, 104, 148, 323
Australian Civil Service, 106, 107, 108
automatic data processing, 82, 97

Bank of England, 307
Beveridge Report (1942), 33, 41, 282
Bridgeman Report (1932), 32, 99
British Board of Film Censors, 308
British Broadcasting Corporation, 246–7, 305, 307

British Leyland Ltd, 307
British Petroleum Ltd, 307
British Railways Board, 307
British Steel Corporation, 151, 249, 307, 312
Brownlow Committee on Administrative Management (USA), 157, 159, 213, 214
bureaucracy, 159–62; representative, 79–80

Cabinet, 128, 202, 227, 241, 246, 252, 262, 266, 269, 275, 277–8, 285, 306, 333
Cabinet committees, 41, 53, 128, 208, 247, 322
Cabinet Office, 35, 91, 97, 245, 250, 267, 270, 279, 280, 333, 334
cabinets, ministerial, 107, 329–30, 332
Cambridge University, 62, 77, 78
Canadian Civil Service, 107
career structure(s), 86–91, 103–5, 187, 188, 297
Carnegie Corporation of New York, 308
Carnegie Institute of Technology, 180, 189
Central Health Service Council, 207
Central Policy Review Staff (CPRS), 109, 245–7, 251, 260, 281, 282, 333–5; report on overseas representation (1977), 108, 141, 246–7
Central Statistical Office, 97, 250, 333
Centre for Administrative Studies, 81
Chief Inspector of Constabulary, 132
Chief Medical Officer, 112, 132
Chief Scientific Adviser, 97, 112

Chrysler UK Ltd, 141, 151
Civil Aviation Authority, 306, 307
Civil and Public Services Association, 71, 94
Civil Research Committee, 28
civil servants: administrative, 68–93; characteristics needed by, 56–8; numbers of, 28–9, 35–6, 36–7, 66–8; political environment of, 125–49; political neutrality of, 88; professional and specialist, 96–122; see also career structure, promotion, recruitment, training
civil service: in the eighteenth century, 21, 26; in the nineteenth century, 21–7; in the years 1900–39, 27–33; in the post-war period, 33–44; in the 1960s, 47–63; in 1977: size and composition of, 66–8; economists in, 97, 109–11, 330; graduates in, 36, 60, 61, 75–8, 106; industrialists in, 111–12; Royal Commissions on, 96 (1912–15), 30, 32, 98 (1929–31), 38 (1953–5), see also Fulton Report; statisticians in, 98, 250; structural requirements of, 58–9; tasks of, 52–9
Civil Service College, 60, 61, 81–6, 103
Civil Service Commission, 23, 42, 43, 50, 73–7, 90, 104
Civil Service Department, 12, 51, 73, 82, 90, 91, 92, 93, 102, 156, 220, 267, 272, 274, 276, 280, 281–2, 287, 296, 328, 333, 334
Civil Service National Whitley Council, 72, 93, 165, 336
Civil Service Selection Board, 74, 323
Civil Service Superannuation Scheme (1972), 87
Civil Service Union, 72
classical theories of management, 156–62
clerical staff, 25, 68, 69, 70, 73, 75
Coalition Government (1940–5), 33, 34, 271
Colonial Office, 273
Commonwealth Office, 268, 273, 277
Comptroller and Auditor General, 140, 303
Conservative Government (1951), 34
Conservative Government (1970), 139, 245, 269, 276, 330
'content theory', 170, 171
contingency theory, 166–7
coordination, 25, 40–2, 287–91, 332–5
cost-benefit analysis, 158, 207, 259, 261, 290

Crichel Down, 39
Criminal Policy Planning Unit, 244
critical path analysis, 158
Customs and Excise, 24, 212, 245, 307

Davies Report (1969), 77
decision-making: bounded rationality in, 178–80; collective, 182; descriptive theory of, 176–8; incremental theories of, 191–2; levels of, 192–3; normative theory of, 174–6; priorities in, 188–91; search activity in, 183–5; selective perception in, 180–3; stages in, 177–8; structural influences in, 186–8; uncertainty absorption in, 185–6
Defence, Ministry of, 66, 67, 98, 99, 102, 141, 241, 245, 267, 277, 278, 300
departmental agencies, 102, 301, 306–7
Deputy Secretaries, 38, 70, 101, 104, 242, 244
devolution, 149, 231, 272–3, 280, 333

École Nationale d'Administration, 84–5
École Polytechnique, 106
École des Ponts et Chaussées, 106
Economic Advisory Council, 28
Economic Affairs, Department of, 50, 51, 192, 267, 269, 271, 272, 273, 274, 276
Economic Affairs, Ministry for, 35
Economic Planning Board, 36
Economist Group, 98; see also civil service
Education, Board of, 27
Education, Ministry of, 272, 284
Education and Science, Department of, 127, 141, 241, 242–3, 245, 263, 267, 270, 271, 278, 279, 286, 287, 289, 330
Employment, Department of, 67, 268, 304, 306
Employment Policy, White Paper on (1944), 34
Employment and Productivity, Department of, 272, 273
Employment Services Agency, 242
Energy, Department of, 202, 268, 273, 278
Environment, Department of the, 71, 73, 90, 98, 102, 104, 109, 130, 149–50, 268, 269, 275, 277, 278, 279, 301
Estimates Committee, 138, 139, 141, 145, 157, 227, 284; report on Classified Roads (1961–2), 101; report on the Home Office (1962–3), 113; report on Recruitment to the Civil Service (1964–5), 50; report on Treasury Control of Establishments (1963–4), 50; report

Estimates Committee – *cont.*
on Treasury Control of Expenditure (1957–8), 48
European Economic Community, 126, 132, 142, 148–9, 231, 333
Executive Class, 32, 61
Executive Officers, 25, 69, 70, 73–4, 75, 76–7, 79, 86, 88, 89, 90, 97, 104
Expenditure Committee, *see* Select Committee on Expenditure

Fabian Society, 50, 123
Ferranti Ltd, 307
Final Selection Board, 74
First Division Association, 71, 72, 92, 148
First World War, 27, 28, 305
Food, Ministry of, 28
Foreign and Commonwealth Office, 242, 268, 269, 270, 278, 288, 289
Foreign Office, 23, 142, 268, 277
'framework theory', 170, 177
French Civil Service, 79, 106, 131, 329, 332
Fuel and Power, Ministry of, 271
Fulton Management Consultancy Group, 51, 121, 255, 295
Fulton Report, 12, 22, 50–1, 57, 58, 59–63, 90, 198, 276, 315, 327, 338; on administrative specialization, 52–3, 60, 325–6, 328; on careers, 62; on class structure, 60–1; on generalists, 59, 91; on hierarchies, 101–2; on hiving-off, 296, 306; on management, 51, 56, 64, 295–6, 299; on planning units, 247–8, 254, 255–6; on professionalism, 59–60; on recruitment, 60, 61; on secrecy, 62, 133; on social background, 62; on specialists, 61, 99–100; on training, 60, 81, 85; terms of reference, 50
functional principle, 279–80

games theory, 175
General Board of Health, 24, 26
generalists, 15, 32–3, 59, 91–3, 105–8, 117–21, 213, 224–5, 262, 321, 322–8, 334; *see also* specialists
giant departments, 71, 126, 130–1, 276–9
Government Accountancy Service, 97
Government Economic Service, 109
green papers, 132–3

Haldane Report (1918), 52, 248, 249, 250, 252, 254, 271, 276, 279, 284, 288, 338
Health, Ministry of, 27, 36, 132, 250, 268, 270, 277, 284, 285

health authorities, 307, 315, 316
Health and Safety Commission, 306
Health and Social Security, Department of, 67, 71, 115, 137, 242, 243–4, 245, 250, 251, 259, 268, 273, 274, 277, 278, 279, 280, 282, 284, 285–7, 289, 291, 302, 330, 331
HM Inspectors of Constabulary, 113, 114, 115
HM Inspectors of Schools, 100, 115, 242
HM Stationery Office, 198, 212, 289, 302
Heyworth Report (1965), 257–8
Higher Executive Officers, 69, 70, 81, 88
Higher Executive Officers (A), 69, 70, 72, 83
hiving-off, 254, 296, 305–15, 316
Home Office, 23, 67, 113, 136, 201–2, 217, 219, 220, 244–5, 261, 267, 270, 273, 284, 285, 287, 288, 291
Home Secretary, 27, 39, 112–13, 114, 115, 201–2, 218, 219, 220, 221, 285
Housing and Local Government, Ministry of, 268, 269, 271, 279
human relations theories, 163–6

incrementalism, 191–2
Indian Civil Service, 22, 79
Industry, Department of, 109, 140, 151, 268, 272, 280
Inland Revenue, 67, 136, 137, 267, 286, 289, 307
Inland Revenue Staff Federation, 71
Institution of Professional Civil Servants, 72, 96, 97, 98, 99, 100, 107, 116, 118, 121, 122, 321
International Computers Ltd, 307

job-rotation, 90–1
job-satisfaction, 164
joint hierarchies, 100–1
junior Ministers, 21, 130, 131, 275, 329
Justice, 134, 151

Labour, Ministry of, 28, 67, 268, 270, 272, 284
Labour Government (1945), 34, 205, 271
Labour Government (1974), 133, 205, 269
Labour Party, 119, 134, 139, 149, 305
Land Registry, 97
lay control, 226–9
laymen in politics, 221–6
Liberal Government (1905), 27
Liverpool Teaching Hospital, 140
local authorities, 27, 34, 113, 217, 220, 222, 240, 289, 316

local government, 35, 108, 116–17, 135, 165, 226, 246, 272, 301
London Passenger Transport Board, 305

MacDonnell Commission (1912–14), 96
maladministration, 135
management, 295–317; accountable, 296, 299–305; as civil service task, 55–6; classical theories of, 156–62; definition of, 295–6; in departments, 296–9; by objective, 301, 302; personnel, 296, 315; scientific, 158; training in civil service, 81
Manpower Services Commission, 302, 306, 307, 312
meta-policymaking, 176, 192
Method II, 74, 77
Metropolitan Police Force, 27
Mines, Ministry of, 28
ministerial responsibility: collective, 53, 120, 122, 143, 332, 336; individual, 54, 120 122, 125–6, 130, 148, 149, 262, 278, 332, 336
Ministers' Powers, Committee on (1929–32), 29
Ministers' relationship with civil servants, 25, 29–31, 37–40, 53–4, 126–34, 147–8, 201, 252, 305, 319–35
Monopolies Commission, 198, 307

National Assistance Board, 283, 284
National Coal Board, 202
National Economic Development Council, 36, 271
National Economic Development Office, 280, 313–14
National Health Service, 34, 132, 135, 144, 205, 272, 274, 282, 284, 285, 290, 307
National Insurance, Ministry of, 271, 282, 283, 284, 285
National Insurance Scheme, 282
National Joint Advisory Council, 36
National Plan (1965), 50, 236, 241, 271
National Physical Laboratory, 108
National Production Advisory Council on Industry, 36
nationalized industries, 35, 36, 165, 198, 200, 205, 238, 240, 305–6, 307, 312–14; ministerial control of, 271, 312–14
naval dockyards, 26, 66
New Zealand, 107, 138
Northcote–Trevelyan Report (1854), 15 22, 23, 25, 26, 27, 52, 60, 96, 338
Northern Ireland, 273

Northern Ireland Office, 268, 273

Office of Population Censuses and Surveys, 251
Official Secrets Acts, 133
Ombudsman: Scandinavian, 134; see also Parliamentary Commissioner for Administration
Open Structure, 70, 72–3, 83, 88, 89, 97, 103, 104
operational research, 158
opportunity posts, 104, 105
ordnance factories, 26, 66, 302
Organization for Economic Co-operation and Development (OECD), 242, 243
organization and methods, 49, 51, 97, 157, 158, 315
organization theory, 13, 15; definition of, 155–6; modern, 166–9; relevance to public administration, 210–15; see also classical theories of management, contingency theory, human relations theories, system theory
output budgeting, 300, 302
Overseas Development, Ministry of, 268, 269–70, 277
Oxford University, 62, 77, 78

Parliamentary Commissioner for Administration, 126, 134–8, 145, 146, 151, 199, 254; administrative implications of, 145–9
parliamentary committees, 138–45; administrative implications of, 145–9; see also select committees
Parliamentary Private Secretaries, 329
Parliamentary Secretaries, 21, 130
pensions, 35, 87
Permanent Secretaries, 30, 31, 38, 53, 56, 70, 89, 91, 100, 104, 129, 140, 145, 146, 148, 210, 242, 255, 277, 285, 296, 328
planning, 237–63, 320; definition of, 237–40; in departments, 241–5
planning-programming-budgeting (PPB), 300
planning units, 242, 243, 247, 250, 255–61, 333
Plowden Report (Control of Public Expenditure, 1961), 48–50, 55, 238, 240
Plowden Report (Representational Services Overseas, 1964), 242
Police Complaints Board, 135
Police Council for Great Britain, 217, 218, 219, 220

police establishments, 112–16
Police Federation, 216–21
police widow's gratuity, 216–21
policy: authorization of 192, 208–9; central coordination of, 332–5; definition of, 193; and the expert, 109–12; formulation of, 192, 207; making of, 54–5; politicians' contributions to, 229–32; securing consent for 207–8; simplification in making, 205–7; sources of data for, 248–51
Poor Law, 24, 26, 270, 284
Post Office, 24, 26, 29, 32, 36, 66, 99, 136, 172, 268, 306, 310
Posts and Telecommunications, Ministry of, 268, 269
Power, Ministry of, 268
Price Commission, 198, 307
Prices and Consumer Protection, Department of, 109, 268, 272, 278
Prime Minister's Office, 130, 280, 335
Principals, 26, 38, 69, 70, 71, 75, 86, 97; direct-entry, 74
principles of administration, 159
Procurement Executive, 102, 301, 307
Professional and Executive Register, 140
Professional and Technology Group, 68, 98, 102
professionals, see specialists
Programme Analysis and Review (PAR), 245, 247, 281
promotion, 23, 69, 83, 88–90, 91, 103–5, 296
Property Services Agency, 98, 102, 116–17, 118, 269, 289, 301–2, 303, 304, 307
Public Accounts Committee, 117, 138, 140, 231, 296, 303
Public Building and Works, Ministry of, 99, 102, 268, 269
public expenditure, 48–50, 237, 238, 240–1, 274, 277, 300, 333
Public Expenditure Survey Committee (PESC), 240–1, 243, 277, 285, 300, 333
Public Health Laboratory Service, 273
Public Works Loan Office, 24

Rayner Report (1971), 102
recruitment, 50, 60, 62, 73–80, 187, 296
Registrar of Friendly Societies, 282
Reorganisation of Central Government, The (1970), 276–82, 291, 338
Report of the Committee on the Civil Service (1966–68), see Fulton Report

Research Councils, 251, 307
Rolls Royce Ltd, 307
Royal Commissions on the Civil Service, see civil service
Royal Institute of Public Administration, 49, 132, 191, 271
Royal Mint, 303

Sachsenhausen Case, 148
School Health Service, 27, 284, 286
Science Group, 68, 98
Scientific and Industrial Research, Department of, 28, 96, 270
scientific management, 158
Scottish Health Service Council, 207
Scottish Office, 268, 272, 280, 291
Second World War, 33, 52, 96, 99, 236, 271
secrecy, 62, 132–4, 150
select committees, 138–49, 227; advisers to, 143–4, 228; see also specialized committees
Select Committee on Agriculture, 139, 142
Select Committee on Education and Science, 139
Select Committee on Expenditure, 139, 140, 141, 145, 227, 241, 249; sub-committees, 140, 141
Select Committee on Expenditure, Report on the Civil Service (1977), 13, 93, 321, 339; on Civil Service Department, 282; 'minority report', 78, 92; on recruitment, 77–8; on training, 85
Select Committee on National Expenditure, 156
Select Committee on Nationalised Industries, 139, 140, 151, 249, 253, 312, 313
Select Committee on Overseas Aid, 139
Select Committee on Overseas Development, 140
Select Committee on Parliamentary Commissioner for Administration, 134, 135, 136, 138, 140, 148, 199
Select Committee on Procedure, 139, 228
Select Committee on Race Relations and Immigration, 139, 140
Select Committee on Science and Technology, 139, 140, 142
Select Committee on Scottish Affairs, 139
Senior Executive Officers, 38, 69, 70, 86
Senior Professional Administrative Training Scheme, 103, 105

Social Security, Ministry of, 67, 268, 277, 282, 284, 285
Social Services, Secretary of State for, 285, 286, 307
Social Trends, 251
social welfare administration, 282–7
social work, 290–1
Society of Civil and Public Servants, 71, 72, 94, 321
special advisers, 107, 129–30, 131, 244, 261, 330–2
specialists, 15, 32, 43, 224–5; career prospects of, 103–5; definition of, 98; need for, 96–8; in local government, 68, 108, 120; numbers of, 68, 97; role of, 108–21; status of, 98–100; relationship with generalists, 32, 98–103, 105–8, 120, 213, 321, 322, 324, 327
specialized committees, 138–45, 226, 228, 229, 253
staff associations, 23, 63, 71, 89, 91, 297, 304; see also individual associations
Study of Parliament Group, 139, 152
Supplementary Benefits Commission, 284
Supply, Ministry of, 37
Swedish Civil Service, 133
system theory, 167–9

Tavistock Institute of Human Relations, 12
team theory, 175, 195
Technology, Ministry of, 122, 142, 268, 269, 271, 272, 274, 275
Tomlin Report (1931), 44, 98
Trade, Board of, 24, 27, 268, 271, 282
Trade, Department of, 109, 268, 289
Trade and Industry, Department of, 131, 268, 269, 277, 278, 279

trade unions, 36, 205, 231; see also staff associations
trading funds, 301, 302, 303
training, 49, 60, 80–6, 175, 186, 187–8, 190, 238
Transport, Department of, 106, 109, 268, 269, 279
Transport, Ministry of, 99, 101, 103, 116, 268
Treasury, 24, 35, 41–2, 48–51, 90, 91, 109, 127, 192, 206, 217, 220, 241, 247, 250, 266, 267, 269, 271, 272, 274, 275, 277, 280, 281, 282, 296
Treasury Board, 26
Treasury Solicitor's Office, 97
Treasury Working Party on Management Training, 81
Trend Report (1963), 257

Under Secretaries, 26, 38, 55, 70, 72–3, 85, 87, 90, 103, 130, 242, 278
Unemployment Assistance Board, 283
UK Atomic Energy Authority, 307, 311
United States of America, 79, 106, 107, 108, 131, 143, 157, 185, 224–5, 229, 300, 311, 332
University Grants Committee, 307

Vehicle and General Insurance Company, 131

War Pensions, Ministry of, 282
Welsh Office, 268, 272, 280
Western Electric Factory, Chicago, 164
Whitley Council: see Civil Service National Whitley Council
Wider Issues Review Team, 318
workers' cooperatives, 140